CONTENTS

W. E. GLADSTONE by J. McLURE HAMILTON, 1890

(Reproduced by permission of Sir William Gladstone, Bart.)

ROYAL COMMISSION ON
HISTORICAL MANUSCRIPTS

The Prime Ministers' Papers:

W. E. GLADSTONE

1: Autobiographica

EDITED BY JOHN BROOKE
AND MARY SORENSEN

LONDON
HER MAJESTY'S STATIONERY OFFICE
1971

PRINTED IN ENGLAND FOR HER MAJESTY'S STATIONERY OFFICE
BY MCCORQUODALE PRINTERS LTD LONDON

APPENDICES

INTRODUCTION

The papers of William Ewart Gladstone are probably the most extensive ever left by a British statesman. The principal collection (among the Additional MSS in the British Museum) consists of 750 volumes of official, political, and literary papers. To these must be added Gladstone's correspondence with Queen Victoria, her private secretaries, and members of the Royal Family (deposited on permanent loan in the British Museum); personal and family papers in St. Deiniol's Library (estimated at some 50,000 documents); and Gladstone's diary, covering almost the whole of his adult life, in Lambeth Palace Library. John Morley, who was entrusted with the task of writing the authorised biography of Gladstone, is said to have remarked that only two things in life had ever frightened him: his first sight of Dublin Castle, and his first sight of the Gladstone Papers.

This immense mass of documents is a treasure trove to the student of nineteenth-century history—political, religious, and social; and essential material for those who would wish to understand the mind and character of a statesman who consciously tried to apply the principles of Christianity to the practice of politics. But obviously no one can hope to read all these documents, and there is necessarily a great deal of dross inter-mingled with the pure metal. Scholars have dipped their buckets into the bottomless reservoir of the Gladstone Papers, and the student is grateful to those who have published significant selections. D. C. Lethbury edited a selection of Gladstone's correspondence on religious affairs.[1] Paul Knaplund was principally concerned with Gladstone's colonial policy.[2] Philip Guedalla was interested in Gladstone's relations with Palmerston and Queen Victoria, and enlivened his selection of documents with percipient introductions.[3] A. Tilney Bassett arranged and catalogued the manuscripts which came to the

---

[1] *Correspondence on Church and Religion of William Ewart Gladstone*, 2 volumes, 1910.

[2] *Gladstone and Britain's Imperial Policy*, 1927; *Gladstone-Gordon Correspondence, 1851–1896*, 1961.

[3] *The Palmerston Papers: Gladstone and Palmerston*, 1928; *The Queen and Mr. Gladstone*, 2 volumes, 1933.

British Museum, and published extracts from Gladstone's letters to his wife.[1] Miss Agatha Ramm, with scrupulous and conscientious scholarship, edited the correspondence between Gladstone and Lord Granville.[2] Despite the work of these and other scholars, the greater portion of the Gladstone Papers remain (and probably will forever remain) unpublished.

In selecting Gladstone for the first subject in the Historical Manuscripts Commission's series of Prime Ministers' Papers we were guided principally by his long tenure of the office and his concern with so many aspects of nineteenth-century political and religious thought. To understand the nineteenth century it is essential to understand Gladstone, and to understand Gladstone it is best to begin with what he wrote about himself. Much of his writing was autobiographical in character, with no thought of publication. He felt the need to express himself, to explain the reasons for his ideas or his conduct, without regard to whether anyone would ever read what he had written. For over seventy years he kept a diary. Throughout his life, and especially before he became Prime Minister, it was his habit to make memoranda of events and conversations in which he had been concerned. And in extreme old age he began to write his autobiography.

Autobiographical writings, not undertaken for publication and without concern for posterity, are perhaps the best revelation of the mind of the dead. In deciding what to publish from the vast corpus of the Gladstone Papers, we have selected what he called his 'autobiographica', together with the accounts he wrote of current transactions. Gladstone's diary, now being published under the editorship of Professor M. R. D. Foot, will provide a day to day record of his life. The present volumes will contain Gladstone's record of transactions for which there was no room in his diary and his reflections and subsequent accounts.

In 1887 Gladstone received an offer from an American publisher to write his autobiography. Our knowledge of this is derived from a letter Lord Acton wrote to Gladstone on 16 August 1887:[3]

> I should be half sorry if it were to snatch you prematurely from the occupations you meant to turn to at Hawarden. For I think often

---

[1] *Gladstone to his Wife*, 1936.

[2] *The Political Correspondence of Mr. Gladstone and Lord Granville. 1868–1876*, 2 volumes, 1952; *1876–1886*, 2 volumes, 1962.

[3] ADD.MS 44093, ff. 300–301.

of that American proposal which you spoke of at Grillions, and which seems to me full of important consequences.

The influence of your name, your ideas, your career, will be the greatest force sustaining and guiding the Liberal party in the next generation.

How many of those who would otherwise have been its appointed leaders have fallen or drifted away, and of those who have not there are scarcely three or four who have had a grasp of the principle, and have been independent of the uncertain influence of combinations. Our most valuable possession will be the unity—unity of direction and progress—of your political life. That is a thing not at all apparent on the surface and easily missed by overlooking links which are neither obvious nor are generally known.

Of those who have known you and lived near you and had your confidence, not one is left who could do justice to the theme, which besides, is infinitely richer and more varied than this central problem.

The materials will be partly inaccessible, partly unintelligible to anybody but yourself. There is a terrible abundance of your letters, the correspondence of half a century, in unfit hands from which you alone can recover it. And there is much to which no one else has the key.

And this is almost equally true of the religious part of your life, and of the literary, which is only part of the religious.

Lastly, apart from yourself, and from the future of that grand instrument for doing good, the Liberal party, how much other secret history, how much secret biography of eminent men, you hold locked *in infimo pectoris*!

So that I heartily wish success to Mr. Putnam—if it is Putnam—so far as may be wished without detriment to the cause which is before us.

Andrew Carnegie also encouraged Gladstone. 'You may remember', he wrote to Gladstone on 12 January 1891, 'that I once told you how you could make £50,000 by writing your autobiography'; and he suggested that Gladstone should dictate it to a stenographer.[1]

It does not appear that Gladstone accepted this offer, but five years later, in July 1892, he began to write his autobiography. In the following month he became Prime Minister for the fourth time, and the labours of the Premiership, undertaken at the age of 81, resulted in the

---

[1] ADD.MS 44512, f. 200.

suspension of his literary work. For the next two years little was done on the autobiography, apart from his recollections of Arthur Hallam, inspired by the publication of Hallam's literary remains, and an unfinished essay on confession. In March 1894 he resigned office for the last time, and immediately resumed his writing. His eyesight was failing, and on 24 May he underwent an operation for cataract. As soon as he could see, he took up his pen again; and in the summer of 1894 added to his autobiography a retrospect of his early parliamentary life, an account of his political career from 1874 to his final retirement, an essay on Protectionism, and the first of his three essays on his political errors. His handwriting had deteriorated, and his sight was so bad that he did not always realise when his pen was running out of ink. Consequently these documents are hard to read, and indeed at times completely illegible. There is a well-known photograph of Gladstone in his old age, taken in his study, which shows him bending over his work, his face almost touching the paper, quite oblivious of being photographed. These were the circumstances in which he wrote a large part of his autobiography.

Gladstone had intended for the major preoccupations of his retirement an edition of the works of Bishop Butler (which was published in February 1896) and a book on the Olympian religion (which he never wrote). He had thus little time to spare for his autobiography and wrote nothing of it in 1895. A certain amount was done in 1896 but it was not until September 1897 that he resumed serious work upon it. During that month he wrote the greater part of his account of his political career, probably in far less detail than he would have done had he not felt that time was running out. The last section was written on 18 November 1897, shortly before his departure for his final visit to the Continent; and concludes with the following sentences:

> With respect to the other world; my only special call to it was that of my age. The attitude therefore in which I endeavoured to fix myself was as follows. I desired to consider myself as a soldier on parade, in a line of men drawn up, ready to march, and waiting for the word of command. Only it was not to be 'march' but 'die' and I sought to be in preparation for prompt obedience, feeling no desire to go until the work I had in hand was completed, but on the other hand without reluctance because firmly convinced that whatever He ordains for us is best, both for us and for all.

He did no further work on the autobiography; and six months later, on 19 May 1898, he died.

It will be seen from the above account that the autobiography was not written in the chronological order of the events which it narrates. The first sections, written in 1892, deal with the early years of Gladstone's life, and it seems that at this date he had publication in mind. Indeed, in speaking of the development of his religious ideas, he refers to a further 'inner' or 'spiritual' account which he intended to write but not to publish (it seems in fact never to have been written). When he resumed the work in March 1894 he did so with the events leading to his resignation fresh in mind, and was clearly writing to justify himself and not for publication. The criticisms of his former colleagues—Harcourt, Rosebery, and Spencer—could not have been published during the lifetime of any of those concerned. Yet he did not altogether abandon the idea of publication. On 21 January 1897 he wrote his reminiscences of Dr. Keate, headmaster of Eton, in the style of the early part of the work. A few days later, on 1 February, he wrote an account of his last visit to Windsor as Prime Minister, which could not have been published while either he or the Queen were alive.

There were other reasons why the autobiography as Gladstone left it eluded publication. There is a certain amount of repetition, including no less than three versions of what he called his 'recorded errors'. He seems at times to have forgotten what he had written earlier: thus there are four accounts (all substantially the same) of how he came to write his first book, *The State in its relations with the Church*. The controversy over the Navy Estimates of 1894, which led to his final retirement, oppressed him so much that he refers to it on more than one occasion and at disproportionate length. Like many old people, he could better remember what he did forty years ago than what he did the week before, and in one section he tells the same anecdote both at the beginning and at the end. There would, therefore, have had to be a great deal of pruning and re-shaping before the work could have been offered to a publisher as a commercial proposition.

There are also large omissions which would have had to be supplied in a connected narrative of Gladstone's life. He only just mentions his visit to Naples in 1850–1, when he exposed the abuses connected with the detention of political prisoners. He says nothing of the time he spent as High Commissioner to the Ionian Islands in 1858–9. His account of his second Administration omits the episode of General

5

Gordon and the story of British intervention in Egypt. There is disappointingly little about Ireland, considering the amount of time he devoted to her affairs and the immense consequence of his ideas on both British and Irish history. There are few 'revelations' and no 'intimate' portraits of the men he had known in sixty years' experience of politics. Considered as a book of memoirs, this would have been a disappointing work to the book-buying public of the late 1890s.

For the historian, and particularly for the student of Gladstone's mind and character, the autobiography with all its omissions and repetitions is more valuable than the book he might have written had he been concerned to make money or write an apologia for the Liberal party. Gladstone wrote about the things that seemed to him important, and was concerned above all to trace the development of his religious and political ideas. Religion receives almost as much attention as politics. As a young man he wished to take Orders, and only his father's decided opposition had prevented him. It is curious to speculate on what Gladstone might have achieved had he entered the Church: perhaps much less than he expected. In his early years (as he admits) there was an element of fanaticism as well as naivety in his religious thought. He tells us with what surprise he heard for the first time about 1828 the idea that souls united to Christ by faith and love could be saved whatever the fault of their opinions. Politics led him to a clearer conception of the role of the Church than he would have had in her service. Sir John Gladstone surely did wisely when he counselled his son to adopt a secular career.

For many years the Church remained his chief interest in politics, and it was not until Peel gave him practical work at the Board of Trade that he began to understand what government was about. But religion remained throughout his guide. In 1837 he told Manning that he had set before himself the solution of 'that hard and formidable question . . . how the principle of Catholic Christianity is to be applied in these evil and presumptuous days to the conduct of public affairs'.[1] Every idea that Gladstone brought to the practice of politics was in its origin a moral or religious idea—even his passion for economy had a moral basis; and this was the source of so much of his strength as a leader of men. He would have felt pleased at the tribute paid to him by Lord

---

[1] ADD.MS 44247, f. 18.

Salisbury in the House of Lords after his death—'He will leave behind him the memory of a great Christian statesman.'

The importance of the autobiography is less in Gladstone's account of events—most of which are well known to the historian and fully documented from other sources, including Gladstone's own papers—than in the picture of the writer. It is impossible to imagine Palmerston or Disraeli writing such a work. Modesty and humility are its hall marks. There is no 'flashing', no ostentation: he does not fail to reveal his errors, or even to present himself in a ridiculous or unpleasing light. The young Gladstone, who objected to his brother's choice of a wife because she had been brought up as a Unitarian, was something of a prig. The young politician, who hesitated to accept a seat in the Cabinet because of conscientious scruples concerning a proposed re-arrangement of Welsh bishoprics, must have been considered by the worldly-wise as something of a fool. He confesses these and other errors, sadly and with repentance; and shows that though he might have learnt slowly he learnt surely and never stopped learning. There is no rancour as he looks back at his past. Apart from one sentence on Disraeli, there is hardly an unkind word about any of the people he mentions—many of them his determined political opponents. It must be remembered that Gladstone wrote this work expecting within a short time to be called before God to account for his actions. It was his general confession of his sins as a statesman.

Like all statesmen, Gladstone combined idealism with ambition; and sometimes the two are so confused that it is impossible to distinguish one from the other. He tells us that he 'deeply desired an interval between Parliament and the grave', and took the occasion of the Liberal defeat at the general election of 1874 to resign the leadership of the party. He was, he says, 'in some measure out of touch with some of the tendencies of the Liberal party, especially in religious matters'. But his crusade against what he calls 'Beaconsfieldism', and then the Irish problem, kept him in politics longer than he expected; and when the time finally came in 1894 he could hardly bear to go. He was deeply hurt by his failure to win support from the Cabinet against the proposal to increase the naval estimates, and dwells on this episode with undue length and petulance. His pugnacity was unabated, and his last speech in Parliament was, in Morley's words, 'a vigorous assault on the House of Lords'. At the age of 84, he was prepared to go to the country and fight a general election on the issue of the relations between the two

Houses. His first intervention in politics was against the Reform Bill of 1832; his last speech in the House of Commons looked forward to the Parliament Act of 1911. Such was the span of his career and the extent of his development.

Apart from that of the writer, there are few vivid personalities in the autobiography. In the early pages we have a picture of Sir John Gladstone, a self-made man, sensible, kind, charitable, and religious: the best kind of Victorian capitalist. Gladstone was devoted to him—he always writes the word 'father' with a capital letter. In politics, the greatest influence on his career was that of Peel and he remained throughout a disciple of Peel. The picture that we are given of Peel is that of the statesman and administrator. Only once, in a curious story of Peel's nervousness when attacked by Cobbett in the House of Commons, do we see the man behind the politician. Under Peel, Gladstone imbibed the doctrines of Free Trade with moral fervour and intensity, and perhaps it was his loyalty to Peel and Peel's other followers that kept him so long from joining with the Liberals. What he would have really liked was a reformed Conservative party, based on the principle of Free Trade, just as Peel had re-fashioned the party after the Reform Bill of 1832. Gladstone began politics as a Conservative and ended as in some respects a Radical, but he never showed any sympathy with Whiggism.

It has been said that Gladstone's greatest defect as a politician was his insensitivity to people and a consequent crassness in dealing with their personal vanities and idiosyncrasies. He certainly did not always handle men to the best advantage. Perhaps the most revealing sections of the autobiography are those devoted to his relations with Queen Victoria. Gladstone, who had an immense reverence for the Monarchy, was deeply hurt by the Queen's hostility to him; and was unable to account for it—or at least in terms that he could frame in words. The story of their relations is well known from the documents published by Philip Guedalla, but even today, when so much has been written about Gladstone and the Queen, there is still a great deal unexplained.

The manuscripts of this work, which are docketed by Gladstone 'Autobiographica', together with one or two related pieces, were bound by the British Museum in the order in which they were written as Additional MSS 44790 and 44791. They were available to Morley, who quotes from them freely in his biography. In this edition they are printed in full in an order based approximately on the events to which they relate. They have been divided into four sections: Early Life; Politics; Religion; and Last Years. Gladstone's original titles, together with the dates on which he wrote each piece, have been retained.

The appendices contain supplementary material which is mentioned by Gladstone in the text or which he intended to introduce into the work. The longest contains Gladstone's letters to his Eton friend, William Windham Farr (now in the John Rylands Library, Manchester), which present a picture of Gladstone in late adolescence and early manhood. A less pleasing picture is to be found in the letter Gladstone wrote to his father about his future career. The long memorandum, 'Twenty-seven propositions relating to current questions in theology', was intended by Gladstone to be included in the work. We have not been deterred by the pedestrian quality of Gladstone's verse from introducing a specimen, written at a profound crisis of his life.

The volume of autobiographica will be followed by three others containing the memoranda Gladstone wrote on current transactions. It was his habit throughout life to write accounts of important conversations or events, both public and personal, apparently solely for his own use, shortly after they took place. The series begins with Gladstone's account of his election for Newark in 1832, and is particularly important for the period of opposition under Peel and the years following the break-up of the Conservative party. Unfortunately, there are relatively few for the times when Gladstone held office after 1846, when presumably he did not have the leisure to indulge in autobiographical writing. To remedy this gap, other documents of a similar character have been included, in particular Gladstone's notes for his audiences as Prime Minister with the Queen.

The sources of these memoranda are as follows:

1. ADD.MS 44819. This is a quarto note-book containing reports of conversations and discussions, 1832–1843, mainly with the leaders of the Conservative party. On f. 2 it bears the title, in Gladstone's hand: 'Notes or Memoranda of Politics and Men'.

2. ADD.MSS 44777 and 44778. A series of 125 political and auto-biographical memoranda dating from 1832 to 1861.

3. ADD.MSS 44722–44776. These volumes, described in the British Museum catalogue as 'Miscellanea', contain a wide variety of material. From these have been extracted all memoranda of a personal or

autobiographical nature, together with Gladstone's notes for his audiences with Queen Victoria and what can best be described as his working papers as Prime Minister. The documents in the last two categories, being written for his own use only, are usually brief.

One class of documents has been omitted: the themes or essays which he wrote on aspects of theology, politics, literature, history, and other subjects. These are important for the intellectual history of his age and as a revelation of his thought, but they rarely relate to current events. Their inclusion would have added a further two volumes to the series and greatly delayed its appearance.

The memoranda supplement the autobiographica and have also a value of their own. Apart from memoranda concerning events in his own family, Gladstone is for the most part chronicling transactions in which he played only a part, and that not always the most important. Their interest is for the general political and party history of the nineteenth century, and especially for the period of Peel.

In reproducing the text we have adhered to Gladstone's spelling and punctuation, correcting obvious mistakes as he himself would have done had he sent the work to the press. In general, abbreviations have been expanded. His capitalisation, which is erratic, has been reduced and systematised. The dates at which Gladstone wrote the manuscripts have been included, the name of the month being expanded and on occasion the year being supplied. Dockets, unless they contain information not to be found in the documents, have been omitted. All footnotes are the editors', unless specified by the initials WEG.

The Commissioners wish to express their thanks to Sir William Erskine Gladstone, Bt., for permission to print these writings of his great-grandfather, and to the Governors of the John Rylands Library, Manchester, for permission to include Gladstone's letters to W. W. Farr. The work was begun during the lifetime of the late Mr. Charles Andrew Gladstone, and he and Mrs. Gladstone kindly gave permission to Mrs. Sorensen to inspect the manuscripts at Hawarden Castle. We wish to express our thanks to the Rev. Dr. Stewart Lawton, Warden of St. Deiniol's Library, and Mrs. Lawton; to Mr. R. L. Arundale; and to Mr. A. G. Veysey, Flintshire County Archivist, for their kindness and assistance. Professor M. R. D. Foot placed his vast knowledge of Gladstone at our disposal, and helped to solve some difficult problems of dating and transcription.

AUTOBIOGRAPHICA

EARLY LIFE

INFANCY—FAMILY—CHILDHOOD

BEGINNINGS OR INCUNABULA

ADD.MS 44790, ff. 5–25 *8 July 1892*

There are some recollections of my infancy and earliest childhood, which, among others of a cloudier character, are definite and clear.

I remember myself as an infant struggling or fighting my way up a staircase, watched and encouraged by my nurse who stood a little higher on the stairs. I remember the particular staircase: it was covered not with carpet but with oilcloth of a brown pattern. The nurse was a woman I think of sallow or brownish complexion: and she had on a gown of yellow with chocolate spots.

I always understood from an aunt who lived much with us, and who was an accurate person, that this nurse was named Brown, and that she died when I was eighteen months old. I have no other recollection of her: but this one seems to agree with the character of an infant at (say) fifteen or sixteen months, clambering by hands and feet from one step to another. It implies having been stout and healthy. But this was the character of my early life. At six months I believe that croup nearly killed me but this I suppose implies only one peculiar liability. I remember the ordinary diseases of measles and scarlet fever (then I think of a milder type than now) and coming through them well.

My next recollection belongs to the period of Mr. Canning's first election for Liverpool, in the month of October (I rather think) of the year 1812. Much entertaining went on in my father's house, where Mr. Canning himself was a guest: and on a day of a great dinner I was taken down to the dining room, dressed if I remember right in a red frock. I was set up on one of the chairs, standing, and directed to say to the company: 'Ladies and gentlemen'. I am sorry to add that I remember showing in boyhood an uncivilised nature by contending that it ought to be 'gentlemen and ladies'. At this time I was under three, and I have no doubt of the authenticity of the anecdote, which I have been accustomed all my life to recollect and refer to.

I have thirdly a group of recollections, which refer to Scotland. Thither my father and mother took me on a journey which they made I think in a post chaise to Edinburgh and Glasgow as its principal points. At Edinburgh our sojourn was in the Royal Hotel, Prince's Street. I recollect it as having at that time a frontage of five windows, the door in the centre. Mr. D. Macgregor, the present proprietor, has assured me that this is correct, and that he himself removed these windows, no doubt as being old-fashioned, to the rear of the house. But my main fact is that I well remember the rattling of the windows when the Castle guns were fired on some great occasion, probably the abdication of Napoleon, for the date of the journey was I think the spring of 1814.

In this journey the situation of Sanquhar in a close Dumfriesshire valley impressed itself on my recollection. I never saw Sanquhar again until in the autumn of 1863 (as I believe) as I was whirled along the Glasgow and South Western Railway I witnessed just beneath me lines of building in just such a valley and said that must be Sanquhar which it was. My local memory has always been good and very impressible by scenery. I seem to myself never to have forgotten a scene.

At the same period when we were in Glasgow I remember in the drawing room before dinner a minister who was a fine old gentleman with a gold headed stick, dressed in shorts and shoe-buckles, whom I believed to have been a minister of one of the Leith churches, and to have walked over from Edinburgh. On the publication within the last few years of the Memoir of Dr. Johnson of (North?) Leith I ascertained by correspondence that this was probably a true remembrance. I was four years old at the time.

I have however one other early recollection to record. It must I think have been in the year 1815 that my father and mother took me with them on either one or two more journies. The objective points were Cambridge and London respectively. My father had built under the very niggard and discouraging laws which repressed rather than encouraged the erection of new churches at that period the church of St. Thomas at Seaforth and he wanted a clergyman for it. Guided in these matters very much by the deeply religious temper of my mother he went with her to Cambridge to obtain a recommendation of a suitable person from Mr. Simeon, whom I saw at the time. I remember his appearance distinctly. He was a venerable man, and although only a fellow of a college was more ecclesiastically got up than many a Dean or even here and there perhaps a Bishop of the present less costumed if more ritualistic period. Mr. Simeon (I believe) recommended Mr. Jones, an excellent specimen of the excellent Evangelical school of those days. We went to Leicester to hear him preach in a large church and his text was: 'Grow in grace'. He became eventually Archdeacon of Liverpool and died in great honour a few years ago at much past ninety. On the strength of this visit to Cambridge I lately boasted there even during the lifetime of the aged Provost Okes that I had been in the university before any one of them.

I think it was at this time that in London we were domiciled in Russell Square in the house of a brother of my mother, Mr. Colin Robertson: and I was vexed and put about by being forbidden to run freely and at my own will into and about the streets as I had done in Liverpool. But the main event was this. We went to a great service of public thanksgiving at St. Paul's, and sate in a small gallery annexed to the choir just over the place where was the Regent and looking down upon him from behind. I recollect nothing more of the service, nor was I ever present at any public thanksgiving after this in St. Paul's, until the service held in that cathedral, after the highly dangerous illness of the Prince of Wales, under my advice as the Prime Minister of this country.[1]

Before quitting the subject of early recollections I must name one which involves another person of some note. My mother took me in 181 [sic] to Barleywood Cottage, near Bristol. Here lived Mrs. Hannah More with some of her coeval sisters. I am sure they loved my mother who was love-worthy indeed. And I cannot help here deviating for a moment into the later portion of the story to record that in 1833 I had the honour of breakfasting with Mr. Wilberforce a few days before his death, and when I entered the house, immediately after the salutation, he said to me in his silvery tones: 'How is your sweet mother?' He had been a guest in my father's house some twelve years before.

During the afternoon visit at Barleywood, Mrs. Hannah More took me aside, and presented to me a little book. It was a copy of her *Sacred Dramas* and it now remains in my possession with my name written in it by her. She very graciously accompanied it with a little speech, of which I cannot recollect the conclusion (or apodosis). But it began: 'As you have just come into the world, and I am just going out of it', etc.[2]

I return to the opening of life. I was baptised I believe in the parish church of St. Peter, Liverpool, by one of the rectors, my father then

---

[1] Marginal note in pencil: 1872?3?

[2] Following this paragraph is the word 'Malvern' in pencil.

residing in Rodney Street. My god-mother was my elder sister Anne, then just seven years old, who died a perfect saint in the beginning of the year 1829. In the later years she lived in close relations with me, and I must have been much worse but for her. Of my god-fathers one was a Scotch Episcopalian, Mr. Fraser of Caldrethel, whom I hardly ever saw or heard of, the other a Presbyterian Mr. G. Grant, a junior partner of my father's.

Before proceeding to the period of my childhood properly so called I will here insert a few words about my family.

My maternal grandfather was known as Provost Robertson of Dingwall, a man held I believe in the highest respect. His wife was a Mackenzie of Terridan. His circumstances must have been good: of his three sons one went into the Army and I recollect him as Captain Robertson (I have a seal which he gave me, a three sided Cairngorm).[1] The other two took mercantile positions. When my parents made a Scotch tour in 1820, with I think their four sons, the freedom of Dingwall was presented to us all, with my father; and there was large visiting at the houses of the Ross-shire gentry. I think the line of my grandmother was stoutly Episcopalian and Jacobite: but, coming outside the Western Highlands, the first at least was soon rubbed down. The Provost I think came from a younger branch of the Robertsons of Struan.

On my father's side the matter is more complex. The history of the family has been traced at the desire of my eldest brother and my own by Sir William Fraser, the highest living authority. He has carried us up to a rather remote period, I think before Elizabeth, but has not yet been able to connect us with the earliest known holders of the name, which with the aid of charter chests he hopes to do. Some things are plain and not without interest. They were a race of borderers. There is still an old Gladstanes or Gladstone Castle. They formed a family in Sweden in the seventeenth century. The explanation of this may have been that, when the union of the crowns led to the extinction of border fighting, they took service like Sir Dugald Dalgetty under Gustavus Adolphus, and in this case passed from service to settlement. I have never heard of them in Scotland until after the Restoration, otherwise than as persons of family. At that period there are traces of their having been fined, by public authority but not for any ordinary

---

[1] Marginal note: Cost him $7\frac{1}{2}$ guineas.

criminal offence. From this time forward I find no trace of their gentility. During the eighteenth century they are I think principally traced by a line of maltsters (no doubt a small business then) in Lanark-shire. Their names are recorded on tombstones in the church-yard of Biggar. I remember going as a child or boy to see the representative of that branch, either in 1820 or some years earlier, who was a small watchmaker in that town. He was of the same generation as my father but came I understood from a senior brother of the family. I do not know whether his line are extinct as also seem to be some stray Glad-stones who are found at Yarmouth and in Yorkshire.

My father's father seems from his letters to have been an excellent man and a wise parent: his wife a woman of energy. There are pictures of them at Fasque, by Raeburn. He was a merchant, in Scotch phrase, that is to say a shopkeeper dealing in corn and stores, and my father as a lad served in his shop. But he also sent a ship or ships to the Baltic: and I believe that my father, whose energy soon began to out-top that of all the very large family, went in one at a very early age as supercargo, an appointment then I think common. But he soon quitted a nest too small to hold him. He was born in December 1764: and I have a reprint of the Liverpool directory for 178 [sic][1] in which his name appears as a partner in the firm of Messrs Currie, corn mer-chants.[2] Here his force soon began to be felt as a prominent and then a foremost member of the community. A Liberal in the early period of the century, he drew to Mr. Canning, and brought that statesman as candidate to Liverpool in 1812 by personally offering to guarantee his expences, at a time when though prosperous he could hardly have been a rich man. His services to the town were testified by gifts of plate now in the possession of the elder lines of his descendants: and by a remarkable subscription of six thousand pounds raised to enable him to contest the borough of Lancaster for which he sat in the parliament of 1818.

At his demise in December 1851 the value of his estate was I think near £600,000. Almost the whole of this was divided into five portions, the residence and estate at Fasque being taken as one: two went to the eldest son, one with the headship of the mercantile house in Liverpool

---

[1] Marginal note in pencil: at Hawarden.
[2] After 'as' there is a blank in the manuscript, and the remainder of the sentence was added afterwards in pencil.

to the second, the others to my brother John, a captain in the Navy, and to myself, the youngest of my brothers.

My father was a successful merchant, but considering his long life and means of accumulation the result represents a success secondary in comparison with that of others whom in native talent and energy he much surpassed. It was a large and strong nature, simple though hasty, profoundly affectionate and capable of the highest devotion in the lines of duty and of love. I think that his intellect was a little intemperate, though not his character. In his old age, spent mainly in retirement, he was our constant social and domestic life. My mother, a beautiful and admirable woman, failed in health and left him a widower in 1835 when she was 62.

Mr. Smiles, who had been led to form a very high conception of his force, wished some twenty or thirty years ago to be his biographer. But there was a difference of opinion in the family, and to my regret the project did not take effect.

I now turn to the records of my own childhood, the period of which I regard as having terminated in September 1821 when I was first sent to Eton.

I wish that in reviewing this period I could regard it as presenting those features of innocence and beauty which I have often seen elsewhere and indeed thanks be to God within the limits of my own home. The best I can say for it is that I do not think it was actually a vicious childhood. I do not think, trying to look at the past impartially, that I had a strong natural propensity then developed to what are termed the mortal sins. But truth obliges me to record this against myself. I have no recollection of being a loving or a winning child: or an earnest or diligent or knowledge-loving child. God forgive me. And what pains and shames me most of all is to remember that almost and at best I was like the sailor in Juvenal

digitis a morte remotus
Quatuor aut septem.

The plank between me and all the sins was so very thin. I did not love or habitually practise falsehood, meanness or indecency: but I could be drawn into them by occasion and temptation. I do not indeed intend in these notes to give a history of the inner life, which I think has with me been extraordinarily dubious, vacillating, and (above all) complex. I reserve these, perhaps, for a more private and personal document: and I may in this way relieve myself from some at least of the risks of falling into an odious Pharisaism. But no account of my character can be given without including something of its relations to right and wrong. And I am deeply shocked in the retrospect first at my nearness and accessibility to wrong: secondly at the absence of all features of what is conspicuously and nobly right. *Miserere!* I cannot in truth have been an interesting child: and the only presumption the other way which I can gather from my review is that there was probably something in me worth the saving or my father and mother would not so much have singled me out to be taken with them on their journies.

I was not a devotional child. I have no recollection of early love for the House of God and for divine service: though after my father built the church at Seaforth in 1815 I remember cherishing a hope that he would bequeath it to me and that I might live in it. I have a very early recollection of preaching (in St. George's, Liverpool) but it is this; that I turned quietly to my mother and said, 'When will he have done?' *The Pilgrim's Progress* undoubtedly took a great and fascinating hold upon me, so that anything which I wrote was insensibly moulded in its style: but it was by the force of the allegory addressing itself to the fancy, and was very like a strong impression received from the *Arabian Nights* and from another work called *Tales of the Genii*. I think it was about the same time that Miss Porter's *Scottish Chiefs* and especially the *Life and Death of Wallace* used to make me weep profusely. This would be when I was about ten years old. At a much earlier period, say six or seven, I remember praying earnestly but it was for no higher object than to be spared from the loss of a tooth. Here however it may be mentioned in mitigation that the local dentist of those days, in our case a certain Dr. Perry of Seel Street, Liverpool, was a kind of savage at his work (possibly a very good-natured man too) with no ideas except to smash and crash. My religious recollections then are a sad blank. Neither was I a popular boy, though not egregiously otherwise. It so happened that I had several escapes: tumbling into ponds and pools (one of them at the east end of the Serpentine, since altered) and scrambling out of them I know not how though these pits were apt to be pretty deep. But I have no recollection of thankfulness to the kind and gracious Father in Heaven, who delivered me in some cases which were not of mere wetting but I think almost certainly of real danger. As a whole the survey is to me most unsatisfactory and bows me down in deep humiliation. The only palliating touch is this. I was a child of slow, in some points I think of singularly slow development: there was more in me perhaps than in the average boy, but it required greatly more time to set itself in order: and just so in adult, and in middle and later life, I acquired very tardily any knowledge of the world, and that simultaneous conspectus of the relations of persons and things which is necessary for the proper performance of duties in the world.

If I was not a bad boy, I think that I was a boy with a great absence of goodness. To show how easily I might even then have become bad I will mention that when about six or possibly seven I carried a penny marked with an Irish harp to a small confectioner's to buy a cake or bun and being fearful that the harp should be objected to and the penny refused I slipped it through a slit into the till. This was of course observed and the penny was accepted but this in no way excuses me.

I may mention another matter in extenuation. I received, unless my memory deceives me, very little benefit of teaching. My father was too much occupied. My mother's health was broken. We, the four brothers, had no quarrelling among ourselves: but neither can I recollect any influence flowing down at this time upon me, the junior. One odd incident seems to show that I was meek which I should not have supposed, not less than thrifty and penurious, a leaning which lay deep I think in my nature and which has required effort and battle to controul it. It was this. By some process not easy to explain I had, when I was probably seven or eight, and my elder brothers from ten or eleven to fourteen or thereabouts, accumulated no less than twenty shillings in silver. My brothers judged it right to appropriate this fund and I do not recollect either annoyance or resistance or complaint. But I recollect that they employed the principal part of it in the purchase of four knives, and that they broke the points from the tops of the blades of my knife, lest I should cut my fingers.

Where was the official or appointed teacher all this time? He was the Rev. Mr. Rawson of Cambridge who had I suppose been passed by Mr. Simeon and become private tutor in my father's house. But as he was to be incumbent of the church the Bishop required a parsonage and him to live in it. Out of this grew a very small school of about twelve boys, to which I went, with some senior brother or brothers remaining for a while. Mr. Rawson was a good man, of high No Popery opinions. He never showed violence in the school, and he preached twice and performed the services creditably on Sundays: he had also prayers on some or all days in the church during Passion

Week. His school afterwards rose into considerable repute, and it had Dean Stanley and the sons of one or two more other Cheshire families for pupils, but I think this was not so much due to its intellectual stamina as to the extreme salubrity of the situation on the pure dry sands of the Mersey's mouth, with all the advantages of the strong tided action and the fresh and frequent north-west winds. At five miles from Liverpool exchange, the sands, delicious for riding, were an absolute solitude, and only one house looked down on them between us and the town. To return to Mr. Rawson. Everything was unobjectionable. I suppose I learnt something there. But I have no recollection of being under any moral or personal influence whatever and I doubt whether the preaching had any adaptation whatever to children. As to intellectual training I believe that like the other boys I shirked my work as much as I could. I went to Eton in 1821 after a pretty long spell in a very middling state of preparation, and wholly without any knowledge or other enthusiasm, unless it were a priggish love of argument which I had begun to develop. I had lived upon a rabbit warren: and what a rabbit warren of a life it is that I have been surveying.

My brother John, three years older than myself, and of a moral character more manly and on a higher level, had chosen the Navy and went off to the preparatory college at Portsmouth. He was a lad of popular as well as upright character. But he evidently underwent persecution for righteousness' sake at the college, which was then (say about 1820) in a bad condition. Of this, though he was never querulous, his letters bore the traces: and I cannot but think they must have exercised upon me some kind of influence for good.

As to miscellaneous notices, I had great affinity with the trades of joiners and of bricklayers. Physically I must have been rather tough: for my brother John took me down at about ten years old to wrestle in the stables with an older lad of that region, whom I threw. Among our greatest enjoyments were undoubtedly the annual Guy Fawx bonfires for which we had always liberal allowances of wreck timber and a tar-barrel. I remember seeing when about eight or nine my first case of a dead body. It was the child of the head gardener Derbyshire and was laid in the cottage bed by tender hands with nice and clean accompaniments. It seemed to me pleasing and in no way repelled me, but it made no deep impression. And now I remember that I used to teach pretty regularly on Sundays in the Sunday school built by my father near the Primrose Bridge. It was I think a duty done not under constraint: but I can recollect nothing which associates it with a seriously religious life in myself.

I remember that during this period I had I think when about ten years old passing admiration for a handsome girl of about the same age named Jane Blackwell. Her brothers were our local friends. I doubt if she was ever conscious of the flame she had raised: but I remember dwelling on the thought of her and this I am afraid during the church service. I mention this because it connects itself with a defect in my mental organisation or a slowness in its development, which was this. Though I was attracted, as it seems, by beauty in the concrete, I had no conception of it in the abstract. At one time my father had no less than four young ladies, just grown up, staying in his house. One had a very strictly fine handsome face, another had a sweet kindly countenance, but hardly pretty. I admired the latter not the former, and was puzzled when others differed from me. Once I remember when I was riding (for my riding, absolutely untrained, began rather early) a sprinkling of village boys whom I passed cried, 'Ay, what a pretty horse', and I recollect feeling that I did not know what it was in the horse that they meant thus to stamp with their approval.

In an addition to this section (undated, but apparently written in 1896 or 1897) Gladstone elaborated the point made in the last paragraph (ADD. MS 44791, f. 68).

In the review of my childhood, I think that like other children, I had a faculty of imagination from the beginning, but it was one both weak and wild. I used to think or dream of myself as furnished in certain odd ways for certain courses of life which I was then left to prosecute at my will. But there was a great want alike of definite purpose, and of dominant attraction, an emancipation from the rule of reason, without the distinct conception of the rule of beauty, or of any other allegiance. In respect to beauty I remember an odd particular which testified to my deficiencies. I used to ask myself what physical beauty was? and could not get an answer. I recollect that at one time my father had a batch of four nieces or quasi-nieces staying with him for several weeks at Seaforth. One of them was very decidedly handsome: but with rather an immobile countenance. Another was full of smiles and kindly expression without the smallest pretension to good looks. To *this* one in my own mind I awarded the palm of beauty, not recognising the smallest claim to it in the undeniably fine forms of the other.

Notwithstanding all this it has undoubtedly happened that in the course of my life I have become and remained one of the most convinced and uncompromising asserters of the substantive character of beauty, in opposition to those who teach that it is conventional or that it takes rank below the dignity of an independent and changeless principle. It may be that beauty is in metaphysic what pleasure is in ethic.

ETON STAGE

ADD.MS 44790, ff. 66–68   *16 July 1892*

I come now to the Eton stage of my life; which begins to be less trivial and more diversified. It moves also from the shallows towards the depths: but I reserve any notice of this movement for my more interior narrative.

I was sent to Eton in September 1821, to the house of Mrs. Shurey, a dame, the door of which looked down the Long Walk, while the windows looked into the very crowded churchyard: from which I never received the smallest inconvenience, though it was my custom (when master of the room) to sleep with my window open both summer and winter. I went under the wing of my eldest brother, then in the Upper Division, and this helped my start and much mitigated the sense of isolation which attends the first launch at a public school. (At Mr. Rawson's I had been a day boy living at home: and with the intervals of I think two London sojourns for the sessions of 1819 and 1820.)

My tutor was the Rev. H. H. Knapp (practically all tutors were clergymen in those days). He was a reputed Whig, an easy and kind tempered man, with a sense of scholarship, but no power of discipline, and no energy of desire to impress himself upon his pupils. I recollect but one piece of advice received (later) from him. It was that I should form my poetical taste upon Darwin, whose poems (*The Botanic Garden* and *Loves of the Plants*)I obediently read through in consequence.

I was placed in the middle remove fourth form, a place slightly better than the common run, but inferior to what a boy of good preparation or real excellence would have taken. My nearest friend of the first period was W. W. Farr, a boy of intelligence, something over my age, next above me in the school. His friendship however was not all good to me.[1]

At this time there was not in me any desire to know or to excel. My first pursuits were football and then cricket: the first I did not long pursue, and in the second I never managed to rise above mediocrity and what was termed 'the twenty-two'.

There was a barrister named Henry Hall Joy, a connection of my father through his first wife, and a man who had taken a first class at Oxford. He was very kind to me and had made some efforts to inspire me with a love of books if not of knowledge. Indeed I had read Froissart and Hume with Smollett, but only for the battles, and always skipping when I came to the sections headed 'A Parliament'. Joy had a taste for classics and made visions for me of honours at Oxford. But the subject only danced before my eyes as a will of the wisp and without attracting me. I remained stagnant, without heart or hope. A change however arrived about Easter 1822. My 'remove' was then under Hawtrey (afterwards Headmaster and Provost) who was always on the look out for any bud which he could warm with a little sunshine. It was with as much astonishment as delight that I was filled when I learned [unfinished].

DR. HAWTREY

The following section is not part of the autobiography, but was written at the request of Francis St. John Thackeray, author of the biography of Hawtrey in the Dictionary of National Biography, where extracts from it are quoted. See Thackeray's letters to Gladstone of 1 January 1890 (ADD.MS 44509, f. 5) and 18 March 1891 (ADD.MS 44512, f. 178).

ADD.MS 44790, ff. 1–3

My recollections of Dr. Hawtrey are few but they are vivid. I was not his pupil at Eton: and I was only under him in the school for one half of the year 1822, when I was in the upper remove of the fourth form. During that period (I had gone first to Eton in September 1821) he sent me up for good. It was an event in my life: and he and it together then for the first time inspired me with a desire to learn and to do,

---

[1] See Appendix 1.

which I never wholly lost, though there was much fluctuation before it hardened into principle and rule at a later period of my life.

I well recollect however the morning of this (for me) great occurrence. I was ordered to repair to Mr. Hawtrey's house. There I saw him and he went through the verses very carefully with me, making such corrections, or improvements perhaps, as he thought necessary. The novelty of the situation to me was extreme, for he all the way through maintained the kindest manner, and appeared to feel an interest in me, which I, a boy of twelve, thought singular and unaccountable, but at the same time enjoyed with much fluttering and a thrill of new hope and satisfaction.

Though I had no direct intercourse with Dr. (then Mr.) Hawtrey during all my remaining years at Eton, I was very intimate for the later two or three years with Arthur Hallam who boarded in his house, so that we messed together though we lived at opposite ends of Eton, the breakfast being at his room and mine in alternate weeks. Being so much in his house and having in this way formed a friendship with the Dean of Windsor, who also lived there, I naturally had more means of forming an opinion about him than Eton boys in general. I looked upon him as first and best among all the masters of the school at the time.

The late Lord Mount Temple and his elder brother Lord Cowper both I think lived in that house. It might be well to inquire as to Mr. Kinglake, but I will not be positive about him. My brother-in-law Sir Stephen Glynne was among the inmates, and was a favourite pupil, much admitted into the domestic interior.

After leaving Eton I saw a good deal of this excellent and most highly accomplished man, full of taste and knowledge, of liberality, and of modesty. In the love of his pursuits he seemed to forget all self-love. He was thought to be rather smart in dress, with an innocent smartness, and always maintained at a high level the character of a clergyman. In the year 1840, as the colleague of my brother-in-law Lord Lyttelton, I examined for the Newcastle Scholarship, spending that week in his house and when free in his company. I also visited him at other times, and found all intercourse with him delightful.

I recollect well the overboiling so to speak of his pleasure on an election when the numbers on the school list touched 777. He almost danced for joy. He was Etonian to the core. I remember a conversation in which he pointed out how Eton, apparently from the solidity of its traditions, had been and continued less dependent than other public schools upon the celebrity and personal distinctions of its headmasters.

Not very long after I left it in December 1827, Eton underwent without doubt a regenerating process. The popular supposition is that it was swept along by a tide of renovation due to the fame and the contagious example of Dr. Arnold at Rugby. But, though Dr. Arnold was a great man, this in my opinion is an error; Eton was in a singularly small degree open to influence from other public schools. I have always held that there were three persons to whom Eton was more indebted than any others for the new life poured into her arteries, and that these three were, Dr. Hawtrey, tutor, headmaster, and Provost: the contemporary Duke of Newcastle who by a stroke singularly happy founded the Newcastle scholarship: and Bishop George Selwyn, the scholar, Christian, and hero, who had Eton graven on the core of his heart and whose influence during the many years he spent there must have been very great.   *3 January 1890*

P.S. I have forgotten I see to refer to Dr. Hawtrey's library, of which I had some but hardly an intimate or general knowledge. Speaking of the time after 1840, I remember that it had to be accommodated in about twelve rooms of his house. It was a very finished library: in keeping with the character of the owner. I do not recollect an unbound or unkempt book: if there were any such, they were hidden in closets. I think there were many select and some rare works: but I cannot give minute information. It is pleasant to me to speak or write about him. R.I.P.   *3 January 1890*

DR. KEATE 1823 (?)

ADD.MS 44791, ff. 64–67

I must not dismiss the Eton period of my life without a notice of Dr. Keate. To him nature had accorded a stature of only about five feet, or say five feet one: but by costume, voice, manner (including a little swagger) and character he made himself in every way the capital figure on the Eton stage and his departure marked I imagine the departure of the old race of English public school masters, as the name of Dr. Busby seems to me to mark its introduction.

In connection with his name I shall give two anecdotes separated by a considerable interval of years.

About the year of 1823, the eloquence of Mr. Edward Irving drew crowds to his church in London which was Presbyterian and in or near Hatton Garden. These crowds were largely supplied from beyond his own persuasion. It required careful previous arrangements to secure comfortable accommodation. The preacher was solemn, majestic (notwithstanding the squint) and impressive; carrying all the appearance of devoted earnestness.

My father had on a certain occasion, when I was still a small Eton boy, taken time by the forelock, and secured the use of a convenient pew in the first rank of the gallery. From this elevated situation we surveyed at ease and leisure the struggling crowds below. The crush was everywhere great, but greatest of all in the centre aisle. Here the mass of human beings mercilessly compressed swayed continually backwards and forwards, I suppose as the sense of the situation became intolerable in one quarter or another. Judge, if indeed anyone can judge, of my intense and transcendental delight, when amidst the fellow mortals who were undergoing this formidable discipline as the price of their curiosity or devotion I detected the puffed out and rounded and almost dwarfish figure of Dr. Keate! He was at a great disadvantage from being so much below the average stature of those who composed the undulating mass, and the face always red attained, or appeared to me to attain, to a preternatural redness. Such a $\pi\epsilon\rho\iota\pi\epsilon\tau\epsilon\iota\alpha$[1], such a reversal of human conditions of being, as that now exhibited between the Eton lower boy uplifted to the luxurious gallery pew, and the headmaster of Eton, whom I was accustomed to see in the gloomy desk of the Upper School with vacant space, and terror, all around him, it must be hard for anyone to conceive, except the two who were the subjects of it. I do not know whether spiteful fortune infused the last drop of bitterness into his cup of mortification by causing him to recognise under his sad circumstances the exulting countenance of one usually counted among his little slaves, but undoubtedly his position was one far worse than that in the Ashbourne dilly

While the prest bodkin groans and sweats between,

while on the other hand the malignant pleasure I remember to have felt exceeded in its full flavoured intensity any previous experience of my life.

---

[1] 'Turning about', 'reverse of circumstances'.

I will now after the manner of novelists ask my reader to effect along with me a transition of some eighteen years, and to witness another and if not a more complete yet a worthier turning of the tables. In the year 1841 there was a very special Eton dinner held in Willis's rooms to commemorate the four hundredth centenary of the school. Lord Morpeth, afterwards Lord Carlisle, was in the chair. On his right, not far off him, was Dr. Keate, to whom I chanced to have a seat almost opposite. In those days at public dinners, cheering was marked by gradations. As the Queen was suspected of sympathy with the Liberal Government of Lord Melbourne which advised her, the toast of the Sovereign was habitually received with a moderate amount of acclamation decently and thriftily doled out. On the other hand the Queen Dowager either was or was believed to be Conservative: and her health consequently figured as the toast of the evening, and drew forth as a matter of course by far its loudest acclamation. So much was routine; and we went through it as usual. But the real toast of the evening was yet to come. I suppose it to be beyond doubt that of the assembled company the vastly preponderating majority had been under his sway at Eton; and if when in that condition anyone of those had been asked how he liked Dr. Keate he would beyond question have answered: 'Keate? Oh! I hate him.' It is equally beyond doubt that to the persons of the whole of them, with the rarest exceptions, it had been the case of Dr. Keate to administer the salutary correction of the birch. But upon this occasion, when his name had been announced the scene was indescribable. Queen and Queen Dowager alike vanished into insignificance: they were nowhere. The roar of cheering had a beginning, but never knew satiety or end. Like the huge waves at Biarritz, the floods of cheering continually recommenced; the whole process was such that we seemed all to have lost our self-possession and to be hardly able to keep our seats. When at length it became possible Keate rose: that is to say his head was projected slightly over the heads of his two neighbours. He struggled to speak: I will not say I heard every syllable; for there were no syllables: speak he could not: he tried in vain to mumble a word or two but wholly failed, renounced the vain struggle and sat down. It was certainly one of the most moving spectacles that in my whole life I have witnessed. *12 January 1897*

ARTHUR HALLAM 1824?–33

ADD.MS 44790, ff. 84–88   *25 November 1893*

Mr. Le Gallienne has kindly sent me his reprint of the *Remains* in part of Arthur Hallam, with his own singularly discerning preface. I rejoice in this publication. It will tend to the accomplishment of Arthur Hallam's unfulfilled renown. But he was one of those to whom it was more given, I may say yet more given, to *be* than to *do*. Of him as he was I have a very few words to say, *my* stone which I am about to deposit on his *cairn*.

Mr. Le Gallienne well observed that it was the Italian journey, undertaken in the company of his family, after he had left Eton, which produced a great, marked, and principal development of his mind and genius. The world has long been familiar with him through a medium. As it knows that Tennyson is a great fact in literature, so it knows that Arthur Hallam is a great fact in Tennyson, the foundation stone on which is built the unparalleled monument of *In Memoriam*. It would be well for the world to know all about the beautiful, and indeed gorgeous, flower of his life and character, that can be known. I think that Mr. Le Gallienne has done much in this sense. As a witness I can do something; and the evidence that I have to give is entirely my own, and would have been so even had not the ranks of his contemporaries been at this date (November 1893) not so much thinned as laid low by death.

[1]My friendship with Arthur Hallam began about 1824, and was in itself remarkable only during the period when both of us were at Eton which terminated in July 1827. I had sense enough to regard it all along as a high privilege though one which I found it impracticable to turn to adequate account. But to this hour I am unable to conceive how on his side he could have found for it any sustaining amount of *pabulum*. It was without any doubt the zenith of my boyhood; and it must have been the nadir of his.

We were I think at almost all points contrasted more or less. He had been from the first of early and quick development: I very slow in growth. Of philosophy he had already a tinge: I was outside it. In poetry he was I think on the right lines: I, if ever I had a chance, had

---

[1] At the top of page 1 of the manuscript there is a pencilled note by Gladstone: 'Begin on page 2', i.e., with this paragraph.

been seriously damaged by a piece of bad advice, the only advice I think which my poor dear tutor at Eton ever gave me: namely to form my style upon the style of Dr. Darwin. In English history, he was with his father, as well he might be: I was in the camp of Clarendon, if not of Hume. In modern politics we were somewhat nearer; but while I was a worshipper of Mr. Canning, he was a Whig. On my own behalf I will record that I think he had in one point a large advantage over me from without. He had evidently from the first a large share of cultivated domestic education: with a father absorbed in diversified business, I had little or none. I cannot recollect to have had a sense of ever having learned anything, until I went to Eton, and had been there some little time: and it was then entirely due not to my own tutor but to his, Dr. then Mr. Hawtrey, that I first owed the reception of a spark, the *divina particula aura*, and conceived a dim idea, that in some time, manner, and degree, I might come to know. Even then, as I had really no instructor, my efforts at Eton, down to 1827, were of perhaps the purest plodding ever known. Over and above all this he had over me the advantage of an immense moral superiority both original and acquired. With all this, he was of the most tolerant temper imaginable. What I may now know and feel of tolerance has been a lesson drilled into me by the experience of political life.

With all this, strange as it may appear, we became at Eton friends rather exceptionally close. He was a very little, a few places, below me in the school, but I do not know that our intercourse had schoolwork to any great extent for its subject matter. Much more did we deal with the politics of British history; and especially with what may be termed from this point of view the eternal reign of Charles I. Later on he was a Foxite, I a Pittite, as I still am in the main down to 1793: then I was no better than a slave to Bishop Tomline and that congeries of parliamentary reports and little more, which, founding himself upon the scissors, he published as a biography. In religion we had no disputes: I think we were agreed. I mentioned philosophy: and I think it was he who put down in our debating society the question whether mathematics (of which I believe he was incapable) or metaphysics were entitled to a preference. He then told me that his father had written to him: 'Your dispute between *Mat.* and *Met.* is truly ridiculous.'

On the whole I fear my memory is in the main a blank both as to the much I got, and the little I gave, in our joint living. But it is guaranteed by a fact which cannot be mistaken among any who knew the Eton life of that day, or its tradition. We formed, and I think kept to, a practice of regularly breakfasting together, week about in his room and in mine. Such a practice was yet uncommon between boys in the same house. But we were in different houses (Hawtrey's and (Dame) Stansmore's) and the houses lay nearly at the opposite extremities of Eton. His room, at Hawtrey's, does not now exist. But next to it was the room of Gerald Wellesley, Dean of Windsor: and this proximity gave occasion or aid to the formation of another very valuable friendship, which lasted to my great profit for some sixty years, until that light was put out.

Under the influence of Milnes Gaskell, a few of us contracted the habit, besides our activity in the Eton debating society, of conducting private informal debates on the Pitt and Fox period, which was prohibited as too recent for our susceptible minds by the school authorities. A word on Milnes Gaskell elsewhere.

I remember well, and it was probably a forecast of the mournful future, that if ever I entered Arthur Hallam's room after he had been closely engaged in work, I used to find him flushed up to the very eyes, in a way quite beyond his usual colour, which was always high.

In closing this poor and hungry sketch I must say that the life of Arthur Hallam at Eton, so far as I knew it, was an ideal life. I declare that when looking back I do not detect in it a single deviation from the ideal, in temper, word, or act. Tennyson was as happy, in having such material made ready to his hand, as Hallam was in the opportunity of a friendship so lofty, and so fraternal.

As material records of Arthur Hallam, I possess a number of his letters, and a copy of the quarto (and first) edition of his father's *Constitutional History* in which he wrote name [*sic*] on presenting it to me, I think when he left Eton a few months before me.

Little remains for me to tell. The rapid revolution which so soon followed in his case, not only aggravated (so to speak) his superiority, but took him if I may use the expression quite out of shot. His letters perhaps will be found best to tell the story. He endured long and with much longsuffering his halting companion. But by degrees, and wholly from inequality not quarrel, the correspondence fell away. I saw him at Oxford when he came over there as an undergraduate with Sunderland and Milnes (Lord Houghton) on the Cambridge mission of propagandism on behalf of Shelley's fame. I visited him not long after, I think in 1831, at Malvern; when he told me that Coleridge might have been either the greatest poet, or the greatest philosopher, of his age, but that his poetry and his philosophy had been allowed to damage one another. In 1832 I was either abroad or actively engaged in my first political campaign at Newark. In 1833, we were both in London for the session, and I please myself with the recollection that our personal intercourse revived in a way to promise growth. But it ended, alas! for me, with the catastrophe at Vienna. And I conclude with the beautiful verse from Ariosto, which his father used in the privately printed volume of *Remains*

> Vattene in pace, alma beata e bella.

I may some day add a word or two on his father, and on his younger brother.

POLITICS

MY EARLIER POLITICAL OPINIONS

(I) THE DESCENT

ADD.MS 44790, ff. 26–35

It cannot be a matter of wonder if my earlier political opinions, often made the subject of reference, have been ill understood; for they were formed under many and sometimes complex influences, and they form a whole far from congruous.

1. The dominant influence on my first political ideas was certainly that of Mr. Canning of whom my father, previously a supporter of the Whigs, had become a determined follower. In all matters civil and religious I was thoroughly submissive, and unquestioningly believed whatever was taught me, or whatever insensibly filtered into me from my surroundings, to be right. Thus like my father I was when a boy Tory in a general way.

2. But this was subject in Mr. Canning and his followers to three very important heads of exception. First the subject which was by far the most prominently before the public eye was that of Roman Catholic emancipation. On this I was with Canning and had no sympathy with the other party. The second concerned the beginnings of the movement towards freedom of trade, which made Mr. Huskisson (in particular) even more hateful to the Tory party than Cobden or Peel was at its completion. I remember visiting in the year 1828 a silk-manufactory at Macclesfield. The silk handkerchiefs exhibited to the visitors were then just placed in competition with French goods, subject to a protective duty of 30%. Of commercial laws I understood nothing: but the thought which on the view passed distinctly through my mind was 'what wretched productions: why should the law give factitious advantage to the sale of such commodities!' Thirdly there was the hostility of Mr. Canning to the Holy Alliance.

I was not a boy of strong political leanings. I went into the Eton debating society in (I think) 1825, which was the focus of what little thought there was in the school outside our school life. But our nascent energies were repressed by a rule which the authorities had imposed and which precluded our discussing any public question which was not more than fifty years old. And I remember that Dr. Keate complained to me of our debating the Rohilla War of Warren Hastings because it had taken place only fifty-two years before.

But spirits keener or larger (or both) than mine were at work: and although the rule remained the great controversies of Pitt and Fox came to be debated among us (or rather some among these, for I do not think we rose to the French war or the Irish union) at clandestine or irregular meetings, sometimes in the very room devoted to the lawful assemblies, sometimes in the private room of Milnes Gaskell beyond Barnespool Bridge. Only four or five of the more select spirits gathered on these occasions.

Within the society itself Canningism had a certain retrospective working, and we debated with animation the laws and proceedings against recusants which marked the later years of Queen Elizabeth. I severely condemned them but with more zeal than knowledge for I had never examined the question whether they were theological or political. They were defended by George Selwyn, afterwards the noble-minded Bishop of New Zealand.

We were all however of a milder or sterner inclination to Toryism insofar that we rather scoffed at a somewhat heavy boy named Law, a colleger, who defended Radical principles, and who was so imprudent as to make the more than questionable admission that 'the Bible was a Tory book'.

I have had however an opportunity of refreshing my recollections upon the colour of my politics at this time, memory if alone being an insufficient guide. Last spring Messrs. Sotheby informed me that they were commissioned to sell a mass of family papers which had belonged to Mr. W. W. Farr, a Hampshire gentleman, a contemporary and friend of mine at Eton. He left Eton a considerable time before me, and the collection contained I think some 25 or 30 letters of mine addressed to him after he had quitted it. Messrs. Sotheby were instructed to hold back these letters if I should deem their publication objectionable. I read a sufficient portion of them and expressed a desire that they should be withdrawn from the sale, as piecemeal biography, and otherwise. They dwelt much on the proceedings of the Eton debaters, among whom he had been counted: and they exhibited my opinions as Liberal I think to the full extent which Canningism allowed.[1] The

---

[1] See Appendix 1.

subject of Reform, it must be remembered, was practically in abeyance during these years.

Then comes the Oxford stage. And here, during the larger part of my time as an undergraduate, my interests were not political, but were either academical or theological. The records of the Oxford Union, to which I belonged, would show that I was neither a constant nor a frequent speaker there. However, the character and merits of the Duke of Wellington's Government came under review, and I made what was for me a considerable effort against it. I am not now clear as to the main motives which governed me: but I think I was either dissatisfied or even more strongly excited by the wayward and arbitrary expulsion of the Canningite ministers in 1828, and I do not doubt that I disapproved the grounds on which the Duke of Wellington founded his action in promoting the repeal of the disabilities. I also remember sharing the general, and I now suppose unnecessary, indignation upon the advancement of Bishop Phillpotts to the bench. I was in sharp opposition on this occasion to Sidney Herbert, afterwards my warm unfailing friend. I recollect well my introduction to Lady Canning, the widow of the Minister, at breakfast in the rooms of her son Charles, who was then a student of Christ Church. I was struck by her earnestness and intenseness; especially, when she spoke of the relations between her husband and the Tories, her fingers quivered to the tips with emotion. This introduction was followed by her kind and warm friendship in later years.

All this time however I was for the era of Charles I a Cavalier, and used to debate much on the question with my loved friend Arthur Hallam, about whom, and whose condescension in giving me his warm friendship, I must speak elsewhere. He followed his distinguished father, nowhere probably more dispassionate than on this great subject. I read through Clarendon's history, followed his line, and nothing could bring me to believe in the bad faith of the King, a point on which so much depends. The best excuse for me is that the modern elucidations of the epoch had not been available. But it was long before I could entirely shake off these illusions of my first youth and assume the requisite sternness in estimating Charles I.

I was not in sympathy with the high and dry Toryism of contemporary Oxford which I never loved. But what estranged me from it was not I think the true love of liberty, which I had not yet learned: it was its hostility to Evangelicalism which my early training had taught me to regard as another name for Christianity. I remember being taught to regard, and regarding, Mount's Bible as a kind of heretical book. I will not now enter further on this subject which would draw me too far aside. I only name it, because I am sure that while it indisposed me to the Toryism of Oxford it laid in me other foundations of Toryism. I think that I must have had at this time coming upon me some dread of a developed Liberalism as a rebellion against God and a foe to Christianity, which exercised a great and (I think) disorderly influence on the mind of Newman. Strong Protestant opinions (into which Hooker had introduced as I must elsewhere tell some leakage), and the very large hold which religious interests (not at all implying an equivalent amount of religious life or progress) had taken upon me, had prepared me to colour political subjects with fanatical interpretations, and I never before my political life began got beyond Mr. Canning's 'everything *for* the people, nothing *by* the people'.

I gradually became at Oxford a hard worker and read Rousseau's *Contrat Social* which had no influence upon me, and the writings of Burke which had a great deal. I remember heartily assenting to the observation of a good and clever undergraduate friend, a Thornton, when he said 'I want no Toryism beyond that of Burke'. But I was thus as completely under his mastery with regard to the French Revolution as he was (I think) under the influence of a thoroughly one-sided view of French history: while his views of reform in Parliament, in combination with those of Mr. Canning, formed a most dangerous preparation for the coming crisis in the history of my ideas.

This crisis came with the promulgation of the plan of reform prepared by the Government of Lord Grey on March 1, 1831. My prepossessions were against Lord Grey on account of his conduct in 1827 on the Corn Bill of Mr. Canning. I was charged with the Canning and Burke ideas of reform. Mr. Hallam was known to be alarmed. Radicalism was delighted. Sir Walter Scott was against it: and that great magician was with me an authority in all things. Oxford was mad. I was only saved by the strong pressure of work from unchecked political excitement: but this was the year of the schools, and unless for a single speech at the Union I do not think the politics even of reform were allowed dangerously to seduce my thoughts, though I remember some foolish pranks: such for example as printing at my own costs and charges some foolish anti-reform placards based upon the idea, then standing for gospel with anti-reformers, that simply and without qualification reform was revolution.[1] One anecdote I must record against myself. The county election was raging. George Harcourt (whose admirable speaking on the hustings I really admired) was a candidate: and Lord Norreys stood on the Tory side. I was circulating in the mob as a volunteer (like all the other undergraduates) on the side of Norreys. I held forth to a working man, possibly a forty shilling freeholder, on the established text, reform was revolution. To corroborate my doctrine I said, 'Why, look at the revolutions in foreign countries', meaning of course France and Belgium. The man looked hard at me and said these very words: 'Damn all foreign countries: what has old England got to do with foreign countries?' This is not the only time when I have received an important lesson from a humble source.

The Oxford undergraduates were almost to a man carried off their feet by the storm; nay we subscribed our little monies for the anti-reform election fund, with Sidney Herbert for our organ (a man essentially gentle and moderate) who I rather think took it up to London and presented this offering of the political babes and sucklings through his brother-in-law, Lord Clanwilliam. From this epoch dates my early Toryism, and from this source it sprang. And I still go so far as to hold (but no farther) that, by reason of the extraordinary peculiarities of the old system, and the then unknown nature of the region in which we were about to travel, the opposition to the first Reform Bill was less unreasonable than the opposition offered in subsequent years to subsequent measures, when the success of the first great experiment had been established.

Behold me then in a new position. On the one hand bound down to ten or twelve hours a day of academic work—more often I think twelve than ten—on the other hand inwardly possessed with a persuasion that the Reform Bill was to be the ruin of the country.

Where lay the root of this folly? It lay here. Early education, civil or religious, had never taught me, and Oxford had rather tended to hide from me, the great fact that liberty is a great and precious gift of God, and that human excellence cannot grow up in a nation without it.

And yet I do not hesitate to say Oxford had now at this time laid the foundations of my liberalism. School pursuits had revealed little; but, in the region of philosophy, she had initiated if not inured me to the pursuit of truth as an end of study. The splendid integrity of

---

[1] See Appendix 3.

Aristotle, and still more of Butler, conferred upon me an inestimable service. Elsewhere I have not scrupled to speak with severity of myself but I declare that while in the arms of Oxford I was possessed through and through with a single minded and passionate love of truth, with a virgin love of truth, so that, although I might be swathed in clouds of prejudice there was something of an eye within, that might gradually pierce them.

Thus then I stood

Mi ritrovai in una selva oscura   Inferno, I, 2.[1]

How did I escape?   *12 July 1892*

AUTOBIOGRAPHICAL RETROSPECT

ADD.MS 44790, ff. 107–110   *22 June 1894*

The stock in trade of ideas with which I set out on the career of parliamentary life was a small one. I do not think the general tendencies of my mind were in the time of my youth illiberal. It was a great accident which threw me into the anti-liberal attitude which having taken it up I held with energy. It was the accident of the Reform Bill of 1831. For teachers or idols in politics or both I had had Mr. Burke and Mr. Canning. I followed them in their dread of reform and probably caricatured them as a raw unskilled student caricatures his master. But this one idea on which they were anti-liberal became the master key of the situation and absorbed into itself for the time the whole of politics. This however was not my only disadvantage. I had been educated in an extremely narrow Churchmanship, that of the Evangelical party, and though Oxford and Bishop Butler had begun my emancipation it had as yet made but a limited progress. Of the greatest of historical facts, the fact that we had among us a divine society, I had no conception. This narrow Churchmanship was of course morbid and too readily embraced the idea that the extension of representative principles which was then the essential work of Liberalism was associated with irreligion; an idea quite foreign to my older sentiments on behalf of Roman Catholic Emancipation. Thus my politics of the hour were tinged with religious fanaticism. Besides these two elements of a creed and a practice I found myself

---

[1] The quotation should read 'per una selva'.

thrust by circumstances into colonial policy. And this first in its most disagreable shape, that is to say in its connection with what became for the moment the commanding question of slavery. I can now see plainly enough the sad defects, the real illiberalism of my opinions on that subject: yet they were not illiberal as compared with the ideas of the time and as declared in Parliament in 1833 they obtained the commendation of the Liberal leader. But what I have said amply bears out my introductory assertion as to the smallness of my stock in trade. How little I then knew or even dreamed not only of the great domestic subjects which were to come up and of the laborious part I was to bear in them but of that yet wider circumscription into which I was to be carried: of those influences seemingly casual which were to make me more conspicuous in many foreign countries than almost any politician of my time: in connection especially with Naples and Italy first, then with Greece, the Balkan Peninsula and the whole question of the Turkish Empire so truly and largely *welt-historisch*.

MY EARLIER POLITICAL OPINIONS

(II) THE EXTRICATION

ADD.MS 44790, ff. 36–65

'Work, work, work' occupied me throughout 1831. I carried out with me some little book printed or manuscript even when I rode for my short hour of exercise. But one streak of Toryism, singular enough in itself, lies across the history of that year. I decided that, before encountering the final schools, it was necessary for me to have one week's holiday. And I determined to go up to London and, if I could possibly get orders of admission to the House of Lords, to hear every hour of the debate in that House on the second reading of the Reform Bill. I went: it was the month of October 1831.[1] The orders were forthcoming but had to be hunted out in the mornings. There was no such thing as chair or stool. But there were certain iron horizontal railings covered with red cloth (it was in the old House of Lords before the fire), between half an inch and an inch thick, on which I used from time to time to clamber up when the feet were too weary, and enjoy a partial and *cutting* repose. I

---

[1] The date was added afterwards in pencil.

heard very nearly the whole debate, sat up I believe the whole of the Friday night, and on Saturday morning when it ended walked up to Hatchetts and returned to Oxford by an early coach. So far as I can remember the reason of the case seemed to me, in the debate, to lie throughout with the opponents of the Reform Bill.

While my opinions were in this hopeless condition, my thoughts were not turned into the road of politics. I resumed my work at Oxford and passed through the schools; whereupon I at once (this statement shall be tested by the dates) wrote a letter to my father expressing my desire to become a clergyman. He wrote back in very affectionate terms pressing me to follow a secular career. I subjoin my actual words.[1]

This matter having been settled by my compliance, it was arranged that I should travel with my naval brother John for six months on the Continent. In July 1832, to my unbounded astonishment, I received in our hotel at Milan a letter from my father transmitting to me an offer from the Duke of Newcastle made through him, to give me the Newcastle influence at Newark for the coming election. This offer could. . . .[2] The seat was in Liberal hands but was deemed recoverable. I wrote back Aye. In the month of September [1832] I was summoned from Torquay to begin my canvass and after a forty hours journey I arrived at Newark on the top of the High Flyer coach at midnight. Friends were there to welcome me and at eight next morning I turned out from the Clinton Arms for the canvass with band, flags and procession. I spent much time in the town before I was landed at the head of the two days poll on the [13th] of December 1832. My opinions were I think considered up to the mark by the constituency, but not in any way beyond it. I give details elsewhere of this curious piece of experience, for such it was to a youth in his twenty third year, young of his age, who had seen little or nothing of the world, who resigned himself to politics, but whose desire had been for the ministry of God. The remains of this desire operated unfortunately. They made me tend to glorify in an extravagant manner and degree not only the religious character of the State, which in reality stood low, but also the religious mission of the Conservative party. There was, to my eyes, a certain element of AntiChrist in the Reform Act and that Act was cordially hated, though the leaders soon perceived that there could be no step backwards. It was only under the

---

[1] See Appendix 2.
[2] This sentence is left incomplete in MS.

(second) Government of Sir Robert Peel that I learned how impotent [and] barren was the conservative office for the Church, though that Government was formed of men able, upright, and extremely well disposed. It was well for me that the unfolding destiny carried me off in a considerable degree from political ecclesiasticism of which I should [at] that time have made a sad mess. Providence directed that my mind should find its food in other pastures than those in which my youthfulness would have loved to seek it. I spoke in 1834 on university tests, in 1835 on the Irish Church (which I thought was indefensible except as a witness to divine truth), in 1837 on Church rates, and in 1840 on education. All this was done in concurrence with the general views of the Tory party. But I went beyond them in State Churchism: for I recollect voting, very early in the day, against Maynooth, against the admission of the Jews (notwithstanding my opinions on the Roman Catholic disabilities, as I held in the matter the rather shallow views of Arnold). It was my opinion that as to religions other than those of the State, the State should tolerate only, and not pay. So I was against salaries for prison chaplains not of the Church, and I applied a logic plaster to all difficulties. I believed in the personality of the State, and in its ownership of the taxes, without which ownership I admitted that the exclusive appropriation would have been unjust. So that Macaulay, judging from acts of this kind, and the book before him, was justified (though he put in exaggeration) in treating me as belonging to the ultra section of Tories, had he limited himself to ecclesiastical questions.

It was not however to these but to colonial affairs that the chief part of my parliamentary time and attention were given during my first stage of active life from 1832 to 1841. When I came into Parliament the slave question was uppermost, and I was thrust into connection with it whether I would or not, for my father was a prominent West India proprietor, and Serjeant Wilde warrantably worked the question against me without stint during the three months of prolonged conflict at Newark. It was on this subject that I made my maiden speech on June 3, 1833. I have perused it lately, as it was printed in the *Mirror of Parliament* with dissatisfaction. But, apart from all changes of political complexion, the advance of social opinion generally on that dreadful subject has been immense. For the time, it was not wholly bad. It argued (I think justly) for compensation, but did not say a word, I think, unfavourable to the great change. At any rate it was, on the same or a subsequent evening very warmly commended in debate by Mr. Stanley (Lord Derby), the

Minister in charge of the bill. I rather think also that it was favourably noticed by Lord Althorp.

In 1835, during the short government of Sir R. Peel, I was under-Secretary of State for the Colonies, with Lord Aberdeen for my chief. In that or the following year I worked on a South African committee and took up the cause of the Cape farmers against Downing Street. In 1838 I defended the apprenticeship which was supported by the Whig government. The speech was an elaborate, and I believe a moderate statement. Meanwhile the large and significant question of Canada came upon the stage. I had not yet attained to a full conception of the true colonial policy, but I must have moved in the right direction, for, under the Melbourne government, Lord J. Russell, who led the way in Liberal ministerial thought, passed an eulogium on my speeches with regard to that particular question. I myself remember that one Painter printed a Canada speech of mine as a 'Conservative' speech, and that I wondered what there was in it which he considered as in a distinguishing sense Conservative. What a mercy it was, though I did not then know it, which thus directed my mind, not without earnestness of purpose, to subjects with regard to which its action was in no way fettered by any ingrained prejudice.

Inasmuch as it was my authorship, and not my speeches in Parliament, which stamped me with a certain kind of ultraism, and set me up to be gibbeted by Lord Macaulay, I ought to explain how it was that I came to be an author. I had read Coleridge, Locke, Warburton, and Paley, but was not anxious to meddle. But a *furore* for Church establishment came down upon the Conservative squadrons between 1833 and 1838, due especially to the activity of the Presbyterian Established Church of Scotland, then not disrupted, and especially to the zealous and truly noble propagandism of Dr. Chalmers, a man with the energy of a giant, and the simplicity of a child. He came to London I think in the spring of 1837. At or about that time we had a movement for fresh parliamentary grants to build churches, I think in Scotland. The leaders did not seem much to like it but had to follow it. I remember dining at Sir R. Peel's with the Scotch deputation. It included Collins, a church bookseller of note, who told me that no sermon ought ever to fall short of an hour, for in less time than that it was not possible to explain any text of the Holy Scripture. Dr. Chalmers, originally I think a Liberal, drifted with the religious movement to the side of the Conservatives. He delivered in the Hanover Square Rooms a series of lectures on church establishments, in the broadest of broad accents, but with a warm and catching enthusiasm. The Tory party attended them largely: I for one devoutly, and from end to end. But though I had a great reverence for Dr. Chalmers I could not quite endure the breadth and positiveness of the religious distinction which he drew. Parliament, he said, was bound by its duty to God to establish and endow a religion. He met all allegations as to the difficulty of its choosing a religion in this way. Undoubtedly it was not competent to deal satisfactorily with the minuter differences between church and church, system and system. But there was no occasion to look into any such differences. There was but one difference worth noting, or worthy to be noted. That was the difference between Popery and Protestantism. As long as the Parliament established only Protestantism it was certain to be right: for Protestantism was 'the word of God', while Popery was 'the word of man'.

I was not at this time far advanced in my ecclesiastical studies, but I could not stand this crude and raw method of distinction, and I believed in the historical character and authority of the Church. It was the idea that Dr. Chalmers, cooperating at that period with Conservative politicians, had propounded a false theory of Church and State which coming from him was likely to make way among them that prompted me to set about working out the subject on a basis which seemed nearer to the truth and more practicable as it allied the State with an institution and not merely with a creed.

Colonial subjects had as I have shown made a first breach in my Toryism. Before I proceed to describe a second and larger irruption I will mention an incident which at least prefigured the impressions which the case of Ireland was to make upon me. Comparing Jewish emancipation, not yet embraced, with that of 1829, I said, at some very early date which I cannot remember, 'But then Ireland had groaned under centuries of oppression.' There followed a tempest of Liberal cheering. I had been seriously impressed in some ways: and first by a saying of Sir George Sinclair, a good, kindly and cultivated man, not always a wise politician. I said to him very foolishly, 'Now is it not hard that this majority consisting of some thirty Irish Roman Catholics should dispose of the fate of the Irish Established Church?' He replied, 'If three hundred English and Scotch Protestants may lawfully vote against the Irish Church, why may not thirty Roman Catholics do the same?' A deeper seed was sown by Lord John Russell whose genuine humanism made him at times a John the Baptist for Ireland. In reply to Tory attacks he used deep words to this effect. 'It seems to me, Sir, that the whole of this Irish case may be summed up in one single proposition. It is that as England is inhabited by Englishmen, and Scotland by Scotchmen, so Ireland is inhabited by Irishmen.' But this movement of mind was indeterminate as yet.

Another of a very determinate character began in 1841. Sir Robert Peel had given me a forward position in the party though he was repelled and dismayed when my book on Church and State appeared. (I remember that when I came back from the Continent in January 1839, he (not rudely) shirked me in the street and I went after him and spoke to him.) When the crisis of 1841 approached, I without having any desire or idea of the Cabinet cherished the wish to be Secretary for Ireland. When he was forming his Administration in August 1841, and I was sent for in my turn, he offered me the Vice-Presidentship of the Board of Trade. It was really at the time a much more important appointment than the other, which also would have placed me in Tory if not Orange associations, his executive in Ireland being anti-popular. I did not appreciate duly the fact that for years Protection was to form the hinge of British politics. And I was painfully conscious of the fact that I was totally ignorant of trade and political economy. I had been accustomed when riding into Liverpool as a boy to see the waterside carts with hogsheads, puncheons, and bales and I knew what these were as did every ragged urchin in the streets. But of every scrap of the true and wide knowledge which the office required my mind was absolutely disfurnished. Sir Robert Peel told me my President would probably be Lord Ripon 'whom you will find a perfect master of the subject'. On this point I was early undeceived: and indeed I am of opinion that the whole Cabinet were much in the dark (except Sir James Graham) and that Peel himself had still almost every thing to learn.

Upon principles however of simple obedience, I accepted his offer without a moment's hesitation: and I instantly set to work to learn my business with as much diligent application (I think) as if I had been reading once more for the schools at Oxford. Consequences began to emerge ere long. I found that I had no guide in my good-natured but timid chief: the ordinary business of the department soon fell into my hands to transact with the Secretaries, one of them Macgregor, a loose-minded Free Trader, the other Lefevre, a clear and scientific one. And in that autumn I became possessed with a desire to relax the corn law which formed I believe the chief subject of my meditations.

Hence followed an important consequence. Very slow in acquiring relative and secondary knowledge, and honestly absorbed in my work, I simply thought on and on as to what was right and fair under the circumstances. In January 1842, and near [not long after[1]] the opening of the session Peel made known to me a bill which he had prepared for the mitigation of the existing corn law which was based upon the sliding scale, a method of taxation devised apparently as an approach to Liberal ideas, but actually venomous in its working. It was probably as much as the Cabinet or the party would adopt. The Duke of Buckingham, the chief representative of agricultural ideas, had resigned his office in the ministry, but Sir Edward Knatchbull, who played the second fiddle, still held good. It was he who said, 'If the corn laws are to be repealed, how are the landlords to pay the interest upon their mortgages?' To these particulars I had little regard. On examining the bill in draft, I considered the relaxation to be less than it ought to be. I wrote or stated this opinion to Sir Robert Peel and begged him to allow me to resign my office into his hands.

Undoubtedly in this proceeding I was absolutely without comprehension of the political situation, and acted like a schoolboy which indeed I still was to no small extent. He received my proposition as was natural with strong hostility. He knew that the point of the fortifications at which I was stationed was τὸ κάμνον[2], and what I had deemed as insignificant (the action not having yet commenced) as a change of sentries, he regarded like the default of a right wing in battle, and to my perfect amazement he hinted even at the abandonment of his task by the dissolution of the government. Manifestly an exaggeration, yet not a mere piece of insincerity. He might I think have gained me more easily by a more open and supple method of expostulation. But he was not skilful I think in the management of personal or sectional dilemmas, as he showed later on with respect to two important questions, one the Factory Acts, and another the crisis of the Sugar Duties in 1844 which but for a rallying and rattling speech from Lord Derby (then Stanley) would probably have wrecked his Administration. He did not argue the number of shillings with me; and in this he was right, for I might have been tenacious. As it was, I went home, after seeing him, well

---

[1] Added above the line in pencil.
[2] i.e., the point at which his own side was hardest pressed in the battle. Euripides, *Suppliants*, 709.

intimidated, and in very low dumps indeed. Thinking the matter over, I think it was on a Saturday and the early part of a Sunday, I gave in.[1] My motives were I think these. In matters of trade I was an ignoramus or a novice. I had not given up Protection in principle; it was a matter of degree. On the other hand I estimated very highly the Conservative interests, and also the financial credit and efficiency, associated with the maintenance and solidity of the government, and these ideas were evidently entitled to preponderate. I made this known to Peel and he became all sunlight.

Immediately or very shortly thereafter, Lord John Russell proposed his eight shilling duty upon corn. Peel desired me to reply to him. This I did, and with my whole heart, for I did not yet fully understand the vicious operation of the sliding scale on the corn trade, and it is hard to see how an eight shilling duty could even then have been maintained.

Then came the formation of the new tariff of 1842. Peel took I think a good deal of part in framing it. I am sorry to say it was a bungling business. Macgregor our adviser had no practical competency. Nowhere was there any knowledge of the trades of the country. Peel had some equitable general ideas, for example about raw materials. But we proceeded very much at haphazard. And late in the proceeding we adopted, under encouragement from Macgregor, a most absurd plan of generally reducing duty in the case of articles brought from the colonies. I am sorry to say the plan included an export duty upon coals, which according to my recollection was the device of Peel himself.

But soon came a most valuable and important part of my economical education. Peel conceived and worked the income tax, long before conceived and recommended to his infinite credit, by Herries, but never before the subject of official countenance. While this however was the cardinal act of the really great financial scheme, the tariff was in bulk and detail the main matter. This it fell to me (as the index to Hansard would show) to work in the House of Commons. On its publication, all the protected interests took alarm, and sent deputations to the Board of Trade, which it was my business to receive. And they were invaluable to me: for, by constant close questioning, I learnt the nature and conditions of their trades, and armed with this admission to their interior, made careful notes and became able to defend in debate the propositions of the tariff and to show that the respective businesses could be

---

[1] See Appendix 5.

carried on, and not ruined as they all said. And I have ever since said that deputations are most admirable aids for the transaction of public business, provided the receiver of them is allowed to fix the occasion and the stage at which they appear. This choice however is rarely allowed. So they generally air themselves in an interminable series of speeches, and are paid off in generalities of no practical value, for which they courteously render thanks.

It also became my duty to introduce early in the session a bill for the regulation of the trade (if I remember right) between our American and West Indian colonies and the United States. Here I recollect that it was proposed to abolish altogether in certain cases the duty on the foreign articles, and that Labouchere (afterwards Lord Taunton), a Whig ex-Minister, and an excellent and liberal-minded man, mildly expostulated with me (a Tory) about this, but did not oppose it in debate. Sir Robert Peel I think to the last clung to the idea of what he called a registration duty: but I had begun it seems to embrace the idea of absolute freedom. I had one advantage over him: my training in practical political economy began at thirty one, his not till he was well over fifty. What was best in him, after his strictness of conscience in public business, was the firm and relentless grip with which he kept hold of whatever he had once attained. He never I think took a backward step: which cannot quite be said of Lord J. Russell's more impulsive nature.[1]

What I had in view in that and other following operations was the attainment of the great advantages which I saw consequent upon freedom of industry, rather than any fully formed theory, or any faith in freedom itself as such. Yet I was working for liberty, and got enlisted in her army, almost without knowing it.

I ought however in this branch as in others to state frankly as far as memory helps me the whole head and front of my offendings. The records of Parliament supply but scanty records of my Protectionism. Never I think, but in a single speech of 1841, on the West Indian sugar duties, was the subject touched: and there it was mixed with, and I think overshadowed by, an important question of philanthropy, for the proposal of the Liberals mainly went to the admission of sugars raised by the labour of countries dependent on an active slave trade. To this Peel strongly objected. I thought in the same strain.

---

[1] This sentence was added later.

But in the year 1840 the seat for Walsall fell vacant: and my excellent naval brother John was chosen as the Conservative candidate. The Anti-Corn Law League was now active; and it must be remembered that the Whigs had as yet taken no objection to the sliding scale. But with the League in the field the election at Walsall turned wholly or mainly on the corn law. My brother had no experience whatever in public speaking: and unfortunately for me I was at a moment's notice plucked away from Hawarden to do the chief part of the platform work. Knowing absolutely nothing, I, as in duty bound, believed everything that was maintained by those in whom I had confidence. It must be remembered too that Cobden had not yet possessed the public mind, and the corn law was ordinarily assailed with what may be termed the mere manufacturer's argument for cheap goods through cheap bread and low wages. Anyhow I was furnished suddenly with a batch of pamphlets favourable to the corn law, and they supplied I believe the staple of my Walsall speeches. We carried the seat. Some while after this event, Cobden challenged me when at Hagley, to a public discussion. This, as I imagine, would have been in the Black Country, where I should not have had a chance. (I think that Mr. Fryer, one of the first Members for Wolverhampton, spoke in his place in Parliament, of 'those damned, infernal corn laws'.) I was probably justified in declining. But I have a vague recollection of writing an impertinent letter to him who was afterwards my master, and of therein denouncing the Anti-Corn Law League as 'a big boroughmongering association'.

I think that before quitting the critical period of 1842 and the educating deputations, I ought to name a deputation of a demonstrative character on account of one who formed part of it. It was received not by me but by Lord Ripon, in the large room at the Board of Trade, I being present. A long line of fifteen or twenty gentlemen from the Lancashire district occupied benches running down and at the end of the room, and presented a formidable appearance. All however that I remember is the figure of a person in (I think) black or dark Quaker costume, seemingly the youngest of the band. Eagerly he sat a little forward on the bench, and intervened in the discussion, which I believe I did not. I was greatly struck with him. He seemed to me rather fierce, but very strong and very earnest. I need hardly say this was John Bright. A year or two afterwards he made his appearance in Parliament.

Following the history of my commercial opinions I may say that they went on developing: and I think that in substance I held by Protection during the Peel government as an accommodation to temporary circumstances. Unquestionably in the beginning of 1843 I made a speech which created much uneasiness behind the Treasury Bench. Graham spoke from that bench later in the evening: it was F. Baring who then said that in consequence of my dangerous address Graham was put up 'to make a stout speech'. An equivocal article in a review, which I had not written, was persistently ascribed to me, and I had to deny the authorship in my place. And at this time I recollect that the Duke of Richmond described me, I believe in the House of Lords, as a deserter from protective principles. But trade improved, and inside Parliament at least the controversy became gradually less acute until the crisis came. At that time I desired that the short intermediate Corn Act should impose a low fixed duty and not a reduced sliding scale. Graham, certainly our best authority, was, as Peel told me, of the same opinion: but our head would not give way.

Later on I tried to accelerate the repeal of the navigation laws, but the Russell government would not accelerate the movement. The American government, at that time a most important factor in the case, had offered I think to open their whole trade including the coast, on the basis of reciprocity, and I was for proceeding on this basis for reasons which I explained in a long speech. But the government declined. I withdrew my proposal, and voted for the bill. In the autumn of 1859, Cobden came to Hawarden to sound me on his proposed French treaty. Neither he nor I were in favour of commercial treaty negotiations generally, which had proved an utter failure. But there were great specialities in this case which doubtless moved him to stand the possible reproaches of *doctrinaires* such as Lord Grey. I went into his plan at once and with my whole heart and never felt more confident that I was bearing loyal service to free trade. Of the stern and stiff battles of 1860 and 1861 I may speak in my general narrative.

The third head of emancipation had reference to religious tests and to the relations of Church and State. The mode was on this wise. The criticisms on my book in 1839 showed me that I had[1] not sufficiently explained myself if I had not in some particulars overshot the mark. So I expanded[2] it into two volumes published in 1841 with some little

---

[1] MS: have.
[2] MS: explained.

softening of effect. This was not much. In 1844 was brought forward the Act for confirming the title of the modern Unitarians to the old Puritan chapels where they had been holding them (I think) for a certain time. I went into the subject laboriously and satisfied myself that this [was] not to be viewed as a mere quieting of titles based on lapse of time, but that the Unitarians were the true lawful holders because though they did not agree with the Puritan opinions they adhered firmly to the Puritan principle which was that Scripture was the rule without any binding interpretation and that each man or body or generation must interpret for itself. This measure in some way heightened my churchmanship but depressed my church-and-statesmanship: and Sheil in the debate predicted that I should soon be entirely free.

In the summer of that year Peel told me he intended to propose an increase in the grant to the College of Maynooth. I felt that as I had declared against any thing of the sort in my book I could not honourably be a party to the initiative as a Minister of the Crown but must by resigning my office place myself in a position to consider the subject with fair presumptions of independence. Peel argued with me, and even let slip that the inconsistency would not be observed, which was neither true nor relevant, and which he did not insist upon. I did not argue against the measure but only on my own personal position. Lord Stanley, afterwards Derby, very kindly made an effort to persuade me; and particularly insisted that if I resigned I should be compelled to oppose: a proposition curiously illustrated by his own declarations and conduct on the corn law eighteen months later. He did not in any way shake me. The measure stood over until 1845 but whether my personal difficulty had to do with this I know not.

When I had resigned I was solicited by Sir Robert Inglis to lead the opposition to the bill. I declined to oppose it. In the course of the conversation he went back to the fatal! character and consequences of the Act of 1829: and wished that his advice had then been taken which was that the Duke of Cumberland should be sent as Lord Lieutenant to Ireland with thirty thousand men. As that good and very kind man spoke the words my blood ran cold, and he too had helped me onwards in the path before me.

It was for me a great occasion: and in quitting the official work of friends to whom I was cordially attached I had paid a great price for the freedom which the occasion gave me. I supported the bill on the second reading in a speech of much argumentation which quite conformably to my book and my ideas gave up in principle the Church of Ireland without entering into detail. All my fetters were at once thrown off. But Ireland had suffered terrible defeat and miscarriage since the days of Drummond. New ideas and schemes were in course of being hatched invisibly and underground. Parliamentary methods were and were long to remain out of vogue. I had not the smallest idea that the Established Church of Ireland was in danger, or would be so for many years to come. I however separated myself in mind from all attempts to rearrange or curtail it or compound for a fresh lease of existence on its behalf. My principle had been and continued to be all or nothing. I never gave countenance to motions for committees or other half measures or I believe spoke on the subject until 1864 or 5, when I denounced it in principle and said that when opportunity came it must be removed. In short after Maynooth I had no great or serious mental change to make.

Milnes told me, I hope correctly, that my speech on Maynooth gave very great pleasure to Bishop Thirlwall.

In 1847 when I had become a candidate for the University of Oxford, the question was put to me through my committee whether I should support the Irish Church. The answer given with my concurrence was I believe to the effect that I did not anticipate any proposal hostile to it which would receive my support. A perfectly safe reply: for at this period the opponents were either wholly silent, or proposed wretched compromises with which I had no sympathy.

As Member for Oxford, and even in 1866 after I had been expelled from my seat, I declined to open the universities by the admission of persons of all religions into the governing body. I had been voting from the outset for the admission of the Jews to Parliament. But I did not fully admit the doctrine of controul over the universities, and I was sincerely afraid of the confusion which I feared that discrepancies of religious communion would introduce into the governing body of a teaching institution. The test for the taught was abolished in 1854. Gradually I found that a process of disintegration had been making way by strides in the university from causes deeper than variations in avowed belief. When in 1869[1] I joined with Lord Coleridge in carrying an Act to abolish tests in all existing colleges, not only did we leave the foundation of future colleges entirely free as to the profession of particular creeds,

---

[1] The date was added afterwards in pencil.

but I was strongly of opinion that in the actual state of things the admission of living religious convictions generally would tend to strengthen the moral and spiritual fibre of the place, and even to cause a rally among the professors of the Church of England. I must elsewhere speak of the Oxford University Act of which I was the principal framer. I sought by it, in opposition to the recent Commission, to make the teaching and ruling university really a self-governing body, and it was the weakness and distraction of the religious life which brought about the re-casting of the statutes of colleges in a sense little favourable to theology or to religion and not the provisions or the spirit of the Act of Parliament.

Excepting the case of the Test Act, I think that from this time onwards I was always on the side of religious liberty: and during the government of Lord Palmerston in 1862 or 3 I got Lord Russell to join me in defeating by threats of resignation a most astute scheme for giving a new lease of life to the Irish Church. What I have however condemned all along and still condemn is the tendency to cook up some *caput mortuum* of Christianity by arbitrary excisions, to call it undenominational religion and to honour it with the patronage of the State. More has been done already in this sense than I like: and I could not have proceeded even as far as the Education Act of 1870 in respect to creeds, had there been any tolerable rally of the Church or even the Conservative opposition, until the bill was too far advanced, on behalf of denominational liberty.

There is but one more emancipation which I need record and that very briefly. It relates to the extension of the franchise. I started from the period of the Reform Act (1832) with something like a horror of it. I remember some feeble lingering of prejudice as late as about 1848. But I at no time spoke a word against it. By 1854 I was thoroughly with Lord J. Russell in his proposal, and should not I think have disliked a larger measure. I had indeed a 'sneaking kindness' for close boroughs on account of what they had done in the first introduction of great and Liberal statesmen into Parliament. But in the year 1859, on the Derby Reform Bill, I declared loudly for the lowering of the franchise. And at a later date I had a controversy with Lord Sherbrooke[1] in the pages of the *Nineteenth Century* where I defended it on very broad principles indeed. In 1866 we went out singly by reason of our attachment to it: and in

---

[1] MS: Sherborne.

1867 when Mr. Disraeli propounded household suffrage we really contended with Bright at our side for a much wider enfranchisement than he did.

Of the various and important incidents of my life which associated me almost unawares with foreign affairs, in Greece (1850), in the Neapolitan kingdom (1851), and in the Balkan Peninsula and the Turkish Empire (1853), I will only say that they all contributed to forward the action of those home causes, more continuous in their operation, which without in any way effacing my old sense of reverence for the past, determined for me, by the process I have endeavoured to describe, my place in the present, and my direction towards the future.

Writing thus has been an effort of introspection and necessarily of egotism. I have endeavoured to write without favour, or reserve, or exaggeration. But I am sensible that underneath and behind my resolution to that effect, the subtle powers of self-deception may have been at work, and may impair or vitiate the relation between my narrative and the absolute truth of the case.

Braemar

16 July 1892

EARLY PARLIAMENTARY LIFE 1832-52

1833-4 IN THE OLD HOUSE OF COMMONS

ADD.MS 44791, ff. 70-102

I am the only commoner now living who sat in [the] old burned House of Commons: I also dined with the Speaker (Manners Sutton—first of the seven whose subject I have been) in St. Stephen's Chapel, then his dining room. I look back upon it with a warm interest and reverence on account of its grand oratorical traditions in particular.

Elected to Parliament on (I think) December 13, 1832, I took my seat at the opening of 1833: provided unquestionably with a large stock at least of schoolboy bashfulness. The first time that business required me to go to the arm of the Chair to say something on business to the Speaker (who was something of a Keate), I remember the revival in me bodily of the frame of mind in which a schoolboy stands before his master. But apart from an incidental recollection of this kind, I found it most difficult to believe with any reality of belief that such a poor and insignificant little worm as I could really belong to, really form a *part* of an assembly which, notwithstanding the prosaic character of its entire visible equipment I felt to be so august.

What I may term its corporal conveniences were, I may observe in passing, marvellously small. I do not think that in any part of the building it afforded the means of so much as washing the hands. The residences of Members were at that time less distant: but they were principally reached on foot. When a large House broke up after a considerable division, a copious dark stream found its way up Parliament Street, Whitehall, and Charing Cross.

I remember that there occurred some case in which a constituent (probably a maltster) at Newark sent me a communication, which made oral communication with the Treasury, or with the Chancellor of the Exchequer (then Lord Althorp) convenient. As to the means of bringing this about, I was puzzled and abashed. Some experienced friend on the Opposition bench, probably Mr. Goulburn, said to me, 'There is Lord Althorp sitting alone on the Treasury bench: go to him and tell him your business.' With such encouragement I did it: Lord Althorp received me in the kindest manner possible, alike to my pleasure and my surprise.

I think that the first occasion on which I had really to open my mouth in the House of Commons was supplied by an attack of Lord Grey's (he was then Lord Howick) on Mr. Stuart, the manager of my father's estates in Demerara, whom he denounced as 'the murderer of slaves'. Whether Lord Howick was justified in making an attack so intimately affecting the father of two fellow-Members of Parliament without any notice to them to give opportunity of defence; or whether the defence with which I was supplied was as I assumed at the moment, sound and sufficient, I cannot now say, but I remember that Lord Althorp, leader of the House, recommended our assailant not to persevere with some motion that he had made, and that he complied. I must say however that even before this time I personally had come to entertain little or no confidence in the proceedings of the resident agents in the West Indies.

Though I was a steady and close attendant, I made only twice what could be called speeches: the 'maiden speech' (June 3, 1833) on the Slavery Abolition Bill: and a speech in 1834 against the proposal for the admission of Nonconformists to the universities. The first of these was warmly commended in debate by Mr. Stanley, who had charge of the bill in this I think the most brilliant portion of his career: and I have an idea that the speech was reported to and noticed by the King. At some later period I have perused it (in a corrected report) and found its tone much less than satisfactory. But of course allowance is to be made for the enormous and most blessed change of opinion since that day on the subject of negro slavery.

I remember a curious incident which concerns Sir Robert Peel. Cobbett made a motion alike wordy and absurd, praying the King to remove him from the Privy Council as the author of the Act for the re-establishment of the gold standard in 1822. The entire House was against him, except his colleague Fielden of Oldham, who made a second teller. After the division I think Lord Althorp at once rose and moved the expunction of the proceedings from the votes or journals: a severe rebuke to the mover. Sir Robert in his speech said, 'I am [at] a loss, Sir, to conceive what can be the cause of the strong hostility to me which the honourable gentleman exhibits. *I* never conferred on him an obligation.' This severe stroke was not original as I long afterwards learned from a notice in Lecky's 'History of the Irish Debates'. But what struck me at the time as singular was this, that notwithstanding the state of feeling which I have described, Sir R. Peel was greatly excited in dealing with one who at the time was little more than a contemptible antagonist. At that period, shirt collars were made with 'gills', which came up upon the cheeks: and Peel's gills were so soaked with perspiration, that they actually lay down upon his neckcloth.

In one of these years, I think 1833, a motion was made by some political economist for the abolition of the Corn Laws. I (an absolute and literal ignoramus) was much struck and staggered with it. But Sir James Graham—who knew more of economic and trade matters, I think, than the rest of the Cabinet of 1841 all put together—made a reply in the sense of Protection, whether high or low I cannot now say. But I remember perfectly well that this speech of his built me up again for the moment, and enabled me (I believe) to vote with the Government.

The year 1833 was, as measured by quantity and in part by quality, a splendid year of legislation. In 1834 the Government, and Lord Althorp far beyond all others did themselves high honour by the new Poor Law Act, which rescued the English peasantry from the total loss of their independence. Of the 658 Members of Parliament about 420 must have been their general supporters. Much gratitude ought to have been

felt to this great Administration. But from a variety of causes, at the close
of the session [of] 1834 the House of Commons had fallen into a state
of cold indifference about it.

3 June 1897

1838-9 MY FIRST BOOK:

THE CHURCH IN ITS RELATIONS WITH THE STATE[1]

The primary idea of my early politics was the Church. With this was
connected the idea of the establishment as being every thing except
essential. When therefore Dr. Chalmers came to London to lecture on
the principle of Church establishments, I attended as a loyal hearer. I
had a profound respect for the lecturer with whom I had had the honour
of a good deal of acquaintance during winter residences in Edinburgh,
and some correspondence by letter. I was in my earlier twenties, and
he near if not in his sixties, with a high and merited fame for eloquence
and character. He subscribed his letters to me 'respectfully' (or 'most
respectfully') yours, and puzzled me extremely in the effort to find out
what suitable mode of subscription to use in return.

Unfortunately the basis of his lectures was totally unsound. Parliament as being Christian was bound to know and establish the truth. But
not being made of theologians it could not follow the truth into its
minuter shadings, and must proceed upon broad lines. Fortunately
these lines were ready to hand. There was a religious system which taken
in the rough was truth. This was known as Protestantism: and to its
varieties it was not the business of the legislature to have regard. On
the other side lay a system which taken again in the rough was not truth
but error. This system was known as Popery. Parliament therefore was
bound to establish and endow some kind of Protestantism, and not to
establish or endow Popery. It was easy for Parliament to choose when
the choice lay between the word of God, and the word of man. Popery
was the word of man: but Protestantism was the word of God.

I could not 'stand' the undisputed currency in Conservative circles
of a theory like this. I made no declaration of controversy: but, by

---

[1] Gladstone here makes a common error. The correct title of the book is
The State in its relations with the Church.

reaction, out of Dr. Chalmers's lectures there sprang my *Church in its relations with the State*. My doctrine was that the State was a person with a conscience. The Catholic Church founded by our Lord was what the State ought to establish and to establish alone: but I made accommodations to meet existing cases which went beyond this line. These accommodations were largely unfolded anew in the fourth edition of the book (1841?) after Macaulay's slashing article. And my position was finally explained long after in *A Chapter of Autobiography* which had a very large sale, quite contrary to my expectations.

I do not know how I acquired sufficient boldness to send my original manuscript to Mr. John Murray: but I remember that his reply came to me in the shape of a packet of proof sheets. In the summer I went abroad. On account of the state of my sight, I went abroad in the summer, after consulting Dr. Farr of Charterhouse Square, who pleased [me] by saying, 'Mr. Gladstone, it is not the Whigs who will save the country, and it is not the Tories who will save the country: it is the *mothers* of England, who will save the country.'

James Hope, afterwards Hope Scott, was very intimate with me at this time. He encouraged and if I may so say egged me on in writing the book: but specified that it did not in his opinion go far enough. When I went abroad in the summer, he kindly took charge of the business of managing the proofs, and it was published while I was in Sicily. I think I heard of the publication at Catania: and I remember that the news very strongly impressed me with a peculiar feeling. I felt as if in laying such a body of opinion on my own behalf before the public, I had been parting with actual portions of myself. It seemed to be a kind of actual parturition.

The first chapters dealing with Establishment drew forth premature praise from many who condemned the chapters that succeeded them and dealt with the Church. On coming home, I found the book warmly approved by such Churchmen as Bishop Blomfield and Dr. Hook. Among my political friends it excited misgiving or dismay (on my behalf); I mean such as were merely political. Sir Robert Peel I believe was astonished that I could thus at my time of life commit political suicide. But Sir R. Peel who was a religious man was wholly anti-church and unclerical, and largely undogmatic. A parliamentary crisis having occurred in 1839, in which he had occasion to take counsel with friends, Lord J. Russell referred to the broaching of dangerous ideas respecting the Church and State when Sir Robert Peel replied that he was not aware of the prevalence of such ideas in the minds of any of those with whom he had consulted. Quite true, I not being one of them. I feel that Sir R. Peel must have been greatly perplexed in his treatment of me after the publication of the book. Partly through his own fault for by habit and education he was quite incapable of comprehending the movement in the Church, the strength it would reach and the emergencies it would entail. Lord Derby I think early began to escape from the Erastian yoke which weighed upon Peel. Lord Aberdeen was I should say altogether enlightened in regard to it and had cast it off: so that he obtained from some the soubriquet (during his Ministry) of 'the Presbyterian Puseyite'.

After the opening of the session of 1839, on a certain evening it happened that O'Connell passed by me behind the Speaker's Chair. He laid his hand in a friendly way on my shoulder and said, 'We claim the half of you.'

The publication of the book may have been an honest error. But it was a stone contributed to the great cairn of that Church movement, of which neither this generation nor the next will probably feel the latest pulsation.

11 September 1897

1840

4 July 1895

Twenty years of my life or thereabouts (besides much outlying matter and time) had for their weightiest employment the commerce and finance of the country. My real knowledge of these subjects, whatever it may be, or has been, had its true beginning when Sir Robert Peel sent me, rather reluctant, to the Board of Trade in August 1841. During the whole of this period, my action may be said to have been on the right side, though the first two or three years represented a stage of transition, and a mind which had not then, even if it has now, accommodated itself to the habit of accepting broad issues before they have become ripe and clear for the mass of the community. The object of what I now write is not to describe that transition stage, but to record as well as I can my political sins against the principles of Free Trade.

My father was an active and effective local politician and the

Protectionism which I inherited from him and from all my youthful associations was qualified by a thorough acceptance of the important preliminary measures of Mr. Huskisson of whom he was the first among the local supporters. Moreover for the first six years or so of my parliamentary life Free Trade was in no way a party question, and it only became strictly such in 1841 at and somewhat before the general election, when the Whig Government, itself rather *in extremis*, proposed a fixed duty upon corn. The chief apology however for my Protectionism is to be found in the nature of the popular and parliamentary argument on which the advocates of Free Trade, antecedent to Cobden (and apart from the pure economists who made no wide impression) appeared chiefly to rely. It was the manufacturer who was supposed to speak, and his language to be this. During the war we had the monopoly of the sea, and so he could compete with the cheap bread countries of the Continent: we have now lost that monopoly and the competition will ruin us unless we have cheap corn. The answer was, then we understand that cheap corn means lowered wages for without these you would derive no advantage from the change. There was therefore a belief, *bona fide* if irrational, that the champions of the Corn Law were also the champions of the British labourer. I think that this belief had possession of my thoroughly uninstructed mind, and that it was encouraged (though I may possibly have done him injustice) by the speeches of Mr. Villiers.

During the great controversy of 1846 and the following years, I never saw any parliamentary speech of my own quoted in proof of the inconsistency of the Peelites. Indeed I had made but one speech touching trade. That was in the debate on the sugar duties in 1841, and the argument turned chiefly on the question of slave-trade sugar from Cuba and elsewhere, not on mere competition as affecting the West Indies.

But, in or about the beginning of 1840 a vacancy occurred in the representation of Walsall. One of my brothers was asked to stand for it; and I was requisitioned to go and support him. The election was to turn mainly on the Corn Law question, which by this time was *aflame* in the Staffordshire district. My brother had been a naval officer, and had no opportunity of acquiring the art of public speaking. Upon me, in a conflict short and sharp, seemed to fall the principal stress of the occasion. I either provided myself, or I was furnished from head quarters, with a packet of pamphlets in favour of the Corn Laws. These I read and I extracted from them the chief material of my speeches. I dare say it was sad stuff, furbished up at a moment's notice. We carried the election.

Cobden sent me a challenge to attend a public discussion of the subject. Whether this was quite fair, I am not certain, for I was young, made no pretension to be an expert, and had never opened my lips in Parliament on the subject. But it afforded me an excellent opportunity to decline with modesty and with courtesy as well as reason. I am sorry to say that to the best of my recollection I did far otherwise, and the pith of my answer was made to be that I regarded the Anti-Corn Law League as no better than a big borough-mongering association. Such was my first capital offence in the matter of Protection: released from public condemnation only by obscurity. I will not say that there may not be another at the general election of 1841, when Lord J. Manners (now Duke of Rutland) and I were returned as Protectionists. But it was an election of small local animation: until the 'eleventh hour' we expected to get through without a contest, and when the battle came it was with a foregone conclusion. My speeches were of absolute dulness but I have no doubt they were 'sound' in the sense of my leaders Peel and Graham of the party.

Not a word of all this had life in it to be remembered or cited against me. The very next stage in my career was my becoming Vice-President of the Board of Trade in August 1841. That assumption was followed by hard, steady, and honest work and every day so spent beat like a battering ram on the unsure fabric of my official Protectionism. By the end of the year I was far gone in the opposite sense: I had to speak much on these questions in the session of 1842 but it was always done with great moderation. From one cause or another my reputation among the Conservatives on this question oozed away with rapidity: it died with that year, and early in 1843 a Duke, I think the Duke of Richmond, speaking in the House of Lords described some renegade proceeding as a proceeding conducted under the banners of the Vice-President of the Board of Trade. When in May 1843[1] Sir R. Peel sent for me on the occasion of my becoming President and entering the Cabinet, he referred to the change in his own views, and said that in future he questioned whether he could undertake the defence of the Corn Laws on principle. His words were addressed to a sympathizing hearer. My speeches in the House had already excited dissatisfaction if not dismay.

15 September 1897

---

[1] The date was added afterwards in pencil.

THE SUGAR DUTIES IN 1844

3 September 1897

There was a short and sharp parliamentary crisis in 1844 brought about by the question of the sugar duties. I think it certain that the diaries of Sir James Graham (which will I suppose see the light ere long) contain a much better account of that crisis than any I can give. We were both members of the Cabinet, but his position in it was much higher than mine, and in truth he might at that time be called Sir Robert Peel's right-hand man.

In 1841 the Whig Government raised the question of the sugar duties and proposed to substitute a protective duty of 12/- per cwt for the actual or virtual prohibition of foreign sugars which had up to that time subsisted. They were strongly opposed, and decisively beaten. The argument used against them was I think twofold. There was the protection plea on behalf of the West Indians whose estates were now worked only by free labour. And there was the great and popular contention that the measure not only admitted sugar the product of slave labour, which we would not allow our own colonies to employ, but that our new supplies would be derived from Brazil, and above all from Cuba and Porto Rico, where the slave trade was rampant, and was prosecuted on an enormous scale.

The Government of Sir R. Peel largely modified our system. Its general professions were the abolition of prohibition, and the reduction of protective duties to a moderate rate. In 1844 it was determined to deal with the sugar duties, and to admit sugar at I think a rate of 10/- per cwt beyond the rate for British grown. But we had to bear in mind the arguments of 1841, and it was determined that the sugars so to be admitted were to be the product of free labour only. There was some uncertainty from whence they were to come. Java produced sugar largely, under a system involving certain restraints, but as we contended essentially free. The whole argument however was difficult and perplexed, and a parliamentary combination was formed against the Government. The Opposition, with perfect consistency, mustered in full force. The West Indian interest, which, though much reduced in wealth, still subsisted as a parliamentary entity, was heavily arrayed on the same side. There were some votes attracted by dislike, perhaps, to the argument on our side which appeared to be complex and over-refined.

A meeting of the party was held in order to confront the crisis. Sir Robert Peel stated his case in a speech which was thought to be haughty and unconciliatory. I do not recollect whether there was hostile discussion, or whether silence and the sulks prevailed. But I remember that when the meeting of the party broke up, Sir Robert Peel said on quitting the room that it was the worst meeting he ever had attended.

It left disagreeable anticipations as to the division which was in immediate prospect. At that time the Court had come to be warmly interested in the fate of the Government: and I have always understood that when the debate came on it soon came to be deemed certain that we should be beaten, and that accounts were sent to Windsor as late as nine o'clock that on the next morning the Ministry would probably have to resign.

The Opposition in general had done what they could to strengthen their momentary association with the West Indian Conservatives. Their hopes of a majority depended entirely upon Conservative votes. Of course, therefore, it was vital to confine the attack to the merits of the question immediately before the House, as an attack upon the policy of the Government generally could only strengthen it by awakening the susceptibilities of party and so reclaiming the stray votes to the Administration. Lord Howick (who afterwards lived to so advanced an age as Lord Grey) entering into the debate as the hours of enhanced interest began, made a speech which attacked the Conservative policy at large, and gave the opening for an effective reply. Lord Derby, then I think Lord Stanley, perceived his opportunity and turned it to account with great force and adroitness. In a strictly retaliatory speech, he wound up Conservative sentiment on behalf of Ministers, and restored the tone of the House. The clouds of the earlier evening hours dispersed, and the Government were victorious. Two speeches, one negatively and the other positively, reversed the prevailing current, and served the Administration. I have never known a parallel case.

The whole honour of the fray, in the Ministerial sense, redounded to Lord Stanley. His career in the earlier years of the reformed Parliament had been one of peculiar brilliancy. But I doubt whether in the twenty-six years of his after life, he ever struck such a stroke as this.

1846-52 AN INTERVAL—NO. 1

In December 1845 I accepted the Colonial Department in succession to Lord Derby who had resigned rather than support the repeal of the Corn Laws but who expressed to me (as well as I believe to the Queen) his fixed intention to do all in his power to expedite the passage of the repealing measure. My deep obligation to the Duke of Newcastle for the great benefit he conferred upon me not only by his unbroken support but far above all by his original introduction of me to the constituency, made it my duty at once to decline some overtures made to me for the support of my re-election, so it only remained to seek a seat elsewhere.

Shortly after the opening of the session of 1846, it became known that the Protectionist petition against the Peelite or Liberal sitting Member for Wigan was likely to succeed in unseating him. Proposals were [made] to me to succeed him, which were held to be eligible. I even wrote my address: and on a certain day I was going down by the mail train. But it was an object to our opponents to keep a Secretary of State out of Parliament during the Corn Law crisis: and their petition was suddenly withdrawn. The consequence was that I remained until the resignation of the Government in July a Minister of the Crown without a seat in Parliament. This was a state of things not agreeable to the spirit of parliamentary government: and some objection was taken, but rather slightly, in the House of Commons. Sir R. Peel stood fire. No heavy colonial question came before Parliament.

An incident happened of small importance which threw light upon the astounding obstinacy or firmness of Lord George Bentinck's character: the prolongation of whose life might have seriously affected the course of our parliamentary history, and even the condition of our country.

It was a duty of routine for me as Secretary of State to sign the appointments of judges appointed, on the responsibility of the Board of Controul, for India. My function was absolutely technical, and there are now analogous cases in our system of Government. But it seems that a thing was mentioned in the patent as *done*, which was only determined to be done. It seems that Mr. Hume quoted this in Parliament as a falsehood told by me, I being in fact wholly ignorant of the matter. (And it is certain that a great officer of State in multitudes of cases ought not to read the papers which he signs. Nor would my reading have made in this case the smallest difference.) Lord George Bentinck seriously urged the point. He when in the Guards had been kind to me as a boy at Eton, and I remember then dining with him at a Salthill party. The matter was ludicrous as the basis of serious dispute. I invoked the aid of

Lord Derby, his political ally: which was freely given. But Lord Derby failed as I had done to move him: and he adhered to the statement made probably in jest by Mr. Hume. A strange idiosyncrasy. It was an affair of smoke.

A Peelite, unless with a Government to support him, had little chance of an opening at a bye-election; and I remained without a seat until the dissolution in June 1847. But several months before this occurred it had become known that Mr. Estcourt would vacate his seat for Oxford and I became candidate. It was a serious campaign. The constituency, much to its honour, did not stoop to fight the battle on the ground of Protection. But it was fought and that fiercely, on religious grounds. There was an incessant discussion, and I may say dissection, of my character and position in reference to the Oxford Movement. This cut very deep, for it was a discussion which each member of the constituency was entitled to carry on for himself. The upshot was favourable. The Liberals supported me gallantly, so did many zealous Churchmen, apart from politics, and a good number of moderate men so that I was returned by a fair majority. I held the seat for eighteen years, but with five contests and a final defeat, which in the opinion of many was due to voting by papers. My continuing parliamentary lines kept the Tories eagerly in arms against me except in 1859, when I served under Lord Lytton in the Ionian Islands.

(And the speech I made (1864 or 5) on the Irish Church justified, in the last issue, their wrath.)

On one point I had gone with the high Tory party in the university. I opposed the Oxford Commission: not because I disapproved, though I did disapprove, of the spirit of the report; but on the constitutional ground that the Crown, without Parliament, had no title to institute an inquiry of this kind, unless by the consent of the parties: which was given when Lord Aberdeen's Government issued a corresponding commission for the public schools. I rather think that Sir Robert Peel accepted my argument.

The opposition to me in 1852 was somewhat cruel. The Tory Government was in a minority: and in concert with Sidney Herbert I had exerted myself to organise the Peelites, who turned the scale at that time (the 108 'Janissaries' being still about forty) to prevent the summary extinction of the Ministry and secure for it a fair trial or leave to produce its plans. Sir James Graham took the other side. My only offence as I believe had been voting for the admission of the Jews to Parliament.

But the whole life time of the Parliament of 1847–52 was one, during which my political life was in partial abeyance. In November 1847 had come the great smash in the affairs of the Glynne family, and the seemingly all but hopeless struggle to maintain the estate and repair the disaster had commenced. The whole burden of conducting it fell upon me: and I should say that for those five years it constituted my daily and continuing care, while parliamentary action was only occasional. It supplied in fact my education for the office of Finance Minister. In the discharge of that office which I held so long (for I proposed in all thirteen Budgets) I owed perhaps a disposition to sail too near the wind, of which my dealings with the South Sea stock supplied an unfortunate example. I have always imagined that this fault was due to my experience in the affairs of the Hawarden and Oak Farm estates: when it was an incessant course of sailing near the wind, and there was really no other hope.

But in this continuing activity there were of necessity many interstices caused by public exigencies, not to speak of the anxious and at times absorbing demands of Church affairs, which never were more critical or less hopeful.

The year 1850, bringing with it a family affliction in the loss of darling Jessy, carried us to Naples in the autumn, and then by a process never anticipated introduced me to a new and very important chapter of my public life in the advocacy of the rights of the oppressed abroad. On this I need not here dwell, and I only refer to my letters to Lord Aberdeen on the subject.

It was the habitual course of parliamentary business that in these years I failed to follow: but great occasions were not neglected. Of these the principal ones were the following, besides the Oxford Commission, the case of the Jews, and the dealings with the Derby Government in 1852 which have been duly noticed.

1. The Navigation Laws.
2. The Hudson's Bay Company.
3. The Greek debate of 1850.
4. Burdens on land.
5. The attack on the Bishop of Bath and Wells.
6. Increase of episcopate.
7. Colonial Church Bill.

Of these I reserve for No. 2 the subjects connected with the Church.

I warmly favoured, and spoke copiously for, the repeal of the Navigation Laws. I desired however to accept a recent overture from America which offered every thing, even their vast coasting trade, upon a footing of absolute reciprocity. I gave notice of a motion to that effect. But the Government declined to accept it; and although the argument for reciprocity at sea is very much stronger than in land trade, I will not say that they were wrong. In the actual situation, my motion would have endangered their bill. I accordingly withdrew it. Of this the Protectionist Opposition who would have supported me I believe complained. I certainly should have done better never to give my notice. This is one of the cases illustrating the extreme slowness of my political education. It did not occur to me that by my public notification I had given to the Opposition generally something *like* a vested interest in my proposal.

When they moved for a committee to consider the incidence of the burdens upon land, the whole Free Trade party opposed the motion; but I voted and spoke in its favour. It was a question of real difficulty. The support of the poor was legitimately a burden upon all property. And this liability was recognised for many years after I entered Parliament by an annual bill to exempt stock in trade from rating. The justification for passing by personalty at large—now by far the largest part of the national property—lay simply in the impossibility of rating it. Since that time the land or rather the rate has been subject to a new burden under the Education Act. But by constant aggressions upon the consolidated fund the land has surely obtained enormous compensations: while the rate other than landed remains seriously burdened. It was with a rather fraudulent ingenuity that the landed folk, per Lopez and Co., availed itself of the case of the town rate-payers to obtain under cover of that case boons to which on the merits of their own case they were less clearly entitled, considering especially the very large benefits which the new Poor Law had conferred.

The question of the Hudson's Bay Company was rather bravely and very warmly taken up by Lord Lincoln and myself with the support of the few but able friends of freedom in colonial government. I always thought the case very strong, and the subject full of interest. We obtained a parliamentary committee, and bothered the Governor of the Company (Sir G. Simpson) very much, for he had to maintain the worthlessness of the territory except for Hudson's Bay purposes and in answering our questions had to call in the aid of incessant coughing. His contention was a mockery. But he was strongly supported. Mr. Ellice, strangely called the Bear, was in the heart of his cause, and what was more he secured Lord Grey the Colonial Secretary, who opposed us with perverseness but with effect. Our object was to obtain a judicial decision upon the claims of the Company. I never could believe, especially considering the prior decisions of the Courts on monopolies, that it was legally in the power of Charles II to mark off a vast portion of a continent, and invest a handful of his subjects with power to exclude from those territories all other subjects of the Crown. At last we obtained from the Colonial Office what we thought was a promise that such a decision should be obtained. But we were eventually put off, in this really great case, by what I thought a rather impudent proceeding. The opinion of the Law Officers was taken as a fulfilment of the promise to us. Our weakness lay in this, that we could obtain no support from Sir R. Peel or Sir James Graham. I remember when Lincoln and I had an interview with Peel on the subject. He did not express any dissent from our opinions; but declared his aversion to any proceeding which might endanger the position of the Government. His reason was that if they went out they would be succeeded by the Protectionists, who in their frantic zeal for the restoration of Protection would probably convulse the country. A wonderful misjudgment. As long as Lord G. Bentinck was alive, there was a possibility that with his portentous will he might carry his party to dangerous lengths. When he was gone, to suppose that Lord Derby and Mr. Disraeli would play such a game was (for different reasons in the two cases) nothing less than absurd. For my own part I desired the accession of the Protectionists to office, as the sure means, and the only means, of effectually drawing the claws and fangs of Protectionism. But so it was that we were defeated by Lord Grey acting on behalf of E. Ellice and the Hudson's Bay Company.

It was in the Greek debate of 1850 which involved the censure or acquittal of Lord Palmerston, that I first meddled in speech with foreign affairs, to which I had heretofore paid the slightest possible attention. Lord Palmerston's speech was a marvel for physical strength, for memory, and for lucid and precise exposition of his policy as a whole.

A very curious incident on this occasion evinced the extreme reluctance of Sir R. Peel to appear in any ostensible relation with Disraeli. Voting with him was disagreeable enough, but this with his strong aversion to the Palmerstonian policy he could not avoid: besides which it was known that Lord Palmerston would carry the division.

Disraeli not yet fully recognised as leader of the Protectionists was working hard for that position and assumed the manners of it, with Beresford, a kind of whipper-in, for his right-hand man. After the Palmerston speech he asked me on the next night whether I would undertake to answer it. I said that I was incompetent to do it from want of knowledge and otherwise. He answered that in that case he must do it. As the debate was not to close that evening, this left another night free for Peel when he might speak and *not* be in Disraeli's neighbourhood. I told Peel what Disraeli had arranged. He was very well satisfied. But, shortly afterwards I received from Disraeli a message (I think so it was this time, a simple announcement) through Beresford, that he had changed his mind, and would not speak until the next and closing night, when Peel would have to speak also. I had to make known to Peel this alteration. He received the tidings with extreme annoyance: thinking I suppose that if the two spoke on the same side and in the late hours just before the division it would convey the idea of some concert or co-operation between them which it was evident that he was most anxious to avoid. But he could not help himself. Disraeli's speech was a very poor one, almost like a 'cross', and Peel's was prudent but otherwise not one of his best.

8 September 1897

1846–52 AN INTERVAL—NO. 2

During the Government of Lord Russell, Sidney Herbert and [I], acting in concert but with no party view, determined to make an effort on behalf of the Church. He undertook the question of the chapters; I proposed an increase of bishops. In jest I called them little bishops. If I remember right, the plan was this.

1. No change whatever as to the bishops who were peers of Parliament.
2. The Ecclesiastical Commissioners might from their funds advance *not exceeding* £1500 a year.
3. Against private contributions (I think to the same amount, and probably with some provision as to a residence).
4. These bishops to have no seat in the House of Lords.

I made my proposal: but it never went beyond a single discussion. Lord John Russell received it kindly, but would not take it up and was not prepared with a substitute. Mr. Ainley was more adverse: he smelt in it danger to Church and State and [there] was no support from the Tory quarter. A flash in the pan: but an indication of what was to come.

A case which might have been very serious arose in the year 1852. The Oxford Movement was at its *nadir*. The Gorham judgment and the crowd of misunderstandings, which clustered around it, were in full force and freshness. The Manning and Hope secessions, with many more, had recently occurred. Mr. Bennett, got rid of at St. Paul's, Knightsbridge, had been presented by Lady Bath to Frome in the diocese of Bath and Wells. Except a prevailing popular prejudice against the whole movement, there was not a word to be said against him. For the Bishop to object would have been monstrous in principle and futile in effect.

Mr. Horsman, whose *rôle* in the House of Commons had been markedly anti-ecclesiastical, gave notice of a motion for a select committee to inquire into the conduct of the Bishop of Bath and Wells in instituting Mr. Bennett to the parish of Frome.

Application was made, as I *understood*, to the Government (that of Lord Derby, weak in numbers and led by Disraeli in the Commons) to defend the Bishop. It was a trial of their rectitude and pluck. All the Bagots I may add were strongly Tory. But they flinched. I admit their difficulties; but was not their refusal shabby beyond description? They announced no leaning or intention either way.

Application was also made to Lord Russell, who declined to interfere. He had no special relation to the case. He declined: and I do not say that he was to blame.

I could not however bear this running down the Bishop and determined on an endeavour to defend him. This was an occasion the first if not the only one, on which I showed something like parliamentary sagacity. I looked up the precedents and found one much to my purpose. Somewhere about the reign of Anne, a motion similar in effect was met by an amendment requiring that the mover 'do lay upon the table' the charges which it is his intention to prove against the said bishop before the select committee.

I went down to Brighton to see the Bishop (whom I had known in earlier years) on the subject. He came into the room with the fingers of one or both hands covered with black silk sheathing: sad to see. He was suffering as I understood under a most painful disease: the fingers as I understood were mortifying joint by joint. All this enhanced the cruelty of the attack, but Mr. Horsman perhaps did not know these particulars.

Notice was duly given of my amendment. Horsman made his speech and I replied. He withdrew his motion which he perhaps could in the then existing state of circumstances have carried. But he probably shrank from certain failure before the committee.

(I was reading at Cuddesdon with Saunders, afterwards Dean of Peterborough, when Bishop Bagot first visited it. He was Rector *ex officio*. I knew that he was also Dean of Canterbury, Rector of Blithfield and I think rector of something else. I was already a strong anti-pluralist (and had my first quarrel with George (Archdeacon) Denison on this subject). I had therefore a strong prejudice against him: which his fine appearance did not suffice to remove. But Sunday came: and the Bishop preached on 'All things work together for good to them that love God and to them who are called according to his purpose'. It was one of the most beautiful and most evangelical sermons I ever heard. I was simply carried off my feet. All my prejudice melted into the thinnest air.)

The condition of the colonial church was [at] this time hampered and perplexed by the conflicting evils of arbitrary rule, impotence, and ambiguity. The colonial legislatures did not regulate or concern themselves with it. I had consulted Archbishop Howley during his lifetime, and found him desirous to give up what was for them a pure fiction of establishment which held them to be the church of all the people of the colony, subject to the freedom of those who desired to separate. I was very desirous to obtain a liberating measure which should place these churches in a condition legally to make resolutions for the government of their own affairs on the same footing as other religious bodies, that is by pure compact or consent. Thesiger (Lord Chelmsford) assisted me in 1851 with his advice: next year when in office he forgot that he had given it and condemned what he had recommended. But he was perfectly honest, and the ground was slippery. In 1852 I brought in my bill. Pakington, the Colonial Secretary, was weak and not very well affected. Bethell, extremely hostile, contended that the bill set up a new church with state authority. I think only Page Wood (Lord Hatherley) supported me. It may be that the language of my bill was not well chosen. I was obliged to withdraw it. One or more efforts were made in subsequent years. In one of these Bethell himself was concerned. It proved to be a curious case of *solvitur ambulando*. No new act was passed either at home or in the colonies *generally*. But the churches acquired self-consciousness and corporate feeling: and thus, aided by high individualities such as Bishop George Selwyn, Bishop Medley of New Brunswick and later on

Bishop Gray, each colony set about doing for itself what it required and built for itself its own house which in spite of all storms has with support from the growth of church feeling at home proved weathertight. I believe the abortive bill of 1852 did good, in giving what was probably the first definite impulsion to the cause.

9 September 1897

1847–52 AN INTERVAL—NO. 3

The relations between Sir R. Peel and his colleagues were never broken off under the Government of Lord J. Russell, but they were paralysed for general purposes by the exclusiveness of his regard to preventing the Protectionists from obtaining office. Hence all the effect of his high character, power, and position was negative as regarded Lincoln, Herbert, and myself who were not similarly tied to merely negative purposes.

When the sad and unexpected death of Sir R. Peel occurred in 1850, it became necessary to consider whether his followers still constituted a party. They were not in general prepared for absorption in either of the two great parties, the Government and the Protectionists. One among us, namely Lord Lincoln, was so sanguine as to believe that we were destined to be a lasting and a growing party: that we were to attract the best men from all sides, and after a time to govern the country. These high[1] expectations I never shared nor in any manner encouraged. Lord Aberdeen as a peer was less concerned with ideas of this kind; and Sir James Graham stood rather aloof from us, and was more readily prepared for what would have been for him simply a renewal of his old and original party alliance with the Whigs or Liberals.

In the autumn of 1850, the few leading Peelites were rather widely dispersed: I had repaired to Naples on account of a question of health in our family. It was certainly remarkable that when Lord J. Russell produced his most unhappy scheme of legislation against ecclesiastical titles (with an exception eventually in favour of the Scottish Bishops!) all these Peelites with either little or absolutely no communication determined against it. There were Lord Aberdeen, Sir James Graham, Lord Lincoln now Duke of Newcastle, Sidney Herbert, and Mr. Cardwell: perhaps one or two more, and I think the opposition made by the

---

[1] MS: I.

minority in the House of Commons to this wise measure was a creditable opposition: and though it was not successful at the moment within the walls of Parliament it crippled and paralysed the new law morally in such a way that it was at once reduced to impotence and even covered with ridicule.

It had in the meantime become essential for the Peelites, if we were to have even for the shortest time a separate existence, to be under a leader. I found that the Duke of Newcastle coveted this post. It appeared to me that Lord Aberdeen was on every ground the person entitled to hold it. I made my views distinctly known to the Duke. He took no offence. I do not know what communications he may have held with others. But the upshot was that Lord Aberdeen became our leader. And this result was obtained without any shock or conflict. What I knew and thought of that admirable man was fully set forth by me in a letter to his surviving son (now Lord Stanmore) written soon after his death which took place at the close of 1860.[1]

9 September 1897

PROTECTIONISM, 1840–1860

ADD.MS 44790, ff. 120–130   *12 July 1894*
When I entered Parliament in 1832, the great controversy between Protection or artificial restraint and Free Trade, of which Cobden was the hero, did not enter into the popular controversies of the day and was still in the hands of the philosophers. My mind was in regard to it a sheet of white paper but I accepted the established traditions in the lump and could hardly do otherwise. In 1833 or 4 the question was debated in the House of Commons and the speech of the mover against the Corn Laws made me uncomfortable: but the reply of Sir James Graham restored my peace of mind. The question was[2]
I followed the affair with a languid interest. But I remember being struck with the essential unsoundness of the main argument (I write from memory) of Mr. Villiers. It was this. Under the present Corn Law our trade, on which we depend, is doomed; for our manufacturers can-

---

[1] Gladstone's letter, dated 21 April 1861, is printed in Morley, ii, 639–644.
[2] The remainder of this sentence has been overwritten and is illegible.

not possibly contend with the manufacturers of the Continent if they have to pay wages regulated by the protective price of food, while their rivals pay according to the natural or free trade price. The answer was obvious. 'Thank you. We quite understand you. Your object is to get down the wages of your work people.' It was Cobden who really set the argument on its legs: and it is futile to compare any other man with him as the father of our system of Free Trade.

However as ill luck would have it, I had in 1840 to dabble in this question, and on the wrong side of it. A vacancy occurred at Walsall. My excellent brother John stood for it: and I was summoned from Hawarden at a moment's notice to speak for and support him. Bad seasons began to disclose the vices of the sliding scale, and the Anti-Corn Law League had I think been founded. But the controversy had not yet taken hold of the public mind in its depths, and the Melbourne Government was fast falling into a discredit partly just and partly unjust. My resource lay in a bundle of pamphlets written to defend the Corn Law: and I talked nonsense with a good conscience and with impunity. Cobden sent me a challenge to debate which I refused with the impertinence of youth. The matter passed from my mind: full of churches and church matter in which I was now gradually acquiring knowledge especially from large perusal of Saint Augustine when in Scotland, and the influence of two remarkable friends, Hope and Manning: the first one of the most fascinating among men, the second possessed of some great and remarkable gifts. In 1841 the necessities of the Government led to a further development of this great controversy: but I interfered only in the colonial part of it in connection with the colonies and the slave trade to Porto Rico and Brazil: our West Indians were now great philanthropists!

When Sir Robert Peel assumed the Government he had become deeply committed to Protection which in the last two or three years had become the subject of a commanding controversy. I suppose that at Newark I followed suit but I have no record. On the change of Government I had vaguely and imprudently hoped I might be Secretary for Ireland: not then likely to be a Cabinet office. Peel with much judgment offered me the vice-Presidentship of the Board of Trade. The offer made my blood run cold. I felt that about casks and packages I knew absolutely nothing: my interest was in men. Nor did Peel himself I think know very much. He told me the President would probably be Lord Ripon and that I should find him a perfect master of the business.

On sound principles of party discipline I took the office at once and having taken it I set to work with all my might as a learner. In a very short time I came to form a low estimate of the knowledge and information of Lord Ripon and of the Cabinet (Sir James Graham I think knew most). And now the stones of which my Protectionism was built up began to get uncomfortably loose. In January 1842 when Peel made known to me his modification in the existing Corn Law which he meant to propose I was so forward as to think it quite inadequate: and placing a very low estimate on myself, and the place I filled in the Government, I requested his permission to resign. On this and many other occasions I was misled by defective knowledge of the world and of its ways: but I was open to instruction. Peel received my overture, which I thought a very slight affair, with what I may call a sulky displeasure. Still it dawned upon me that I was unknowingly in the act of striking a blow which I did not intend and in a choice of difficulties I undertook to support his bill as against a fixed duty, the scheme of the Whig semi-Free Traders. He was now all radiant. And when we came to the larger plan and larger question of the tariff, we were all nearly on a par in ignorance and we had a very bad adviser in Macgregor, Secretary to the Board of Trade. But I had the advantage of being able to apply myself with an undivided attention. I learned the cause of the different trades out of the mouths of the deputations which were sent up to remit our proposals. So that by the close of the session I began really to know something about the matter and my faith in Protection except as a system of transition crumbled rapidly away.

From this time down to 1860 or thereabouts the question of Protection mainly determined the parliamentary history of the country and it became my fate to bear a very active part in it especially after the death of Sir Robert Peel: until in the year last named it came in my judgment to involve also through the French treaty the question of peace and war: for such was the irritation of men and parties in that year at the acquisition by Louis Napoleon of Savoy and Nice for France, that the choice lay between closer bonds of amity through the treaty, and a tension of relations almost certain to result in a rupture. With this treaty, the movement in favour of Free Trade reached its zenith. Since that time we have witnessed a strong and almost universal reaction. For my part I am a Free Trader on moral no less than on economic grounds: for I think human greed and selfishness are interwoven with every thread of the Protective system.

This real though limited evangel of [*illegible*] is now committed to the care of Britain. But we have persevered: we feel that we can hold our own. One argument which I made at Dundee in 1891 or 2 would I think have had the approval of Cobden. If we have courage and persistence in the right (as so often in the wrong) we shall convert the world.

It has been a blessed thing to share the work of those who scatter plenty in a smiling land and in essentially if not yet sufficiently changing the position of my labouring fellow countrymen. I owe it not to myself, who in ignorance eschewed the subject, but to Peel and to the Providence which sat and wrought behind him.

Thus was I introduced to the third of six great subjects which have mainly supplied the material of my political action. The first two were the Church and the colonies. Freedom of trade the third. This discussion upon finance, the fourth. Then came the emancipation of subject races the fifth. And finally Ireland the sixth. And so pass my sixty years and more.

There were some excellent points in the political creed of Lord Palmerston: but he was no genuine Free Trader. In the matter of the French treaty, from the time when the skies darkened he pursued a course I think of latent hostility or armed neutrality, to the French treaty. But Lord Russell remained as always loyal.

In this great controversy Peel as I think displayed perfect honesty and inflexible courage: but was open to remark in point of sagacity in foresight. From the language he held to me in December 1845 I think he expected to carry the repeal of the Corn Law without breaking up his party. But meant at all hazards to carry it.

A miscalculation followed which was more difficult in my opinion to explain. The opposition to the repeal depended chiefly on three men. The first was George Bentinck, a man of iron will, whose whole soul was in the matter and whose convictions were profoundly engaged. The next Lord Derby. He was a man brilliantly endowed: but his gifts of character were I think hardly equal to his talents. From the high position which he occupied he was a most ornamental leader. But he was not a man to fight doggedly for a losing cause. The third and not least remarkable was Disraeli. From first to last he simply played with the subject.

As long as George Bentinck lived, he was the animating principle of the party: and he would certainly have urged it, I may say constrained it, to go all lengths for its purposes. But in 1848 he was removed by an

early and sudden death. The change thus brought about was fundamental. The Protectionists were from thenceforth a house built upon the
sand. Their leaders were two men, one of whom had no stomach for a
desperate fight, while the other never dreamed of fighting at all, except
for his career. Under these circumstances it was with astonishment that
I listened to Peel when he said to me, 'I foresee that there will be a
desperate struggle made for the restoration of Protection', and 'I think',
he added, 'it will convulse the country'. Therefore in 1846–50 he made
it the main principle of his parliamentary action to support the Whigs
(without becoming himself a Whig or Liberal) and to keep out the
Protectionists. I held this to be an hallucination. In my estimation Protection was certain to thrive and flourish so long as it continued irresponsible and could only be brought to its deserved extinction by being
subjected to the touch of office, of governing the country, when as by the
wand of a magician it would at once dissolve. Such was the issue to
which it was brought in 1852[1]: and the issue is before the world.

SECOND STAGE OF PARLIAMENTARY LIFE 1853–65

1852–3 AND THE ABERDEEN GOVERNMENT

ADD.MS 44791, ff. 103-130

In December 1852 I had with other leading Peelites a share in the actual
formation of the Cabinet: in which it may be thought that the Whigs,
whose party was to supply five-sixths or seven-eights of our supporters,
had less than their due share of power. It should however be borne in
mind that they had at this juncture in some degree the character of an
used up and so far a discredited party. Without doubt they were sufferers
from their ill-conceived and mischievous Ecclesiastical Titles Act. Whereas we the Peelites had been for six and a half years out of office, and had
upon us the gloss of freshness.

The Government of Lord Aberdeen lifted me more into the public
view than the preceding years had done.

---

[1] The MS is difficult to read but the date appears to be 1854. Presumably,
however, Gladstone was referring to the assumption of office by the Protectionists in 1852.

It fell to me to follow Disraeli in the concluding debate which overthrew the Derby Administration. I rose very late: could it be at three
in the morning, and spoke long and keenly. Having run away from Protection, as it was plain from the first they would do, they had little to
offer to the land but that little their minority was ready to accept. But
the flagrantly vicious element in Disraeli's Budget was his proposal to
reduce the income tax on Schedule D to fivepence in the pound, leaving
Schedule [A] at sevenpence. This was no compensation to the land: but,
inasmuch as to exempt one is to tax another, it was a distinct addition
to the burdens borne by the holders of visible property. It was on Disraeli's part a most daring bid for the support of the Liberal majority,
for we all knew that the current opinion of the Whigs and Liberals was
in favour of this scheme: which on the other hand was disapproved by
sound financiers. The authority of Pitt and Peel, and then my own study
of the subject, made me believe that it was impracticable, and probably
meant the disruption of the tax with confusion in finance as an immediate *sequitur*. What angered me was that Disraeli never had examined
the question. And I afterwards found that he had not even made known
his intentions to the Board of Inland Revenue. The gravity of the question thus raised made me feel that the day was come to eject the Government; and we overthrew them by the small majority of sixteen(?)[1]
Graham would not take the financial department, and after the share
I had had in bringing about the crisis I had no choice but to accept it:
although as it plainly appeared my first duty would be the conversion
of our own party on the most crying financial question of the day.

But, before the period for the annual Budget, a remarkable opening
was given for the foundation of a two and a half per cent stock. The
idea though in those days novel was very favourably received. The three
per cents stood at   on the   of   .[2] I produced my plan. Disraeli offered it a malignant opposition. He made a demand for time:
the one demand that ought not to have been made, however it may
always seem to be. In proposals of this kind, it is allowed to be altogether
improper. In 1844 Mr. Goulburn was permitted I think to carry through
with great expedition his plan for a large reduction of interest. When Mr.
Goschen produced his still larger and much more important measure,
we the Opposition did our best to expedite the decision. There are no

---

[1] 'Sixteen?' added afterwards in pencil. The correct figure was 19.
[2] Blanks in MS.

complications requiring time on such an occasion. It is a matter of *a giorno*. But when time is allowed the chapter of accidents allows an opponent to hope that a situation known to be unusually happy will deteriorate. Of this contingency Disraeli took his chance. Time as it happened was in his favour. The course of public affairs (I think in the east?) removed the magic touch that had brought about such a felicitous conjuncture. It was no question of the substance of the plan, but a moderate change in the political barometer which reduced to two or three millions a subscription which at the right moment would have been twenty or thirty. I was probably wrong in acceding to the request: but in such a case the chief power lay with the maker of it. Even as it was the stock was created, and it was a very important step, though at the time of small pecuniary result, to have a basis laid for further and more extended operations.

I must say of this Cabinet of Lord Aberdeen's that in its deliberations it never exhibited the marks of its dual origin. Sir W. Molesworth, its Radical member, seemed to be practically rather nearer in colour to the Peelites than to the Whigs. There were some few idiosyncrasies without doubt. Lord Palmerston, who was Home Secretary, had in him some tendencies which might have been troublesome but for a long time were not so. It is for instance a complete error to suppose that he asked the Cabinet to treat the occupation of the Principalities as a *casus belli*. Lord Russell shook the position of Lord Aberdeen by action most capricious and unhappy. But with the general course of affairs this had no connection; and even in the complex and tortuous movements of the Eastern negotiations, the Cabinet never fell into two camps. That question and the war were fatal to it. In itself I hardly ever saw a Cabinet with greater promise of endurance.

With reference to the war I may give a curious example of the power of self-deception in the most upright men. The offices of Colonial Secretary and War Minister were, in conformity with usage, united in the hands of the Duke of Newcastle. On the outbreak of war it became necessary to separate them. It evidently lay with the holder to choose which he would hold. The Duke elected for the War Department, and publicly declared that he did this in compliance with the unanimous desire of his colleagues. And no one contradicted him. It was obviously impossible to contradict him. We could only 'grin and bear'. I cannot pretend to know the sentiments of each and every Minister on the matter. But I myself, and every one with whom I happened to communicate were very strongly of an opposite opinion. The Duke was *well* qualified for the colonial seals, for he was a statesman: *ill* for the War Office, as he was no administrator. I believe we all desired that Lord Palmerston should have been War Minister. It might have made a difference as to the tolerance of the feeble and incapable administration of our army before Sebastopol. Indeed I remember hearing Lord Palmerston suggest in Cabinet the recall of Sir Richard Airey.

In that crisis one man suffered most unjustly. I mean Sidney Herbert. To some extent perhaps his extraordinary and most just popularity led people to refrain from pouring on him those vials of wrath to which his office exposed him in the eyes especially of the uninformed. The duties of his department were really financial. I suppose it to be doubtful whether it was not the duty of the Secretary of State's department to deal with the question of supply for the Army, leaving to him only the management of the purchasing part. But I conceive it could be subject to no doubt at all that it was the duty of the administrative department of the army on the spot to anticipate and make known their wants for the coming winter. This if my memory serves me they wholly failed to do: and, the Duke of Newcastle's staff being in truth very little competent, Herbert strained himself morning noon and night to invent wants for the army and according to his best judgment or conjecture to supply them. So was laden the great steamer which went to the bottom in the harbour of Balaclava. And so came Herbert to be abused for his good deeds.

I will proceed here with what little I have to say of this distinguished and delightful man: a man of such qualities that any one possessed of them must always be without a rival in his generation. I remember my first sight of him in the building and on the occasion when the University of Oxford met to petition Parliament against the Roman Catholic claims in 1829. The beauty and grace of his appearance, exhibiting him as one of Nature's nobles, made an indelible impression upon me.

'A lovelier and a sweeter gentleman,
   Framed in the prodigality of Nature
   The spacious earth hath not to show again.'

Years after his death and that of the Duke of Newcastle, I found that it was intended that a life of the Duke should be written by a certain Mr. Carlyle. The intention has never yet been executed; which all things considered is perhaps as well, though he had great gifts and qualities together with sad and profound misfortune. He was a fast friend to me, and was the means perhaps of fixing my profession, certainly of introducing me into Parliament through his father and the constituency of Newark.

I conceived that his biographer would almost certainly even though unconsciously be unjust to Sidney Herbert in dealing with the Crimean winter. This made me readily fall in with the desire of Lady Herbert for a memoir of her husband. When one or more proposals had failed, I recommended Arthur Gordon (Lord Stanmore) for this charge. Long years ago: I have not an idea why the volume has never appeared.

When the second Cabinet of Lord Palmerston was formed in 1859, Sidney Herbert fell under the influence of the prevailing French panic. He behaved with extraordinary kindness to me in the adjustment of income and charge for the year 1860-1, which was a critical affair. There arose however a correspondence between us in which views were fully declared by each of us. He warned me that I was in danger of overlooking a great danger, that of invasion from France. I on my part dubbed him 'the captain general of alarmists'.

We spent at Wilton the last Easter of his life, and were full of alarms about him: more full I think than Lady Herbert herself. Had his life been prolonged, I think it would have secured his family against that woeful dispersion and confusion in matters of belief which was progressively exhibited, and which made his own portion of the splendid church he built for a long time nothing (I believe) but a desert: I must however say for Lady Herbert that after her own secession she either fitted up or continued the use of a suitable apartment for well conducted family prayers: and she herself regularly played the organ for the hymns.

14 September 1897

1855-8

During the period of my life from 1855 to 1858, I was again to some extent in a false position. On the one hand my opinions became progressively more liberal, while the ties that had bound me even to my original party retained force, and in some degree even resumed it. Before the formation of the Aberdeen Cabinet I did not share the opinion of Newcastle who thought it was the destiny of Peelism to found an intermediate party and policy and attract to it elements sufficient to hold the conduct of affairs. I was disposed to cooperate with each party in each case according to the merits, and so be guided by experience; but I did not see that we had attractive force to rally a party round ourselves in our own name or Peel's or that there was a ground lying between the positions of the two old parties and having anything like the breadth and solidity required to sustain a new body and a new form of action. My share in the Aberdeen experiment was tentative or empirical. But on most subjects the Peelite element in the Aberdeen Cabinet was in advance, I do not say of Lord John Russell or of Granville, individually, but of the Whig element as a whole. We had Molesworth, a doctrinaire *Radical*, in the Cabinet, and we were certainly more in harmony with him than the Whigs were. A spirit of administrative activity and reform had been derived by us from Peel: and on the important subject of colonial policy in particular we were and had long been in thorough agreement with the propounders of autonomy.

When that Government was overthrown by the motion of Mr. Roebuck for a committee on the condition of the army in the Crimea, and by the conduct of Lord Russell on that motion, this stroke produced in me a political reaction favourable to Conservative reunion, provided that reunion were a reunion of a body with a body: for I never at any time contemplated replacing myself as an individual in the Conservative ranks. Strong sympathy with Lord Aberdeen and resentment at the treatment he had received lay at the root of this tendency. A strong sentiment of revulsion from Disraeli personally, a sentiment quite distinct from that of dislike, was alone sufficient to deter me absolutely from a merely personal and separate reunion; besides which there would have been no power, unless in company, to give to Conservatism a liberal bias in conformity with the traditions of Peel.

After the downfall, and I think before either Derby or Palmerston had been definitely called in, Lord Lansdowne sent for me to Lansdowne House, and acquainted me that he had received a commission to form a government. He had taken time to consider, and he was endeavouring to feel his way. He asked whether I would continue to hold my office as Chancellor of the Exchequer in the event of his persevering. He said that if I gave an affirmative reply he would persevere with the commission: and I think intimated that except on this condition he would not. I said that the working of the coalition since its formation in December 1852 had been to me entirely satisfactory, but that I was not prepared to cooperate in its continuation under any other head than Lord Aberdeen.

This I think was one of the greatest, perhaps the greatest, error I ever committed. There was no defect in Lord Lansdowne sufficient to warrant my refusal. He would not have been a strong or very active Prime Minister: but the question of the day was the conduct of the war, and I had no right to take exception to him as a head in connection with this subject. His attitude in domestic policy was the same as Palmerston's, but I think he had a more unprejudiced and liberal mind, though less of motive force in certain directions.

I think that the issue I then contemplated was the formation of a Derby Government; and to this, now that the party had been *drubbed* out of Protection I did not in principle object; for old ties were with me more operatively strong than new opinions: and I think that Lord Derby's error in not forming an administration was palpable and even gross. Such, it has I think appeared, was the opinion of Disraeli. Lord Derby had many fine qualities; but strong parliamentary courage was not among them. On receiving the Queen's overture he invited Lord Palmerston to join him, in conjunction with the Peelites (or some of them, I being one) and to lead the House of Commons. When Lord Palmerston (probably with a sagacious discernment of the immediate future) declined, he made no separate offer to the Peelites. Lord Palmerston asked my opinion which was somewhat in favour of his acceptance and of our accepting with him. He acted in the opposite sense. But had Lord Derby gone on, he would have been supported by the country, then absorbed in the consideration of the war. None of the three occasions when he took office offered him so fine an opportunity as this; but he missed it: a Palmerston government was the only available alternative.

Graham, Sidney Herbert, and I reluctantly agreed to keep our seats in the Cabinet; and a new start was made. It was determined in due form to send a commission to the Crimea. But this very proper measure which was intended as a substitute for the Roebuck committee, obviously left a great parliamentary difficulty in its rear. What was to become of the vote for the Roebuck committee given by a large majority? I think it might have been quite possible to induce the House to consent to hold that weapon for a while in reserve. But the mode of proceeding required the utmost deliberation, care, and studiousness of handling. I cannot but think Palmerston was here much to blame. He never invited the Cabinet to consider the best mode of proceeding: but went to the House and set his proposed commission against the committee in so bold a manner, without offering the House any alternative or middle term, that it as it were spontaneously persisted. We three retained our objections: and were accordingly compelled to resign.

We were severely and generally censured for thus deserting Palmerston who had in fact by precipitate and rude handling stranded us. I will not say whether we were right. Graham was our leader in the business; and we acted with him against Lord Aberdeen's opinion, on high, almost romantic grounds. But this I will say without doubt: the final upshot of the transaction, including the Chelsea inquiry, and the eventual refusal of the House to take into consideration the drastic and damnatory report of its own committee was creditable to none of the parties principally *concerned* in bringing it about. For the country the result was this, that three separate and disconnected authorities (committee, commission, and Chelsea board) contradicted one another by laying the blame one on the Aberdeen Government, one on the military administration in the Crimea, and one on the sub-department of the commissariat in the Treasury. And these three verdicts were left by the House of Commons, notwithstanding the immense importance of the issues involved, to knock their heads against one another without any effort to decide between them. Perhaps the very worst miscarriage of public justice since the Reform Act; and one which stands in rather discreditable contrast with the Walcheren inquiry.

FRENCH PANIC AND CRISIS OF 1859–61

31 August and 1 September 1897

The session of 1860 with its complement in the principal part of 1861, was I think the most trying part of my whole political life. It was my nadir in public estimation. To what a point I sank may be estimated from a passage in Greville's Journals referring to the close I think of session 1860, and from an article, I think a jubilant article in *The Times*, on the subject of my extinction.[1]

In the autumn of 1859, Mr. Cobden came to Hawarden to discuss the question of a commercial treaty with France which was then in

---

[1] The references seem to be to the entry in Greville's journal for 12 May 1860, and to the first leader in *The Times* of 6 February 1860.

embryo. My union of sentiment with him on this and I think most other subjects was complete. We were both keenly in favour of such a treaty: and both I think (I myself certainly) were in favour of this particular treaty without intending thereby to signify the smallest disposition to the promotion of tariff treaties in general. I had been an active party to the various attempts under Sir Robert Peel's government to conclude such treaties, and was as far as possible removed from any disposition to the renewal of labour which was itself so profitless, and which was dangerously near to a practical assertion of a false principle, namely that reductions of indirect taxation, permitted by fiscal considerations, are in themselves injurious to the country that makes them, and are only to be entertained when a compensation can be had for them (unless otherwise by way of an exception).

The business of Cobden's mission to Hawarden was therefore soon disposed of: and the correspondence which would in the ordinary course have been exchanged between the Foreign Offices of the two countries was carried through in a series of personal letters between Mr. Cobden and myself. I remember indeed that the Emperor or his government were desirous to conceal from their own Foreign Minister (Walewski?) the fact that such a measure was in contemplation. On our side, the method pursued was only recommended by practical considerations. I contemplated including the conditions of the French Treaty in a new and sweeping revision of the tariff, the particulars of which it was of course important to keep from the public eye until they were ready to be submitted to Parliament.

When I obtained the assent of the Cabinet to the proposed treaty with France, there was no general opposition, but objection was taken on the ground that we ought not to commit ourselves to a sacrifice of revenue until we had before us the income and charge for the coming year. I think that this observation was taken by Sir George Lewis and Sir C. Wood.

It was not devoid of force: but the situation was exceptional. The House of Commons did not then regard the income tax as a fixed portion of the general burdens of the country. It had been in the previous July provisionally renewed at a high rate. The naval and military expenditure were rising. The willingness of Parliament to vote supplies would depend in large measure on its being satisfied with the measures proposed, and there was reason to believe that the French treaty would be very acceptable. I of course believed that (as it proved) the conclusion of it would open much trade and largely enrich the country. But I had a reason of a higher order. The French Emperor had launched his project as to Savoy and Nice. It should have been plain to all those who desired an united Italy, that such an Italy ought not to draw Savoy in its wake: a country severed from it by the mountains, by language, by climate, and I suppose by pursuits. But it does not follow that Savoy should have been tacked on to France: while for the annexation of Nice it was difficult to find a word of apology. But it could scarcely be said to concern our interests, while there was not the shadow of a case of honour. The susceptibilities of England were however violently aroused. Even Lord John Russell used imprudent language in Parliament about looking for other allies. These were hailed and encouraged from the Opposition bench. The progress of this excitement was much aided by the increase of the defensive estimates which however had no reference to the plans of France. A French panic prevailed, as strong as any of the other panics which have done so much discredit to this country. For this panic the treaty of commerce with France was the only sedation. It was in fact a counter-irritant; and it aroused the sense of commercial interest to counteract the war passion. It was and is my opinion that the choice lay between the Cobden treaty and, not the certainty but the high probability of a war with France.

I ought to say that I think both Sir G. Lewis and Sir C. Wood had spoken entirely without *arrière-pensée*.

In the early stages of the contest which followed, the French treaty, and the Budget, of which it formed the most salient feature, carried all before them. Lord Palmerston who had taken a somewhat neutral position, and who never I think was profoundly interested like Cobden or like Peel, in freedom of trade, was delighted with the general situation, and congratulated me on it warmly.

But three causes were at work, which entirely altered by their joint operation the complexion of the scene.

1. Lord Palmerston himself had a favourite scheme for expending eight or nine millions on fortifications at Spithead. This he had hoped to carry early in the session. But I was rather stiffly opposed to it: and the consequence of my resistance (I believe) was its postponement until late in the session. So it hung over us as a difficulty ready to become very serious when associated with other difficulties.

2. Lord Russell, most unhappily, insisted while we were deep in the Budget, on pressing the second reading of his Reform Bill, which the

Opposition hated, and many of the Government party (Lord Palmerston at their head) scarcely loved. He therefore played in the most egregious manner into the hands of the Opposition: who were able in conformity with a widespread though largely latent sentiment in the House to obstruct him right and left, not only by prolonging debate but by refusing so that they were able if I remember right to prolong the proceedings on the second reading of his bill over a number of weeks. When Lord John (as he still was) asked the Cabinet to stop the Budget in order to fix a day for his second reading, I said to him, 'Lord John, I will go down on my knees to you, to intreat you not to press that request.' But he persevered; and this although he was both a loyal colleague and a sincere friend to the Budget and to the French treaty. The Budget itself, involving an entire change of our tariff, required a great deal of time, the expenditure of which the country followed with satisfaction. But for this unhappy error of procedure about the Reform Bill, we should have disposed *midway* in the session of the tariff and of the Paper Duties Repeal Bill, to which at this time there was only a Protectionist opposition without adventitious aid, and which fitted into the finance of the year as it then stood.

3. But as matters stood, when we at length got rid (for the moment) of reform in order to prosecute finance, we had so much to do that in the midst of it there came upon us the news of hostilities in China, which demanded at once an increase of outlay, not very large in comparison [with] expenditures to which ear and mind are now attuned, but yet sufficient to destroy my accruing balance, and thus to disorganize the finance of the year. The opposition to the Paper Bill now assumed most formidable dimensions. It was late in the session when we were able to propose the third reading: and if I remember right, we only carried it by a majority of nine.

4. During a long course of years there had grown up in the House of Commons a practice of finally disposing of the several parts of the Budget each by itself. And the House of Lords had shown so much self-controul in confining itself to criticism on matters of finance, that the freedom of the House of Commons was in no degree impaired. In 1853 on the proposal of Lord Aberdeen the House of Lords passed the bill for the repeal of the soap duties in the face of financial probabilities much more formidable, though less defined, than those which had arisen in 1860. But there was the opportunity of mischief: and round the carcass the vultures now gathered in overwhelming force. It at once became

clear that the Lords would avail themselves of the opportunity afforded them by the single presentation of financial bills, and would prolong, and virtually re-enact a ban, which the representatives of the people had repealed. The important auxiliary causes, to which I have referred, would not, however, of themselves have availed to bring about this daring innovation, had it not been that public opinion had at this time lost its tone, and had fallen into [a] state of demoralization, proceeding from and induced by the manner in which it had tampered with its own conscience and with public policy, in the matter of the parliamentary franchise.

We were agreed in the Cabinet that, viewing the advanced time of year and all the circumstances, no remedy could at the moment be applied: Lord Palmerston, however, recorded his protest in a speech. I followed him and did the same. The tone of the two remonstrances could not be in exact accord: but by careful steering, on my part and I presume on his, all occasion of scandal was avoided.

Then came on the fortifications crisis. I had stated, I believe, repeatedly, my utter objection to the plan: and, satisfied with this, I withdrew myself from the meeting of the Cabinet, on a day when it was to come on anew. Argyll fought my battle in my absence, and I believe did it with great ability and zeal. The plan could not be abandoned by the Prime Minister. It could not on the other hand be accepted by me, and possibly if I had withdrawn one or two more might have done the same. The Cabinet with its small majority was not in a condition to stand a surgical operation such as an amputation of this kind. In some manner which I either did not know or do not now recollect, the plan was recast and the proposal cut down from nine millions to five. This was a large concession; but I had more even than this to consider. The French treaty still hung in the balance. The *ad valorem* duty which France had engaged to impose had to be converted into specific rates. With this vital though subsidiary process I had no personal concern. But Lord Palmerston now completely alienated from the French Emperor had become either lukewarm or hostile about the treaty while he was adverse to the repeal of the paper duties, which indeed some were supposed to have voted against from being informed that such were his secret inclinations. The treaty had few warm friends in the Cabinet. It was exposed to danger at every step from differences of opinion among the negotiators at Paris, and I feared that these would grow when energetic support of the treaty in the Cabinet should have come to a close.

I therefore resolved not to resign (a question of course constantly before me) for any small or secondary matter until the treaty had been steered safely into port. When the fortifications plan had been cut down nearly by one half, I went to Sir James Graham whose aid had been invaluable to me in the whole course of these difficulties, and with whom I had been in agreement throughout. We were both agreed that in the situation such as I have described I ought to vote for the reduced scheme of fortifications rather than (as I thought) endanger the treaty. And I did so.

(This account is I believe rigidly accurate in every important point, and it contains probably the only reply I shall ever make to an account given or printed by Sir Theodore Martin in his Life of the Prince Consort which is most injurious to me without a shadow of foundation: owing I have no doubt to defective acquaintance with the subject.)

The hostilities in China reached a rather early termination, and in the early part of the session of 1861 it appeared almost certain that there would be a surplus for 1861–2 such as I thought would make it possible again to operate on the paper duties. Unfortunately the income tax was at so high a rate that we could not reasonably hope to carry the paper duty repeal without taking a penny off the tax. The double plan strained the probable means afforded by the Budget. In this dilemma, I received most valuable aid from the shrewd ingenuity of Milner Gibson, who said why not fix the repeal of the paper duty at a later date than had been intended, say on the 10th of October, which will reduce the loss for the year? I gladly adopted the supposition, and proposed a Budget reducing the income tax by one penny, and repealing the paper duties from October 10, 1861. With this was combined what was more essential than either: the adoption of a new practice with respect to finance which would combine all the financial measures of the year in a single bill.

We had separate discussions in the Cabinet on the constitutional proposal. It was not extensively resisted there, though quietly a good deal misliked. I rather think the Chancellor Campbell took strong objection to it: and I well remember that the Duke of Newcastle gave valuable and willing aid. So it was adopted.

The Budget was the subject of a fierce discussion, in which Lord Palmerston appeared to me to lose his temper for the first and only time. The plan, however, to my great delight was adopted. It was followed by a strange and painful incident. I received with astonishment from Lord Palmerston, immediately after the adoption of the bill, a

distinct notice, that he should not consider it a Cabinet question in the
House of Commons, when it was known that the Opposition and the
paper makers would use every effort to destroy the plan. I wrote an
uncontroversial reply (with some self repression) and showed it to Granville, who warmly approved and was silent on the letter of Lord P.

The battle in Parliament was hard, but was as nothing to the internal
fighting: and we won it. We likewise succeeded in the plan of uniting
the financial proposals in one bill. To this Spencer Walpole gave honourable support: and it became a standing rule. The House of Lords, for
its misconduct, was deservedly (in effect) extinguished as to all matters
of finance.

1 September 1897

1864 THE DANISH QUESTION

Not only during this year, but before it, the controversy respecting the
succession to the duchies of Schleswig-Holstein was under diplomatic
discussion, and was moving towards a crisis; the duchies being at the
time under the dominion of Denmark, to which power the attitude of
Prussia and Austria was extremely hostile. Probably by way of stalking
horse they were by way of supporting against Denmark the title of the
Duke of Augustenburg. But there grew up a suspicion if not a belief
that they meditated the use of force against Denmark.

The session was far advanced when in this state of circumstances
Lord Palmerston took an occasion of touching on the question. He adverted to the contingency of the adoption of military measures against
Denmark, which Denmark would have to resist: and he observed that
if that case arose it would probably be found that Denmark would not
stand alone. It seems that this statement was generally and not unnaturally interpreted as a promise of support from England. Lord Palmerston does not seem to have added any condition or reservation.

Strange as it may appear, he had spoken entirely of his own motion,
and without the authority or knowledge of his Cabinet: in which indeed,
so far as my memory serves, nothing had happened to render likely any
declaration of any kind on the subject. I have no means of knowing
whether he spoke in concert with the Foreign Secretary, Earl Russell,

with whom his communications, agreeable to policy and to established usage, were I believe large and constant.

When the question was eventually disposed of by the war which Prussia waged against Denmark, there was much indignation felt against England for the breach of her engagement to give support in the case of war to the small power so egregiously in need of it. And there was no one to raise a voice in our favour.

In the meantime circumstances of great importance had happened, which so far as I know have never come before the world. As the year advanced, and the prospect of war came nearer, the subject was very properly brought before the Cabinet. I believe that at the time I was not even aware of Lord Palmerston's declaration which, owing to the exhausted period of the session, had I believe attracted no great attention in England. I do not know whether this....[1] Whether my colleagues were as little aware of what happened as myself I do not know but unquestionably we could not all have missed learning it. However we did not as a body recognise in any way the title of the Prime Minister to bind us to go to war. We were however indignant at the conduct of the German powers, who as we thought were scheming piracy under cover of pacific correspondence. And we agreed upon a very important measure, in which Lord Palmerston acquiesced, when he failed, if I remember right in inducing the Cabinet to go further. We knew that France took the same view of the question as we did, and we framed a communication to her to the following effect.

We were jointly to insist that the claim of the Duke of Augustenburg should be peacefully settled on juridical grounds: and to announce to Prussia and Austria that if they proceeded to prosecute it by the use of force against Denmark, we would jointly resist them with all our might.

This communication was accordingly made to Louis Napoleon. He declined the proposal. He said! that the question was one of immense importance to us, who had such vast interests involved, and that the plan was reasonable from our point of view: but that the matter was one of small moment for France whom accordingly he could not ask to join in it.

The explanation of this answer, so foolish in its terms, and so pregnant with consequences in its matter, was I believe to be found in the pique

---

[1] This sentence was left incomplete.

of Louis Napoleon at a reply we had then recently given to a proposal of his for an European conference or congress. What the subject of it was to be, I cannot at this moment recollect. But I remember that we all thought his plan was wholly needless and would in all likelihood lead to mischief. So we declined it in perfect good faith and without implying by our refusal any difference of policy in the particular matter.

Had Napoleon acceded to our proposal, would the German powers have persevered? There was a chance that they might not: Austria might have flinched: I do not think Bismarck would have been on that side; but he might have shrunk from isolation. Had they persisted, the matter would have been most grave as a question of military operations. A good deal would have depended on Russia, whose bias was towards the side which we had taken. In any case, οὐγε ἂν ἀνιδρωτί γ' ἐτελέσθη [1]. But there is far more in question than this. Prussia would have had to spend in this conflict the resources which she husbanded till 1870. Our alliance with France would have become far closer and more stringent than that of the German war. The quarrel, Danish in its inception, would have absorbed the whole question depending between Prussia and France. Russia would most probably have gone against the German powers: in any case, France with Great Britain on her side never would have undergone the crushing defeat which she had to encounter in 1870-1, with the territorial alienations involved in it. That is to say the whole course of subsequent European history would in all likelihood have been changed.

2 September 1897

FIRST PERIOD OF LEADERSHIP

THE RESIGNATION OF 1866 AND HOUSEHOLD SUFFRAGE IN TOWNS

ADD.MS 44791, ff. 131-166
In the Parliament of 1865, while the Tory party was known to be utterly opposed to an extension of the franchise, there was a considerable fringe of professing Liberals, who were not less hostile but were not willing to

---

[1] Homer, *Iliad*, xv, 228. 'Ev'n pow'r immense had found such battle hard' (Pope).

confess to their hostility before their constituencies. Lord Russell on the other hand adhered with great tenacity to his ideas, in which he was strongly supported by me as his leader in the Commons, and by Granville and others of the Cabinet. Bright, the representative man of popular ideas, behaved with an admirable combination of discretion and loyalty. Lowe was an outspoken opponent, so superstitiously enamoured of the ten pound franchise as to be thrown into a temper of general hostility to a government which did not recognise its finality and sanctity. He pursued our modest Reform Bill of 1866 with an implacable hostility, and really supplied the whole brains of the Opposition. So effective were his speeches that, during this year only, he had such a command of the House as had never in my recollection been surpassed. Nor was there any warrant for imputing to him dishonesty of purpose or arrière-pensée. But his position was one for the moment of personal supremacy, and this to such an extent that, when all had been reconciled and the time for his peerage came, I pressed his viscountcy on the Sovereign as a tribute to his former elevation which though short-lived was due to genuine power of mind, as it seemed to me that a man who had once soared to those heights trodden by so few ought not to be lost in the common ruck of official barons.

I inclined to believe that we too readily accepted our defeat by an infinitesimal majority as a ground for resignation. There were at least four courses open to us: first, resignation; secondly, dissolution; thirdly, to deny the finality of the judgment and reverse the hostile vote on report; fourthly, to take shelter under a general vote of confidence which Mr. Crawford, M.P. for the City of London, was prepared to move.

Of these the last was the worst as disparaging to political character. Lord Russell, secretly conscious I suppose that he had arrived at the last stage of his political existence and desirous that it should not be abbreviated, inclined to adopt it. Granville and I were so decidedly set against it that we allowed ourselves I think to be absorbed in its defeat, and set up against it what was undoubtedly the readiest and simplest expedient; namely immediate withdrawal. To dissolve would have been a daring act, an appeal from a shuffling Parliament to an unawakened people. Yet it is possible, even probable, that such an appeal unhesitatingly made would have evoked a response similar though not equal to that of 1831. Or again a retrial of the question with a call of the House would in all likelihood have resulted in victory. By our retirement we opened the door for that series of curious deceptions and intrigues within the Tory party which undoubtedly accelerated the arrival of household suffrage; the old constitutional scot and lot with such variety of application of the principle as public convenience required.

When the Parliament reassembled in 1867, parties and groups were curiously distributed. The two great bodies were the regular supporters of the Tory Ministry, and those grouped around us who had been expelled. The first did not know what course they would have to take; but depended on the secret counsels of another mind. To keep to the *drapeau* was the guiding motion, as it has ever been since the creed and practice of Peel were subverted by the opposite principles of Disraeli, who on a franchise question had his peer colleagues at his feet. Besides these, other decisions had to be recognised. The Salisbury secession from the government supported by Sir W. Heathcote and Beresford Hope was high in character but absolutely insignificant in numbers. There was Lowe, so great among the Adullamites of 1866, but almost alone among them in the singleness and strength of his opposition to reform. These were the bulk of the Adullamite body, unable to place themselves in declared opposition to the Liberal mass, but many of them disposed to tamper with the question, and to look kindly on the Tory government as the power which would most surely keep down any enlargement of the franchise to its minimum.

It would be idle to discuss the successive plans submitted by the government to the House of Commons with an unexampled rapidity. The governing idea of the man who directed the party seemed to be not so much to consider what ought to be proposed and carried as to make sure that whatever it was it should be proposed and carried by those in power. The bill on which the House of Commons eventually proceeded was a measure I should suppose without precedent or parallel, as on the other hand it was for the purpose of the hour, and as the work of a government in a decided minority, an extraordinary piece of parliamentary success.

Our position on the other hand was this.
1. We felt that if household suffrage were to be introduced into the boroughs, it ought to be real household suffrage.
2. The existing state of our legislation under which a large majority of the householders made no disbursement of rate but paid them without distinction in their rent, showed that a bill professedly for household suffrage but taking no notice of compound householding would be in the first place a lottery and in the second an imposture. Some towns

would have large enfranchisement, some none [at] all, and no principle but the accidental state of local law would determine on which side of the line any town was to be found. And the aggregate result would be ludicrously small as a measure of enfranchisement. Of such a measure we could not approve.

We did not wish to make at once so wide a change as that involved in a genuine household suffrage (always in our minds involving county as well as towns) and we could not fairly separate ourselves from Bright on such a point.

3. So we adhered to our idea of an extension considerable but not violent, and performing all it promised.

But the Adullamite spirit went to work, and finding that the bill had the popular recommendation of a great phrase, combined with the recommendation to them of a miserably narrow sphere of practical operation, determined to support the principle of the bill and abandon our plan, although our mode of operation had been warmly approved at party meetings held at my house: Mr. Roebuck himself I think having by speech joined in this approval and afterwards abandoned it.

The result was in a tactical sense highly damaging to us. Perhaps we ought to have recognised that the idea of household suffrage when the phrase had once been advertised by a government as its battleground, was irresistible, and that the only remaining choice was whether it should be a household suffrage 'cabined, cribbed and confined' by the condition of personal ratepaying, or a household suffrage fairly conforming in substance and operation to the idea which the phrase conveyed. The first was in our view totally inadmissible: the second beyond the wants and wishes of the time. But the government it must be admitted bowled us down by the force of the phrase; and made it our next duty to bowl them down by bringing the reality of the bill into correspondence with its great profession.

This we were able to do in some degree when we reached the committee for some of the restrictions included in the measure were such as the double facing Liberal fringe did not venture to uphold against the assaults of their own party.

But the grand question of compound householding which was really to determine the character of our legislation, was one on which we could not reckon upon either the conscientious or the intimidated and prudential support of our Liberal fringe. The government were beyond all doubts at least for the moment masters of the situation. The question was raised, if not in its fullest breadth yet in a form of considerable efficiency by a proposal from Mr. Hodgkinson, Member for Newark and a local solicitor little known in the House. I went there to support it but without an idea that it could be carried, and anticipating its defeat by a majority of a hundred. Never have I undergone a stronger emotion of surprise than when as I was entering the House our Whip met me and stated that Disraeli was about to support Hodgkinson's motion. But so it was, and the proposition was adopted without disturbance as if it had been an affair of trivial importance.

How it came about I partially learned at a later date. A Cabinet was held after the fact, which Sir John Lambert, the great statistician of the day, was summoned to attend. The Cabinet had had no idea that the Hodgkinson amendment was to be accepted; the acceptance was the sole act of Mr. Disraeli: and when it had been done the Ministers assembled in order to learn from Sir John Lambert what was the probable addition which it would make to the constituency.

I do not suppose that in the whole history of the 'mystery-man' (as Bright had called him from the title of an official of the Ojibbeway Indians) this proceeding can be surpassed. The Tories having been brought to accept household suffrage on the faith of the limitation imposed by personal payment of the rates found at a moment's notice that that limitation had been thrown overboard and that their leader had given them a bill virtually far larger than any that Mr. Bright had sought to impose upon them. It was certainly no business of ours to complain: and they made it no business of theirs.

I imagine that they still relied upon rectification of the bill by the House of Lords. And the Lords did rectify it largely; but these rectifications were all rejected when the bill returned to us, except the minority, which Mr. Disraeli was strong enough to secure by means of the votes of a body of Liberals who approved it, while he detested it, and made as Bright said the best speech ever delivered against it.

So came about the establishment of an effective household suffrage in the cities and boroughs of England: seminally at least contained in the proceedings of Parliament, the mode of settlement depended on the men who conducted it. Half a century ago, had the thing been practicable, the manner would have been different: for the men of that day would not have stooped to employ the methods of this.

18 September 1897

FIRST CABINET 1868–74

I look back with great satisfaction on the internal working of the Cabinet of 1868–74. It was a Cabinet easily handled; and yet it was the only one of my four Cabinets in which there were several members who were senior to myself: the Lord Chancellor (Hatherley), Lord Clarendon, with many other men of long ministerial experience. When this Cabinet was breaking up in 1874 I took the opportunity of thanking them for the manner in which they had uniformly lightened my task in the direction of business. In reply Halifax, who might be considered as the senior in years and experience taken jointly, very handsomely he said the duty of the Cabinet had been made more easy by the considerate manner in which I had always treated them. Some of them were as colleagues absolutely delightful from the manner in which their natural qualities blended with their consummate experience. I refer especially to Clarendon and Granville.

An odd incident had happened as to the first. At the time when the coming ministerial change was beyond doubt, though the actual moment for it had not arrived, the Queen intimated to me I think through Lord Halifax, that there were two names which she did not desire to have submitted to her for offices they had formerly held: those of Lord Clarendon and Lord De Tabley. The second of these raised no difficulty. De Tabley was an ex-Lord in Waiting, and a promotion in the Household would at once be convenient to him on the ground of income, and to the Queen as giving him less occasion to appear in her presence. The case as to Clarendon was very different. He had already held with credit and success for a lengthened period the seals of the Foreign Office, and his presumptive title to resume them was beyond dispute. He was a man of free and entertaining, and almost jovial conversation in society, and possibly some remark culled from the dinner hour had been repeated to the Queen with carelessness or malignity. I do not know much of the interior side of Court gossip but I have a very bad opinion of it, and especially on this ground that while absolutely irresponsible it appears to be uniformly admitted as infallible. In this case, it was impossible for me to recede from my duty, and no grave difficulty arose. So far as I can recollect the Queen had very little to say in objection, and no keen desire to say it. Clarendon was the only living British statesman whose name carried any influence in the councils of Europe. Only eighteen or twenty months remained to him: they were spent in useful activity. My relations with him were, as they were afterwards with Granville, close, constant, and harmonious.

It has recently appeared, from Purcell's *Life of Manning*, that, during the Council of the Vatican, Lord Odo Russell, who then irregularly but with much talent represented us at Rome, frequently or habitually made known to that Cardinal and through him to the Papal Court, all the confidential communications among the diplomatists at Rome. This is an unquestionable, but an amazing disclosure. I do not think that the British Government as a whole could have authorised it without gross breach of duty to other states. I am sure that Clarendon had no authority to enjoin or permit anything of the kind even with or still without my knowledge and concurrence and I have the most absolute moral certainty that he never would have done or did any thing of the kind. Such communications as I have had with his successor tend to show that nothing of the sort was ever done by him. But if Lord Odo Russell acted thus of his own motion, he committed an error which amounted to a crime, and deserved the severest censure, if not the ultimate penalty of recall.

While the governing instrument was thus in good order, my mind had of course been largely occupied with the work it would have to perform. In England it remained to perfect the work of enfranchisement for the towns by a fresh bill with regard to compound householding, but in the actual position of affairs there was no reason to believe that this proceeding could entail serious difficulty. It was Ireland which mainly and almost entirely filled the political horizon. In the view of the public there were three great objects to be dealt with: the Church, the land, and the higher education. In my own mind there were two other subjects of moment. Firstly I was anxious to inquire whether it would be possible and advantageous to establish some closer relation of property or otherwise between the State and the railways in Ireland, the development of which appeared under the actual system to be slow and feeble. The last of the five subjects touched the higher relations between the countries, and involved the whole question of the position of the Royal Family in regard to Ireland, and of any consequential changes therewith connected.

The subject of the Church requires little notice. We allowed[1] the Lords to plunder to a certain extent the residuary fund of Church

---

[1] MS: advised allowed. Presumably Gladstone forgot to delete the first word.

property as the lesser of two evils. But I never have been concerned in bringing about a legislative change on which I look back with more lively or more unqualified satisfaction.

Our land legislation of 1870 was so singularly favoured by current circumstances that for a time there was even an appearance that it might suffice. As it was it supplied for the subject an effective introduction to the arena of legislation: and by our compensation for disturbance (a suggestion originally due I think to Lord Carlingford) we laid broadly, but perhaps with no very clear consciousness of it the foundations of the doctrine of tenant right for all Ireland.

As regards the subject of the higher education in Ireland, the rejection of our bill was a cruel massacre of our excellent measure. There is no bill in which I have ever been concerned, and for which I am more desirous to claim my full responsibility. Unless its principle be resumed, all legislation on this subject must remain mere costly patchwork. The Tories temperately and wisely determined to accept it. Delane, editor of *The Times*, said to Manning when they were leaving the House of Commons, "This is a bill made to pass." Manning himself heartily acquiesced in it. What notion induced the Roman Catholic Bishops of Ireland to decide on opposing it, I have never been able to conceive. As to the reasons alleged against it they were on the merest matter of detail. But *hic jacet* with much else that is good.

As respects the railways it was impossible to make way unless aid could be had from preliminary inquiry by persons of weight. I was able to man a good commission, with the Duke of Devonshire at its head, and Lord Derby as his coadjutor. But this commission did not venture to force any considerable change, and as they would not move, I who might be held in a manner to have appealed to them, could do nothing.

My attempt to bring about an altered attitude of the Royal Family towards Ireland may have been a daring one; but I think it was right, although it also involved, as I framed the scheme, important changes in England. It was not (although an Irish) an exclusively Irish proposal. Since the death of the Prince Consort, the Court, properly so called, had virtually dropped out of existence, and a valuable and important instrument of public influence on behalf of the monarchy was thus placed in abeyance. It certainly was not possible to hope that the commission of new means and responsibilities to the Prince and Princess of Wales would wholly fill the vacuum: yet it seemed that something in this direction might be done, and useful in more respects than one.

It has always been my belief that the Prime Minister had particular responsibilities of his own, little shared by his colleagues, in advising the Sovereign on matters of general position and conduct where the public interest was concerned. On this principle I proceeded, and I did not consult in this matter with my colleagues, except probably with Granville. I consulted very freely with the Duke of Cambridge, whose views upon the matter appeared to me to be loyal, shrewd, and sound. I did the same with Colonel Ellis who I think in the first place made his ideas known to me. Except within these narrow bounds, I have kept the matter profoundly secret for a quarter of a century, and the time has not yet come for divulging it, though come it must. I do not enter on a description of my project so to call it: for the papers *in extenso* which are not very bulky, may properly form part of these notes, as they have their proper place in any full account of our relations with Ireland.[1] My way as will be seen was absolutely blocked by Her Majesty; and the case was one in which this obstacle was insurmountable. I thought also that she much disliked the English part of the arrangements, as an interference, which it undoubtedly was with her personal conduct, and the new, and less beneficial, framework of her public life.

23 September 1897

DISSOLUTION OF 1874[2]

No trustworthy account of the dissolution of Parliament which took place early in 1874 has ever been published. I remember that when the new Parliament met Mr. Stirling of Keir (as he then was), a most kind as well as accomplished man, censured my conduct in a rather disparaging manner: and that Disraeli following in the debate

---

[1] See Gladstone's account of an audience with the Queen, 25 June 1871 (ADD.MS 44760, ff. 40–45); and his correspondence with the Queen, 5 July–11 September 1872 (Philip Guedalla, *The Queen and Mr. Gladstone*, i. 351–381).

[2] This is the first of two accounts which Gladstone wrote with this heading. It has a note in pencil in Morley's hand: 'Another account written in September 1897'.

generously excepted to this method of treatment and referred to the success which the Liberal party had previously obtained under my leadership.

When I proposed the dissolution to the Cabinet, they acceded to it without opposition or I think even discussion. In setting it before the public in my election address, I associated it with the repeal of the income tax, which indeed became its soul when it was resolved upon. The Parliament had recently entered on its sixth year, and so, according to usage, had but one year more to run. But, as far as the repeal of that tax was concerned, things might with perfect propriety have been allowed, perhaps, to take their course for the time.

There was another important fact which might have been permitted to weigh powerfully in favour of dissolution, namely that of the very large majority with which we entered office in 1868, no small part, perhaps near a moiety had disappeared as the aggregate result of byeelections. I confess, however, that either I had not observed or I had not fully appreciated the force of this circumstance as an indication that we were losing or had lost the confidence of the constituencies. And the matter was not observed upon by others, so far as I know.

The actual occasion of the measure was known I think only to Lord Granville and Lord Cardwell with myself, it having a sufficient warrant from other sources.

In 1871, the year of the abolition of purchase and of other important Army reforms, I had, in full understanding with Cardwell, made a lengthened speech in which I referred to the immediate augmentations of military expenditure, which the reforms demanded, abatements at early dates through the operation of the new system of relying considerably upon reserves for imperial defence.

When Cardwell laid before me at the proper time, in view of the approaching session, his proposed estimates for 1874–5, I was strongly of opinion that the time had arrived for our furnishing by a very moderate reduction of expenditure on the Army, some earnest of the reality of the promise made in 1871 which had been so efficacious in procuring the enlargement which we had then required. Cardwell, though not an extravagant Minister, objected to my demand of (I think) £200,000. I conferred with Granville, who without any direct knowledge of the subject, took my side, and thought Cardwell would give way. But he continued to resist: and, viewing the age of the Parliament, I was then driven on the idea of dissolution, for I regarded the matter as virtually involving the whole question of the value of our promises, an anticipation which has proved to be correct. But he entered readily into the plan of dissolving, and moreover thought that if my views carried the day with the constituencies this would enable him to comply.

And so came the dissolution, the end of which is known. We were fatally hit in two ways.

First, our remaining British majority was converted into a minority. Secondly, the Irish national party, who since 1868 had acted in and with the Liberal party, became detached from us. Although our proposal was to repeal the income tax, and this proposal was addressed to an electorate including a far larger proportion of income tax payers than now, we were unequivocally defeated. Why was this? There was no matter of principle set up against us. Mr. Disraeli aimed at taking the wind out of our sails by declaring that he had always been opposed to the continuance of the tax. But this could not possibly I think have carried much weight. The serious technical error in our proceedings was the rawness, the novelty of our proceedings. It was indeed old enough: witness the proceedings of 1853: and we had worked our way towards it by gradual reductions of the rate until we had reached a state of things which made the plan perfectly feasible. But between 1858 and 1874 the subject had been removed from the arena of parliamentary discussion and from the public eye, so that it had again grown into a novelty and the country got no effective grip of the idea. Contrast with this the subject of the Beaconsfield foreign policy which we were able to work steadily for four years before 1880. So the defeat came: and with it all my pledges of 1853 completely lost all binding force. Another most important consequence was that with this facile and classic instrument in their hands every government disposed to enlarge expenditure for whatever purpose had a sure and easy road opened to them. As far as mere money is concerned the dissolution of 1874 with its result cost the country scores of millions, and may yet be found to have cost it hundreds. Out of the six million surplus which we handed over, the tax was reduced to twopence in the pound, and the Tories herein did the very least that they could do. In all the conditions which our finance had presented since the year 1874, the repeal of the tax has been wholly out of reach: and we have actually without war raised it to a higher point (8d.) than that at which (7d.) it was fixed by Sir R. Peel in 1842.

10 February 1897

The causes of the dissolution of 1874 have never yet I believe been fully explained to the outside world. I do not recollect whether I have put them upon record privately. In any case I will now do so.

The Parliament chosen in November 1868 had entered upon its sixth year. This was not the reason; but it was an element in the case.

The course of the bye-elections had I believe sufficiently shown that the cause of the Government was declining or lost. But this subject had not been brought prominently into notice.

The finance of the country was most flourishing, and allowed of a great measure. It had become practicable to drop the income tax, subject to certain accompanying measures. I had always felt a great desire for its cessation: specially and personally because of the pledges given in 1853, which it now for the first time had become possible to redeem. But I also wished to have done with its funds, its inequalities, and the vast facilities which it has afforded for the augmentation of expenditure.

All these matters would in their due course have come forward at the close of 1874, which may be called the natural period for dissolving the Parliament of 1868. Still the time of their obligatory force had not yet arrived.

The choice of the moment for dissolution, and a very sudden choice it was, sprang from different quarters; but it was also due to a question of old and unredeemed promises which since that time have become I suppose wholly antiquated and obsolete.

The important Army Reform Bill of 1871, framed and carried by Lord Cardwell, which introduced the system of reserves, and provided for the abolition of purchase, increased the military charge of the country. But as we believed the new plans when they came into operation would countervail that increase, and even substitute for it a reduction. To give the firmest assurance in our power to Parliament that these were our expectations, I, as head of the Government, in concert with, and I think stimulated by Lord Cardwell, made a lengthened speech to the House, in which these views were conveyed.

I felt strongly the binding force of the pledge. The years 1871–2 and 1872–3 had passed away, and the time came to frame the estimates for 1873–4. I thought that in honour it was now time to give some earnest of the reality of the expectations, which we had very confidently held out, and I feared that if we did not begin to give a sample of our promised compensation we might probably never begin at all. I therefore pressed strongly upon Cardwell that he should in his estimates arrange for a reduction of (I think) £200,000: a small sum, but sufficient for my purpose. Cardwell stoutly and persistently declined.

I had made known to Lord Granville what had occurred at the time of my proposal. Granville took it for granted that no serious difficulty could arise.

I am not able to say from memory at this distance of time what was the course of the argument between us. But we both adhered to our respective points of view. And Cardwell would I have no doubt [have] resigned rather than give in. This need not have brought about an immediate crisis. But the loss would have been heavy in feeling and in fact.

Sur ce, as the French say, it occurred to me that the Parliament was old and the financial conditions favourable. I therefore broached to the two Ministers I have named the idea of dissolution: which, if adopted, would of course bury in oblivion the dispute concerning the estimates.

The proposal was promptly and I think unanimously adopted by the Cabinet and on the instant carried into action amid no small surprise which however did not yield to prying investigations. The measure of the Government was really an attempt to re-establish the old doctrine that the income tax was a great weapon to be held in reserve for a time of war. The country did not seem to care about the doctrine, nor about the tax, which was low. It is now saddled on the country as a permanent part of our finance, but not by my act; and it has enabled us to treble our expenditure say since 1835, deducting for both years what is incidental to the debt: and, amidst a great prosperity to keep the tax at a rate (8d.) higher than that (7d.) at which it was imposed in 1842 to meet a great emergency.

4 September 1897

1884–5 HOUSEHOLD SUFFRAGE IN COUNTIES

The adoption of household suffrage for the counties, with accompanying change of the franchise in the direction of extension, was adopted by the Cabinet without serious difficulty. My recollection is that

Hartington gave utterance to the apprehensions which were felt on the subject of this extension in Ireland. But Spencer disposed of this objection by stating that the difference of strength which the change would give to the Nationalist party would be insignificant; a very large majority in its favour being certain even with the present constituency.

Nor were the difficulties serious in the House of Commons although it involved what would have been most difficult except for the conjunction of favourable circumstances, an increase (though a small one from 658 to 670) in the numbers of the House. Forster, on the introduction of the bill, though a decided friend to its principle, took every possible objection in a manner which would have been dangerous had he commanded sympathy in any noticeable section of the House. But he did not command it; and neither the retention of the full number of Irish Members as it stood, nor the augmentation of the aggregate, nor the appeal to the metropolis to claim a larger share of representation, produced any noticeable effect. Forster was a sincere and upright man, though with strong prejudices and strong self will; and I daresay he was not aware of his own palpably adverse bias. A person consistently desirous to give effect to the principle of the measure would have reserved the statement, or at any rate the development, of their objections to a later stage.

When the bill was thrown out in the House of Lords, the Government determined on energetic action; and of course entirely set aside the idea of a dissolution which appeared to some persons the proper solution of a conflict of opinion between Lords and Commons. A marvellous conception! On such a dissolution, if the country disapproved of the conduct of its representatives, it would cashier them: but, if it disapproved of the conduct of the Peers, it would simply have to see them resume their place of power to employ it to the best of their ability as opportunity might serve, in thwarting the desires of the country expressed through its representatives.

It is not uncommonly boasted, especially in after-dinner speeches which return thanks for the House of Lords, that that assembly never pushes its resistance to a point which would disturb the peace of the country. The same claim to honour might be advanced by any and every sedition-monger who may exist in the country. He too has powers of political vision sufficient to save him from running into self-destruction: and so we have had no civil war, no disturbance, during the last half-century, either from the sedition-monger or the House of Lords. But the difference is that the one is invested, and the other is not, with the absolute power of intercepting the solemn decisions of the constitutional representatives of the nation.

On this occasion, I took the opportunity of representing to the Queen that a conflict with the Lords, to which the whole strength and credit of the House of Commons were committed, could only end in one way: and that if as was then probable the issue should involve danger to hereditary succession in the House of Lords, hereditary succession to the Throne would become isolated, and might possibly be compromised.

I will not undertake to say what had been Her Majesty's leanings in the earlier stages of this conflict. But undoubtedly I think that in the later stages she shared the views of her Ministers: and even that she exerted herself, perhaps with important effects, in dissuading the Opposition from prolonging a dangerous contest.

We of course were very desirous to avoid a further collision of constitutional powers. The suspicion that, by holding the two subjects of franchise and redistribution apart, we reserved it to ourselves when the franchise had been carried to mutilate its just expression through artificial arrangements, proceeded upon hypotheses as to our intentions which were wholly groundless. This being so it seemed important to employ any means in themselves legitimate for obviating a struggle resting for its justification on suppositions entirely unreal. Accordingly my friend Mr. Algernon West made arrangements by which I might meet my old friend Sir Stafford Northcote, privately and informally, at his house. This meeting took place on a Thursday night [13 November 1884]. Nothing could be more amicable than the tone on both sides; and Northcote said nothing on his behalf of a nature to impress me with the belief that the case was hopeless. It had however too often happened, when I had held conferences with him behind the chair as leader of the opposite party, that when I had thought the tone of the conversation favourable to accommodation, the power of conferring with his friends, which he properly reserved, put a new complexion on the matter, and in fact showed that he could in no degree answer for, or anticipate, the decisions of the party with which he acted.

So it proved on the present occasion, for, on the Friday, I received from him the short but decisive letter which I here subjoin:[1]

---

[1] ADD.MS 44217, ff. 229–230.

30, *St. James's Place, S.W.*

Confidential   *14 November 1884*

My dear Mr. Gladstone,

The only answer I can give to your question is—that the House of Lords will not part with control over the Franchise Bill till it has the Redistribution Bill before it. But it would be perfectly possible to offer guarantees against any apprehended maltreatment of the Redistribution Bill if the result of previous communications be satisfactory.

I remain,

Yours very faithfully,

STAFFORD H. NORTHCOTE

According to the terms of this letter, nothing was to be gained by attempts at friendly conference with the Opposition. It remained to consider whether a public appeal to the members themselves of the House of Lords might afford some hope, however faint, of bringing them to a truer view of their position. It was not a very bright prospect: for the men holding a sort of middle position in the House of Peers, though well inclined, were not men of mark or nerve sufficient to cope with any serious crisis.

The Cabinet met on Saturday the [15th November]: and determined that at the meeting of the House on Monday I should state publicly our views in the terms in which I had made them known privately to Northcote with no other issue than a blank refusal. We were not therefore very sanguine as to the upshot; but it seemed right to try, and I made the statement accordingly, as a last appeal not to the official Opposition, but to the peers.

It was with no less surprise than pleasure that, as we found, an entire change had within the last day or two, been brought about in the views of the Front Bench opposite. One man after another plainly intimated that my statement, which had been launched as a forlorn hope, might be made the basis of a practical accommodation.

And so it proved. We really had no more trouble in the accomplishment of this great change. Lord Salisbury and Sir Stafford Northcote paid repeated visits at my official house in Downing Street: *ils five-o'-clockèrent chez moi*, and with the help of a few cups of tea we went in substance through the whole business of redistribution. On the side of the Government, Lord Granville, Sir C. Dilke, and I were usually present. Dilke showed a great mastery of particulars. Lord Salisbury took the whole matter out of the hands of Northcote who sat by him on the sofa like a chicken protected by the wings of the mother hen. In one matter we made a most important concession. We agreed not to touch in the coming bill the representation of the universities. I am doubtful whether we were right. The compact was kept with great rigour on both sides. Our order of proceeding was maintained. I must admit that the liberty of the House in dealing with the particulars of redistribution was seriously hampered. Dilke showed great ability: and no sort of stain at this time rested on his name.

We made another and greater concession with our eyes open. At least my eyes were quite open to the general consequences of dividing our greater constituencies into single-member districts. For I remembered that in 1835 when the Municipal Reform Act was passed, the Conservative alarms of those days were principally allayed by the consent of the Melbourne Government to divide the great towns into wards. But the question was whether the plan was good, not whether it served this party or that. From this point of view it was decided. I will not say we were fully conscious of its importance, but if we had known it ever so fully, I do not think our line of procedure would have been altered.

And so was disposed the great subject which added several millions to the constituency: far exceeding, in itself, the effect of all former Acts since 1832. The effect of the great Reform Bill was not mainly numerical but moral.

Some day I suppose the world will know what took place between the Friday and the Monday I have mentioned, to determine in a better sense the course of procedure. It is most probable that the Queen had to do with it and possibly her influence in the matter may have been increased by an impression in the Tory mind that the general leanings were now in that direction. It was understood that Lord Cairns and the Duke of Richmond, the former [of] these having the longest head in the party, were at Balmoral on their way south during the short interval.

30 September 1897

THIRD CABINET 1885–6

In view of the dissolution which, after the vast enlargement of the constituency, was particularly appropriate, Ireland was the great object that loomed upon us in the distance. Even apart from the enlarged franchise it was known that the strength of Mr. Parnell would be very largely increased. As matters actually stood, we had to anticipate as a moral certainty a pronouncement of that country by a vast majority on behalf of Home Rule: yet it could not be assumed as a matter of fact while the coquetry of the Tory government of 1885 with the National Party, and the bait held out through Lord Carnarvon, sufficed to secure the Tories for the present against any dangerous approximation between Nationalists and Liberals. It was thought that suggestions with a view to the election were peculiarly needful for the guidance of Liberals, and in consequence while on the cruise to Norway in Lord Brassey's yacht the Sunbeam, I wrote my address which was published with the date of September[1] 1885. On repairing to Midlothian later in the season I magnified in my first speech at Edinburgh the Irish case, and laid it down that the privileges of local government to be accorded to Ireland must have references to the special circumstances of that country, and could not be confined to what was within the usual purport of the phrase. Mr. Parnell, probably still relying on the encouragement given him by Lord Carnarvon (not to mention the extraordinary declaration of Lord Salisbury respecting the case of Austria-Hungary) not unnaturally received my declarations (which were in complete conformity with my speech (on the Address[2] of 1882) herewith) in a hostile manner and invited me to produce my plan.

The election I think quite came up to our expectations. As we computed, the numbers were exactly equal to the combined force of Nationalists and Tories: three hundred and thirty-five against a like number made up of eighty-five Nationalists and two hundred and fifty Tories. This was for a Government a safe Parliament as to the general business of the country, for the two could not be worked together as an efficient Opposition. I appealed, however, to the country to give us a commanding majority of Liberals, as this was the only way in which the constitution of the country could be rendered thoroughly secure against intrigues in connection with Ireland.

I had no means of forming an estimate how far the bulk of the Liberal party could be relied on to support a measure of Home Rule which should constitute an Irish Parliament subject to the supremacy of the Parliament at Westminster. I was not sanguine on this head. The

---

[1] 'September' added afterwards in pencil.
[2] 'Address' added afterwards in pencil.

Viceroy, Lord Spencer, had indeed declared himself in this sense, and was supported by his able non-political coadjutor Sir R.[1] Hamilton. But even in the month of December, when rumours of my intentions were afloat, I found how little I could reckon on a general support. Under the circumstances I certainly took upon myself a grave responsibility. I attached value to the acts and language of Lord Carnarvon, and the other favourable manifestations. Subsequently we had too much evidence of a deliberate intention to deceive the Irish with a view to their support at the election. But in the actual circumstances I thought it my duty to encourage the Government of Lord Salisbury to settle the Irish question, so far as I could do this by promises of my personal support. Hence my communication with Mr. Balfour which has long been in the hands of the public.

It has been unreasonably imputed to me, that the proposal of Home Rule was a 'bid' for the Irish vote. But my desire for the adjustment of the question by the Tories is surely a conclusive answer. The fact is that I could not rely upon the collective support of the Liberals: but I could and did rely upon the support of so many of them as would make the success of the measure certain in the event of its being proposed by the Tory administration. It would have resembled in substance the Liberal support given to Roman Catholic emancipation in 1829, and to the repeal of the Corn Laws in 1846. Before the meeting of Parliament, I had to encounter uncomfortable symptoms among my principal friends, of which I think Sir W. Harcourt was the organ.

I was therefore by no means eager for the dismissal of the Tory Government, though it counted but two hundred and fifty supporters out of six hundred and seventy, as long as there were hopes of its taking up the question, or at all events doing nothing to aggravate the situation.

When we came to the debate on the Address I had to face a night of extreme anxiety. The Speech from the Throne referred in a menacing way to Irish disturbances, and contained a distinct declaration in support of the legislative union. On referring to the clerks at the table to learn in what terms the Address in reply to the Speech was couched, I found it was a 'thanking' Address which did not commit the House to an opinion. What I dreaded was lest someone should have gone back to the precedent of 1833, when the Address in reply to the Speech was advisedly made the vehicle of a solemn declaration in favour of the Act

---

[1] 'R' added afterwards in pencil.

of Union. Home Rule, rightly understood, altered indeed the terms of
the Act of Union, but adhered to its principle which was the supremacy
of the Imperial Parliament. Still it was pretty certain that any declaration of a substantive character, at the epoch we had now reached,
would in its moral effect shut the doors of the existing Parliament
against Home Rule.

In a speech of pronounced clearness, Mr. Elliot endeavoured to
obtain a movement in this direction. I thought it would be morally
fatal if this tone were extensively adopted on the Liberal side; so I determined on an effort to secure reserve for the time, that our freedom
might not be compromised. I therefore ventured upon describing myself
as an 'old parliamentary hand,' and in that capacity strongly advised
the party to keep its own counsel, and await for a little the development
of events. Happily this counsel was taken: had it been otherwise, the
early formation of a Government favourable to Home Rule would in all
likelihood have become an impossibility. For although our Home Rule
bill was eventually supported by more than three hundred Members,
I doubt whether, if the question had been prematurely raised on the
night of the Address, so many as two hundred would have been prepared to speak and act in that sense.

The determining event of these transactions was the declaration of
the Government that they would propose coercion for Ireland. This
declaration put an end to all the hopes and expectations associated with
the mission of Lord Carnarvon. Not perhaps in mere logic, but practically it was now plain that Ireland had no hope from the Tories. This
being so, my rule of action was changed at once: and I determined on
taking any and every legitimate opportunity to remove the existing
Government from office. Such an opportunity was at once afforded by
the amendment of Mr. Jesse Collings which attacked the Speech, quite
justly, in consequence of its silence with respect to agricultural holdings.
We carried his amendment; the Government resigned, and I was
commissioned to form a Government.

Immediately on making up my mind about the ejection of the Government, I went to call upon Sir William Harcourt and informed him as
to my intentions and the grounds of them. He said, 'What, are you prepared to go forward without either Hartington or Chamberlain?' I
answered, 'Yes'. I believe it was in my mind to say, if I did not actually
say it, that I was prepared to go forward without any body. That is to say
without any known and positive assurance of support. This was one

of the great Imperial occasions which call for such resolutions.

In 1884 (I think) Chamberlain had proposed a plan accepted by Parnell (and supported by me) which, without establishing in Ireland a national Parliament, made very considerable advances towards self-government. It was rejected by a small majority of the Cabinet: Spencer and Granville being among those who declined to accept it. Granville said at the time he would rather take Home Rule. Spencer thought it would introduce a confusion into executive duties.

On the present occasion a full half of the former Ministers declined to march with me. Spencer and Granville were my main supports. Chamberlain and Trevelyan went with me, their basis being that we were to seek for some method of dealing with the Irish case other than coercion. What Chamberlain's motive was I do not clearly understand. It was stated that he coveted the Irish Secretaryship, and that the appointment of John Morley was the real cause of his estrangement. To have given him the office would at that time have been held to be a declaration of war against the Irish party.

Selborne nibbled at the offer, but I felt that it would not work and did not use great efforts to bring him in. James, now Lord James, was prepared to go with us if his supporters would allow him: but on going down to Bury he found it impracticable to arrange with them and held aloof.

When the matter was finally adjusted by Chamberlain's retirement, we had against us: Derby, Northbrook, Carlingford, Selborne, Monk[1] Bretton (Dodson), Chamberlain, Hartington, Trevelyan, Goschen, Bright, and for: Granville, Kimberley, Ripon, Rosebery, Harcourt, Childers, Lefevre, Dilke (unavailable).[2]

When I had accepted the commission, Ponsonby brought me a message from the Queen that she hoped there would not be any separatists in the Cabinet. The word had not at that time acquired the offensive meaning in which it has since been stereotyped by the so-called Unionists: and it was easy to frame a reply in general but strong words. I am bound to say that at Osborne in the course of a long conversation the Queen was frank and free and showed none of the 'armed neutrality' which as far as I know has been the best definition of her attitude in the more recent years towards a Liberal Minister.

---

[1] MS: Mount.

[2] This paragraph was added afterwards in the margin.

Upon the whole, when I look back upon 1886, and consider the inveterate sentiment of hostility flavoured with contempt towards Ireland which has from time immemorial formed the basis of English tradition, I am much more disposed to be thankful for what we then and afterwards accomplished than to murmur or to wonder at what we did not.

28 September 1897

1879–94 [1]

ADD.MS 44790, ff. 111–119

In the winter of 1873–4, the general election made necessary the retirement of the Ministry, of which I was then at the head. And I was most desirous of making their retirement the occasion of my own. I had served for more than forty years. My age (64) was greater than that of Sir Robert Peel at his retirement in 1846 or at his death in 1850: and was much beyond that at which most of the leading commoners of the century had terminated their political careers together with their natural lives. And I felt myself to be in some measure out of touch with some of the tendencies of the Liberal party especially in religious matters. I thought they leant to the dethronement of the private conscience and to a generalised religion. Sir A. Clark whom I consulted would give me on medical grounds no encouragement whatever. But I deeply desired an interval between Parliament and the grave, which might in the counsels of God be far or near. And in spite of the solicitations of my friends I persisted. For 1874, there was a sort of compromise 'without prejudice'. As having a title to some rest, I was not a very regular attendant but did not formally abdicate. When 1875 opened I carried the matter to issue and resigned the leadership, Hartington being chosen to fill the vacancy. Through that year and again in 1876 my abdication took real effect and I only acted from time to time as an independent member of the party.

When in 1876 the Eastern question was pressed forward by the disturbances in the Turkish Empire, and especially by the cruel outrages

---

[1] This document is incorrectly arranged. The correct order of the sheets is: ff. 111, 112, 113, 114, 117, 115, 116, 118, 119, The word 'Retirement' in pencil is written at the top of f. 111, apparently in Morley's hand.

in Bulgaria, I shrank naturally but perhaps unduly from recognising the claim they made upon me[1] individually. I hoped that the Ministers would recognise the moral obligations to the subject races of the east, which we had in honour contracted as parties to the Crimean War, and to the peace of Paris in 1856. I was slow to observe the real leanings of the Prime Minister, his strong sympathy with the Turk and his mastery in his own cabinet. I suffered others, Forster in particular, to go far ahead of me. At the close of the session a debate was raised upon the subject, and I had at length been compelled to perceive how the old idol was still to be worshipped at Constantinople, and that as the only person surviving in the House of Commons who had been responsible for the Crimean War and the levelling of the bulwark raised by the treaty of Kainardji on behalf of the eastern Christians I could no longer remain indifferent. Consequently in that debate Mr. Disraeli had to describe my speech as the only one that had exhibited a real hostility to the policy of the Government. I was however at that time an opposition without hope. I went into the country and had mentally postponed all further action to the opening of the next session: when I learned from the announcement of a popular meeting to be held in Hyde Park that the game was afoot and the question yet alive. So I at once wrote and published on the Bulgarian case. It was with some difficulty on account of lumbago which made my body creak as I tried to write but at length I performed the task in bed with pillow props and was able in two or three days. . . .[2] I went up to London to make needful references and to correct the press. From that time forward until the final consummation in 1879–80 I made the eastern question the main business of my life. I acted under a strong sense of individual duty without a thought of leadership: nevertheless it made me leader again whether I would or no. In 1880, Midlothian leading the way, the nation nobly answered to the call of justice and [br]oadly[3] recognised the brotherhood of man. It was the nation, not the classes. These at the close of the session in 1886 [sic] were as usual dispersed in pursuit of their recreation. I thought accordingly the occasion was bad: but it was good, for the nation did not disperse, and the human heart was beating, as it had beat before. When the clubs re-filled in October, the Turkish cause

---

[1] MS: upon me upon me.
[2] The sentence was left incomplete.
[3] MS torn.

began again to make its way. Then came a checquered period: and I do not recollect to have received much assistance from the front bench. Even Granville had been a little startled at my proceedings, and wished me to leave out the 'bag and baggage' from the text of my pamphlet.

Thus it came about that I was fastened down to the resumption of the Premiership in 1880, and I learned in a practical way how difficult a thing it is to retire when by long use a man has become an acknowledged and prominent figure on the public stage.

During the first two years of that Government we had accomplished important purposes in Afghanistan, in South Africa, in the application of the Treaty of Berlin, and in the rectification of finance. The Egyptian entanglement had begun but we did not yet know how serious it would prove. There had however risen from the ground to confront us another formidable figure of which in 1880 we hardly dreamed—the Irish question; and it assumed such grave dimensions that although the engagements of 1880 were fulfilled I found that new ties had been woven around me which absolutely precluded my retirement.

The Irish question lay so near the very heart of the Empire that no claim which it legitimately made could on any account be disregarded. We went or tried to go to the bottom of it in the Land Act of 1881, only to discover that we had not reached the core and the national aspiration was that which really required from us and from the country an Aye or a No. At the outset (I think) of 1882 I had spoken on the principle. By the Franchise Act of 1884–5 we made a long step towards the solution, for we put the Irish people, virtually the whole Irish people, to speak its mind. That mind was spoken plainly enough at the general election of 1885: and it also soon appeared that the Irish demand was capable of being bounded by the limits required under the constitution of the United Kingdom. I could not but entertain some belief in the reality of the manifestations amounting to promises which the Tory Government had held out to the Irish party. And I took the daring step, only to be justified by the circumstances of the case if justified at all, of making known to an adverse Government my readiness to give them all the aid in my power for the settlement of the Irish question. Thus opened the new drama. For another seven years from 1885 to 1892 we fought a national and popular battle—resembling that of 1876 to 1880 for the subject races of the east. And we were probably on the way to a result not less decisive, when the deplorable disclosures in the case of Mr. Parnell introduced discord into the Irish ranks and not only diminished the numerical power and broke up the united vote of nationalism in Ireland, but naturally presented to the British mind an altered view and kept our majority within bounds such as not to abash the courage or audacity of the House of Lords. Immediately after the general election at a conference with the leading Irish I said to them, 'I shall not be in at the death.' And now we are in the winter of 1893–4.

When I saw from my post at Biarritz how the Lords had mown down virtually the whole work of our enormously protracted session, I conceived the idea that a dissolution would be timely and politic. But I found no countenance among my colleagues and I was not strong enough to persevere. They had in general treated me kindly and knew that it was worth their while: but I think that the idea of 'too old' was afloat generally in their minds.

Meanwhile through no choice of mine a double and parallel chain of causes had been set up, quite independent of one another, but either of them charged with death to my official career. On the one side cataract in my eyes had so damaged my reading powers (not to mention a serious growth of deafness) that my physical capacity for office became more and more liable to question. On the other hand a project for a further great increase of the Navy which I thought 'mad and drunk' and which though in sentiment I stood nearly alone, nothing could induce me to share in. I will not here discuss this portentous subject. Suffice it to say had there been no Navy scheme I must have resigned on cataract: had there been no cataract I must have resigned on the estimates. With some difficulty I was able to keep cataract in the foreground. And thus without raising any new political controversy (from which I could anticipate no good), I was allowed by the mercy of God a peaceable escape from my long life of political contention, amidst expressions of goodwill nearly universal (*very* nearly) which I had in no way desired but which I profoundly and thankfully appreciate.

11 July 1894

CRISIS OF 1894 AS TO THE LORDS AND DISSOLUTION

ADD.MS 44791, ff. 55–56

The process of working up to the election of 1892 lasted for six, or I might say for seven years. Before that election I was sometimes asked what majority I expected that we should gain. This was I think after the Parnell scandals which I conceive had an operation not less wide and mischievous than subtle. My answer was, 'I do not know what majority we shall have: but I know what majority will content me: nothing less than three figures.' Apart from the deplorable case of Parnell, I think we should probably have had them. The forty, to which we were reduced, were quite sufficient for the purpose of holding office; but quite insufficient for the purpose of forcing the House of Lords, as we had done with the Irish Church and land. Every opportunity of that kind would have been utterly lost had the Lords been wise enough to keep to that single issue. But they most rashly multiplied the issues: so that, at the moment when they had inflicted a deadly mutilation on the Parish Councils Bill, they (having also refused our measure on employers' liability) had placed themselves in sharp conflict with public opinion on great subjects both in England and Ireland. Scotland could be thoroughly depended upon for general reasons. But here also the Lords had refused a bill in which the public felt a real interest though it only related to salmon fisheries. It was therefore not too much to say that they had destroyed the year's work which had cost the House of Commons two hundred nights of labour. I was at Biarritz when this happened in January or February of 1894. I suggested dissolution to my colleagues in London where half or more than half the Cabinet were found at the moment. I received by telegraph a hopelessly adverse reply. In normal circumstances it would have been my duty to come home at once and urge the adoption of my views. But not only was I aware that I had lost all influence in the Cabinet; I was also fatally as well as directly at variance with my colleagues upon the naval estimates for 1894–5: besides which it was plain that dissolution at that moment would have required some exceptional arrangements in order to provide for the regular course of financial business: this was however a secondary matter. But, fatally crippled as I was, I was compelled to let the matter drop. There was another difficulty also secondary though not unimportant. We were totally unprovided with arrangements and with candidates. Thus there was let slip an opportunity in my opinion nothing less than splendid for raising decisively an issue of vital importance to popular government: an opportunity which if rightly used would have given the Liberal party a decisive preponderance for the full term of one or probably two Parliaments, quite apart from the vast public advantages within reach. The great controversy between Lords and Commons, terrible in 1831–2, formidable in 1860–1, happily averted with the Queen's wise aid in 1884, but commonly at work with serious though not always perceived consequences, would have reached a practical settlement: and the yet graver controversy (as involving character) of seven hundred years with Ireland would have come nearer to a complete settlement by a measure of Home Rule than was promised even by the administration of Lord Fitzwilliam.

13 February 1897

1894 THE FINAL IMBROGLIO

ADD.MS 44791, ff. 23–28

It can scarcely have happened that a physical disturbance in itself highly inconvenient, like cataract in the eye, can have served the purpose of escaping political disturbance so effectually as it did for me in 1893–4. Two causes were in concurrent operation, like two oars worked by a rower: one of them a physical infirmity, wholly independent of my will and mental faculties, the other a most grave dissension between the majority of my colleagues and myself. In one point my simile falls short of precise accuracy. The slow progress of cataract eventually reaches the time of a sufficient ripeness for a relieving operation, but this ripeness cannot be said to arrive on this or that particular day or week: it is perhaps best defined by the cessation of the faculty of effective reading. But a difference on the military or naval expenditure of the year is one the disclosure of which cannot be postponed beyond that early day in the session of Parliament when it becomes necessary to lay the estimates on the table. Their preparation in the department is another matter, for this may at any time be controuled and altered by the Cabinet. Subject to this qualification it is strictly true that I resigned the office of Prime Minister not for one reason but for two; of which only one however was declared to the world at the time, or even to the Sovereign; who however was far too well pleased with the event itself to be fastidious or energetic about inquiry into causes.

In the autumn and even winter of 1893 we were engaged in carrying on, with all the force we could, the business of an unexampled session. We had sent the Irish Government Bill to its fate in the House of Lords, and had thereby raised effectively a large portion at least of the issue between the two Houses of Parliament. But it would not have been prudent to challenge the verdict of the country against the House of Lords on this great measure alone, inasmuch as what was wanted was not only a victory but a crushing and smashing victory, sufficient by its impetus to carry both the question of the Lords and the Irish question as well as some others. Hence we extended the session of 1893 to (I think) some thirteen months.

During the months of the fall, the Tories, with an unexampled disregard of the principles of the constitution, determined to force an increase, and if they could, a great increase of the naval estimates. They knew better than I did what at length the Whip revealed to us, that a section, even a formidable section, of Liberals were of their mind: and I presume that they were also aware of the ideas and intentions of the three Admirals, the professional portion of the Board of Admiralty. The attempt to commit the House at this period, against the executive, on the naval expenditure of 1894 was in principle monstrous. Nevertheless we found that in pleading for our rights and responsibilities as the executive, which ought to have been unanimously admitted, we had only a sufficient breadth of standing ground to give us a majority *below* our normal majority of forty. In these circumstances and apart from the over-ruling attraction of some great interest or measure, to refuse all augmentation of the naval estimates for 1894 would have been to stake our existence on the die and probably to lose it but with the effect of damming in some considerable degree the flood of expenditure.

The position of Spencer was as clear as it was in my judgment deplorable. He accepted the monstrous scheme of the Admirals in a reduced form, pleased to have cut it down from something yet more monstrous. It would have been better to bring it to the Cabinet in its nakedness, where it perhaps would have encountered an effectual smash: for I am doubtful how far they approved what they accepted and threw me out upon.

There were three Ministers who entirely agreed with me: Morley, Lefevre, and Harcourt: the two first had the courage of their opinions, and if I had resigned on the estimates would I think have done the same. As matters went, I did not urge them. The third was Harcourt. When I learned Spencer's intention I at once assured Harcourt as the official dragon of the Treasury of my hearty support in resisting it. His countenance at once fell and I at once found that he had made up his mind to accept it, and accept my impending resignation as part of the arrangement. I do not suppose he was so blind as to expect the succession. But he probably had the notion of graduated death duty in his head, and was so charmed with it as in some degree to excuse the expenditure on its account.

In this state of facts I determined on two things:

1. To make a large offer for the chance of maintaining unity. I offered to take half Spencer's proposal: which would however have broken into it effectually as a progressive scheme.

2. To postpone until the latest moment the acceptance of the estimates by the Cabinet: i.e., until the session of 1893 should have been disposed of and 1894 come into clear view.

It was more important in the public interest to let the Lords take their course with our measures: and then consider whether to raise a definitive issue with them. They had rejected all our important proposals, in a much smaller number of hours than it had taken us days to prepare them. There remained only the Parish Councils Bill to let the cup over-flow.

When (on December   )[1] having stated my insurmountable objections to the naval policy I also requested the Cabinet to postpone their decision. They acquiesced in general: but to my astonishment Rosebery and Harcourt argued against it: but happily without effect. To refuse it, even to a Prime Minister of 83, would in truth have been hardly decent.

The work of the Commons being over, I went, under the friendly convoy of Mr. Armitstead, to Biarritz. In the meantime the Lords proceeded not to reject but *vitally* to mutilate the Parish Councils Bill, which for polemical purposes was equivalent to rejection. It appeared to me that they had thus given us an opportunity, so brilliant as could not have been hoped for, of raising the question between the two Houses by a dissolution. They had in their intemperance committed themselves to a hopeless position. I felt no doubt that an election would give us force enough to settle all the pending problems, together with the added one which was the immediate occasion of the crisis.

I ought here to state that I entertained no idea of any plan for re-forming the House of Lords but thought the road lay pretty plain for a measure to restrain its legislative powers. The inconveniences of sudden

---

[1] The Cabinet meeting to which Gladstone refers seems to have been that of 9 January 1894. See ADD.MS 44648, ff.142 and 154.

action with regard to unarranged candidatures, and perhaps with respect to money, would have been grave; but these were of an order altogether secondary. The appeal to the nation would have worked as it did in 1831.

I signified the idea as to dissolution by letter or telegram to London: but the reply was that all the Ministers in London, and they seemed to be nearly or quite a majority, were against it. The alternative of course was to patch up the Parish Councils Bill, and miss one of the finest opportunities ever offered to statesmen.

Had I not had cataract entailing early disability: had I not been eighty-three years old: had I not had vital controversy with my colleagues on the estimates, such as to break up or dislocate our whole relations, I might have come to London and proved the question of dissolution. But in view of the actual state of facts, and the very small amount of desire (except so far as the indication of kind feeling was concerned) the Cabinet had shown to avert my resignation, it was out of the question.

Otherwise I would, cataract notwithstanding, have fought the battle with them and would have engaged myself at the least to see them well started on their way towards the necessary change in the relation of the two Houses.

Thus it was upon this matter of the Lords that everything eventually turned. They were not so far gone in idiocy as to refuse all concessions on the Parish Councils Bill. At this cheap and insignificant price they were allowed to walk peaceably out of the *impasse* in which they had lodged themselves. I know not whether, proud of seeing themselves surrounded with the ruins [of] our shattered work carried on through (I believe) two hundred nights, there were any misgivings prevailing among them. But I have heard a story which appears to me supported by internal evidence and the likelihood of the case. It is that the Duke of Devonshire, when the Parish Councils Bill lay almost *in extremis*, used language to this effect: that he did not know what Mr. Gladstone would do in the case which had arisen, but he knew very well that, if this opportunity were missed, pretty good care would be taken not to afford such another. Alack! Mr. Gladstone knew well enough what *he* had it in his heart to do, but also knew that he lay fettered if not hamstrung by the difficulties of which the most formidable lay in the disposition, and in the wants of disposition, prevailing among his immediate friends.

10 November 1896

WAY OPENED FOR RETIREMENT

ADD.MS 44790, ff. 101–102

I seem to have awakened, with a slowness which argues a want of quick and lively gratitude, to the fact that a great blessing, which I had for years, almost for scores of years, desired, but had almost ceased to hope, has after all been wrought out for me by ways not of my own seeking or devising, with a completeness which leaves nothing to be desired, and with accompaniments an hundred fold more gratifying than I had either claim or reason to expect.

Politics are like a labyrinth, from the ironic intricacies of which it is even more difficult to find the way of escape, than it was to find the way into them. My age did something but not enough. The deterioration of my hearing helped, but insufficiently. It is the state of my sight which has supplied me with effectual aid in exchanging my imperious public obligations for what seems to be a free place on 'the breezy common of humanity'. And it has only been within the last eight months or thereabouts that the decay of working sight has advanced at such a pace as to present the likelihood of its becoming stringently operative at an early date. It would have been very difficult to fix that date at this or that precise point without the appearance of making an arbitrary choice: but here the closing of the parliamentary session (1893–4) offered a natural break between cessation and removal of engagements which was admirably suited to the design. And yet I think it if not certain yet very highly probable at the least [that] any disposition of mine to profit from this break would, but for what I call the 'mad and drunk' scheme of my colleagues on the naval estimates, have been frustrated by their desire to avoid the inconveniences of a change and by the pressure which they would have brought to bear upon me in consequence. The effect of that scheme (the most wanton contribution in my view to accursed militarism that has yet been made in any quarter, unless possibly by the Crispian Italy) was not to bring about the construction of an artificial cause or pretext rather of resignation, but to compel me to act on one which was rational, sufficient, and ready to hand.

This operation of retirement, long ago attempted, now at length effected, must I think be considered to be among the chief momenta of my life. And like those other chief momenta which have been numerous they have been set in motion by no agency of mine, and have all along borne upon them the marks of Providential ordination.

At the general election of 1892 I had no adverse knowledge except that the sight of my right eye was bad. When soon after Mr. Grainger of Chester announced cataract in both eyes he also said that the sight of the better eye would probably continue for a long time, I think a time measured by years, without material change, and it seems to have been in September of 1893 that I told Lord Acton of my desire to escape, and my total inability to draw a *political* map that would supply for me a way, and of my hope and even expectation that the eye and ears question, especially the conditions of the eyes, might provide what was requisite.

If anyone had then predicted to me the 'mad and drunk' scheme of the present estimates I should have treated the prophecy as that of a pure visionary. But am I *Athanasius contra mundum*? Or am I Thersites, alone in the Achaian Assembly? Three only of the sixteen were in sympathy with me on the *merits* of the scheme. Thirteen against me! But this I must say, I have upon me the responsibilities of the training I have received and the experiences of crises remembered and confronted, under or in concert with such men as Peel, Aberdeen, Graham, Lord Russell, Clarendon, and Granville, and thus I have had more and better teaching and experience in international and European questions than all the thirteen put together.

The withdrawal of the demands, excitements and appliances of responsible office may leave behind at the moment the sense of a blank. But in this matter I cannot plead that I am taken by surprise. It is my deliberate conviction that the political life of the present and the future, so far as I can estimate it, is not to be preferred to the life outside of politics. It is not from inside but from outside the political circle that man if at all is to be redeemed. This is a new and great subject, not now to be opened with any good effect.

19 March 1894

ADD.MS 44790, ff. 96–100
There is a note in pencil in John Morley's hand at the top of the first sheet of this document: 'Imperfect, and for the present irreducible, but apparently meant to introduce the argument on the Naval Estimates of 1894.' It is docketed by Gladstone: 'Autobiographica'.

A proposal in view, though not yet adopted, to raise the navy estimates by $4\frac{1}{4}$ millions over the last normal estimates (or estimates not including the exceptional expenditure under the Naval Defence Act), naturally leads to the inquiry whether any precedent can be found for such expenditure. This question also divides itself into two: the first as to the figures, the second as to their significance with reference to the circumstances of the time, whether of peace, or military expenditure in view of war proximate or impending.

First as to the figures. On a superficial view, the most promising case is that of 1860–1 which in the financial abstract for the time shows a gross increase over 1859–60 exceeding four and a half millions. But there was war expenditure on account of China in both years, which must at once be deducted. In 1859–60 it was 858,000, and after the deduction the military and naval charge for the year stands at 25,931,000. In 1860–1, the charge for the China war was:

As in the financial abstract	3,043,000
As pledged in the estimates	1,600,000
Together	4,643,000[1]

When this war charge has been deducted from the total for the year, there remains a sum of 26,702,000. The increase, thus shown, appears to be, apart from war expenditure, not more than 771,000 and these figures are of course wholly unavailable for establishing a precedent.

When we turn to 1859–60 the case is materially different so far as it depends upon the figures. There was then a gross increase of this expenditure reaching 4,279,000 and of this augmentation only about 72,000 is due to increase of war charge so that the real increase apart from actual war is about 4,200,000 which may be taken roughly as equivalent to the $4\frac{1}{4}$ millions now in view (though I think the total will probably exceed this figure).

These figures have not indeed the whole force which at first appears to belong to them. The increase of $4\frac{1}{4}$ millions is calculated upon the year 1889: but the 13,000,000 of that year itself showed an increase upon preceding years not inconsiderable (excluding the vote of credit passed in anticipation of probable war in 1885). On the other hand the

---

[1] See Mr. Gladstone's Budget statement (special) of July 1860. [WEG]

increase for 1859–60 is obtained by comparison with 1858–9, a reduction gross of 1,275,000 and after deducting war charges of near 700,000.

It was my duty as Finance Minister, just after my accession to office, to propose the definitive plan of charge and income for the year. As far as concerns the figures of charge my responsibility was full and absolute: indeed acting on the sound principle of estimating charge largely, I anticipated an augmentation considerably beyond the actual result, and exceeding 5,000,000. The responsibility though full was not un-divided. The defence estimates for the year showed an increase beyond four millions, of which only one-fourth had been presented in February by Lord Derby's Government. But it is stated in my speech of July that the defence expenditure had gone forward upon a scale beyond that of the voted estimates. It was however, accepted by me fully and warmly, not apologetically. I had already begun to be apprehensive that an era of extravagance was approaching: but I did not look upon the large demands of July 1859 as falling within that description.

What then was the character and significance of these proposals? With some surprise, I find that it stated they were proposals directed by the Government of that day against France and against France only: and that Europe had then already been overrun by the militarism which curses it at the present day.

That European states had then, and many years before, military establishments unnecessarily large, was the opinion of Sir Robert Peel declared in my hearing before the House of Commons in the year 1842. But that was an imprudence of peace rather than a peril or a cause of war. Let any one who doubts this inquire what was the cost of the Prussian army at the time. As far as I remember it was, without any nameable fleet, not over five millions, perhaps not over four. The Crimean War had done little in this respect. It was not until after the war of 1870–1 that the portentous development of this began.

Still more important is the assertion as to France. But here I begin with an admission. The Protectionist party which was now the Tory party never loved the French alliance, and were distinctly hostile to the cause of Italy, which they regarded as a revolutionary cause. But the Liberal party had created, and the Peel connection had maintained, the French alliance. Lord Palmerston had not yet given up his faith in Louis Napoleon: he, Lord Russell, and I were [the] three members of the Cabinet most strongly Italian (Lord Granville sympathising): we were the three persons who almost alone spoke for the Government in the House of Commons on the subject, and who took a not less prominent part in the Cabinet. It is possible that as was usual the (rather silly?) naval reconstruction then going [*unfinished*].

Z RECORDED ERRORS

ADD.MS 44791, ff. 29–44
Mental defects associated with them.
The State in its relations with the Church, 1838.
The abortive resignation of 1841–2.
The quasi-proposal of myself for a Residency at Rome.
Finance of 1853–4. South Sea Stock.
Resignations of February 1855 (?)
Lord Lansdowne's inquiry, February 1855.
Declaration at Newcastle respecting Jefferson Davis and the South.
Appointments of 1892.

To be read with Y.[1]

Record of special errors.

I will now endeavour to set forth what are in my view the most pal-pable errors of my political life. I do not include among them the general misdirections of policy, but only what may be called errors of occasion. Nor do I include cases in which the presumptions of error are obvious, but when they are counterbalanced and thrown into doubt by considerations drawn from other sources, such as was the publication in 1838 of my crude book on the relations of the Church to the State. That book entailed upon me great embarrassments over and above the dissatisfaction of Sir Robert Peel, my political leader and guide, whose confidence I think that I never again quite fully acquired. But it was a stout practical protest, not without influence, against the mischiefs of Erastianism which had so grievously marred English statesmanship, and was a part though a subordinate part of the great and complex movement of the nineteenth century which has vitally altered the conditions of existence for the English Church.

The first of these errors occurred in the beginning of 1842.

In September 1841 Sir Robert Peel wisely desired for me an appoint-ment wholly severed from the regions of religious controversy. I do not

---

[1] In Morley's hand. The document 'Y' may be one of the alternative versions. See Appendix 7.

know what were the motives which governed him; whether he thought of my fitness for the Board of Trade or of my unfitness for a place like the Irish Secretaryship, which I had inwardly coveted but which would have placed me in contact more or less with slippery subjects, and would also in reality have been inferior in real Parliamentary weight. If he proceeded upon the positive idea, it was impossible for any one to be less fitted to represent the Government on questions of trade than I was: for, though I had seen hogsheads of sugar, and bales of cotton, hauled about the streets of Liverpool I had no tastes lying that way, and I was totally ignorant both of political economy and of the commerce of the country. I might have said, as I believe was said by a former holder of the Vice-Presidency (Mr. Courtenay) that my mind was in regard to all those matters 'a sheet of white paper', except that [it] was doubtless coloured by a traditional prejudice which had then quite recently become a distinctive mark of Conservatism. In a spirit of ignorant mortification, I said to myself at the moment, the science of politics deals with the government of men: but I am set to govern packages.

If on the other hand Sir R. Peel was mainly guided by an indisposition to place me in any office where I could have continued to dip my fingers into religious controversy, he was sagaciously right, for on the one hand I was infected with that disposition and on the other hand my training was not sufficiently advanced to have provided me with the necessary safeguards which were afterwards (as I hope) slowly but substantially acquired.

In my condition of ignorance I was prompted by the strongest motives of duty, interest and inclination to set about the business of my economical education. And I did set about it with all my heart and with all my strength.

I find my reluctance recorded with my acceptance in my journal for August 31, 1841. On September 3 I was sworn of the Privy Council. In [my] journal for August 2 I find this record: 'since the Address-meetings' (which were quasi-Cabinet) 'the idea of the Irish Secretaryship had nestled imperceptibly in my mind'.

The effect of a few months of hard work in the office and out of it was to shake terribly such protective ideas as were in my mind. The consequences were not slow to follow. When Sir R. Peel had framed his rather feeble amending Corn Bill for the session of 1842, and obtained (I presume) the assent of the Cabinet (except the Duke of Buckingham) he made it known to me. I was not a repealer but I thought the plan too limited, and I spoke to him expressing my desire to resign. This conversation I recorded at the time. He took it ill, and said he might even have to consider whether to break up the Government. I, poor fool, had not seen anything in the proceeding: nor was I moved by his exaggeration: but I saw what I ought to have seen before, that the retirement in the moment of crisis of the person chosen to represent the Government in matters of trade in the House of Commons *was* a serious matter. I had looked at nothing, and thought there was nothing to look at, but the figures in the bill. Such had been my slowness of education. I now saw my duty differently. This conversation had been on a Saturday. On Sunday morning I wrote a note of retractation: Peel was all sunshine again. There was no such broad ground of difference between my views and his as to justify the step I had taken. Severances upon narrow grounds go far to render government impossible. I subjoin [1]

My resignation in January/February 1845 on the ground of inability to support the intended increase of the grant of Maynooth was right and was rightly followed by my independent and unofficial support of the measure. But it was followed by another blunder: a blunder which was the silliest action probably that I ever committed: due to religious fanaticism, for fanaticism may be very strong in a character which for purposes of religion is very weak. I write from recollection only: and can hardly believe what I write.

It was I think in connection with the augmentation of the Maynooth grant and some other conciliatory measures that as it seemed to me there would or might or should be a change in our relations with the Court of Rome, then as will be remembered still the court of a temporal sovereign; the sovereignty of the Pope not indeed having at the period I am dealing with (1845 or thereabouts) been seriously called in question. Peel had dealt with the Pope for the purpose of obtaining aid in carrying on the government of Ireland, a mistaken proceeding for which however, there were some apologies. It occurred to me that there might be a British resident at the Roman Court. I had resigned on account of Maynooth, and I wrote to Sir R. Peel offering myself for this nonexistent office.[2] I suggested that I should not consider myself entitled to a reply; and reply there was none. Indeed I can conceive Peel's

---

[1] See Appendix 5.

[2] For Gladstone's letter to Peel of 12 July 1844, see *Sir Robert Peel from his private papers*, ed. by Charles Stuart Parker, iii. 160–161.

astonishment on receiving such a letter; and I must own that on this occasion I tried him hard by a most indiscreet proceeding. I cannot now recall the ideas which brought me into such a state of mind as made my proceeding on this occasion possible, but they must I think have been based upon supposed opportunities that might be afforded me for bringing about in Latin quarters a more just estimate of the English Church.

It was perhaps fortunate that in this same year I had an opportunity of rendering a service to the Government. Peel had a plan for the admission of free labour sugar on terms of favour. Lord Palmerston made a motion to show that this involved a breach of old treaties with Spain. I examined the case laboriously and though I think his facts could not be denied I undertook (myself out of office) to answer him on behalf of the Government. This I did and Peel who was the most conscientious man I ever knew in spareness of eulogium: said to me when I sat down, 'That was a wonderful speech, Gladstone'. It was what we used to call an ἅπαξ λεγόμενον,[1] and I allow myself the pleasure of recording it.

In the year 1847, at the moment of the monetary crisis, and under the pressure which it caused, came the great smash in my brother-in-law's affairs which was brought about by the recklessness of one person, his agent, and his own too generous confidence, and systematic non-interference. Upon me devolved the very arduous labour of grappling with the state of things thus brought about with the aid of the various agents. This was the first and severest stage of my financial training: the only training of that kind which I had before becoming Chancellor of the Exchequer for the first time in December 1852. The work was almost desperate: even now it is not quite finished. I mention it here because it gave me I think the habit of sailing rather too near the wind; of which I shall mention an inconvenient result.

From the time when I took office I began to learn that the State held in the face of the Bank and the City an essentially false position as to finance. When these relations began, the State was justly in ill odour as a fraudulent bankrupt who was ready on occasion to add force to fraud. After the Revolution it adopted better methods though often for unwise purposes: and, in order to induce monied men to be lenders, it came forward under the countenance of the Bank as its sponsor, hence a position of subserviency which as the idea of public faith grew up and gradually attained to solidity it became the interest of the Bank and the

---

[1] i.e., Something said once, for the first time, and never again.

City to prolong. This was done by the adoption of amicable and accommodating measures towards the Government, whose position was thus cushioned and made easy in order that it might be willing to give it a continued acquiescence. The hinge of the whole situation was this: the Government itself was not to be a substantive power in matters of finance but was to leave the money power supreme and unquestioned.

In the conditions of this situation I was reluctant to acquiesce, and I began to fight against it by financial self-assertion from the first, though it was only by the establishment of the Post Office Savings Banks, and their great progressive development, that the Finance Minister has been provided with an instrument sufficiently powerful to make him independent of the Bank and City power when he has occasion for sums in seven figures. I was tenaciously opposed by the Governor and Deputy Governor of the Bank, who had seats in Parliament, and had the City for an antagonist on almost every occasion. In 1854, when war approached and was declared, I proposed very early in the season an increase of the income tax, and determined to go through that first year of war without a loan. Instead of this I issued a few millions of Exchequer Bonds for short terms [of] years. The City was obstinate and for some time declined to subscribe. Before the pressure began I had given the legal notice to pay off at par the South Sea Stock, my balance being very large. The proprietors offered to accept other three per cents instead of cash: but having regard to the state of the public credit which had enabled me to create (I think) some $2\frac{1}{2}$ per cents I declined. Then the pressures came, and I had to pay off at par when the Funds had fallen considerably below it. I think that the balances were in a condition to bear a considerable part of it: had it been otherwise there might have been a loss of half a million. A small loss actually occurred. This was owing to 'sailing too near the wind': my fault was not in the original notice but in my oversanguine refusal to accept the exchange offered by or for the holders of South Sea Stock.

I shall next insert a case in which I did not act alone but in concurrence with two most honourable and scrupulous politicians, Sir James Graham and Sidney Herbert.

During the winter of 1854 the soldiery of the army before Sebastopol suffered heavily: and their sufferings were presented by the daily press in such a manner that the nation could hardly be expected to remain passive. A motion for a committee of inquiry was made by Mr. Roebuck and carried by two to one. Lord Aberdeen and the Duke of Newcastle disappeared from the Government, Lord John Russell had resigned so as to anticipate the storm. After various *andirivieni* Lord Palmerston reappeared as head of the Cabinet, in company mainly with what Disraeli wittily called his 'reburnished colleagues'. The Cabinet determined to replace the committee by a Royal Commission. But this delicate operation was as I thought treated by Lord Palmerston with a hand both rude and careless, and the committee, which the Cabinet of Lord Aberdeen had with unanimity thought itself bound in honour to resist, thus remained upon its legs. We three adhered to the judgment formerly arrived at, and possibly overacting the part of parliamentary chivalry resigned our offices. For this we were generally condemned as 'deserters'; but whether we were right or wrong this seems hardly the proper term for those who simply held their ground and desired upon that footing to continue their service as ministers.

We thought that men on trial before a parliamentary committee could not prosecute a great war and uphold a critical alliance with due dignity and energy. We drew arguments from the Walcheren case. I leave open the question whether our judgment was sound. Quite apart from this, the history of the subject is painful for the people of England were in homely phrase bamboozled.

The commission (a very able one) inquired on the spot: and laid the blame on the authorities of the Army. The committee with inferior means inquired and censured the Government or some departments of it. The military caste obtained the appointment of some Generals, to meet at Chelsea, to get rid of the report of the commission. They acquitted the military and I think censured the commissariat which was then under the Treasury and directed *de super* by its permanent officers. In view of these conflicting authorities and of the gravity of the case, Mr. Roebuck, after presenting the report of the committee moved that the House should take it into consideration. We three deserters voted with him. But the House rejected his motion and the case remained without any conclusive or final verdict. A discreditable and for those who feel a stain like a wound a disgraceful history. If lives were wasted before Sebastopol, no reparation whatever was offered to the dead.

But I leave the accuracy of the judgment formed by the expelled Ministers as an open question.

During the excitement, but before the inquiries, most serious administrative changes were very precipitately made. I have never felt satisfied about them.

I have, however, deviated from chronological order. It has been noticed that there were some abortive movements between the death of Aberdeen and the first start of the Palmerston Government: for Lord Palmerston was taken as a *pis aller*, not being acceptable at Court, the Court of those days.

On the [2nd] of [February] I received a request from Lord Lansdowne that I would call upon him; and I drove up to Lansdowne House accordingly. The story is soon told. He made it known to me that he had been requested by the Queen to undertake the re-formation of the Ministry. He desired to know whether I would continue to serve in it as Chancellor of the Exchequer. If I declined he would not persist in his effort: if I agreed he would.

And now I committed one of the most important as well as least pardonable errors of my political life—I declined at once and positively. I said that the Coalition under Lord Aberdeen had worked to my entire satisfaction, but that I was indisposed to partake in it under any other form. He was naturally vexed, but did not enter into particulars and remained carefully reticent.

I wished very soon that he had persevered for as a head of the Government he would have been preferable to Lord Palmerston. He shared with Lord Palmerston the fault of timidity concerning the enlargement of the parliamentary franchise, though he had avoided the rather grave error which Lord Palmerston committed in resigning when the proposals of 1854 were adopted by the Cabinet and then simply resuming on request, without any concession made to meet his views. His mind was temperate and statesmanlike: I should call him a great gentleman. He would not have shared in full the superstition of Lord Palmerston concerning the rehabilitation of the Turkish Empire, and would have had a greater regard for principle as against expedients. He would have had less sympathy with the military party, certainly not less, perhaps more, of zeal for practical improvements. He would not have worked the Church preferments with such a flagrant disregard of governing qualities in the persons preferred. Be it remembered that if Lord Palmerston had never been resisted or baffled his results would have exibited this characteristic in a yet higher degree.

I ask myself what was my motive in this vexatious refusal? It was not any dislike or any dread of Lord Lansdowne himself and I confess it appears to me inconsistent with my consent, and almost immediately afterwards, to continue to hold my office under Lord Palmerston. The best account I can give of it is this. Although in point of opinion I had departed far from the Conservative and Protectionist party, and entertained no idea of coalescing with it unless as one of a body, yet my sympathies lagged much behind my opinions: my wish on the whole was that Lord Derby should form a government, and I was unwilling to do anything that would block him out of the field.

And I am certainly still of the opinion I then held, that in declining to form one he missed a great opportunity. He commanded as large a following in the House of Commons as the Liberals, for the working majority of 1853–5 depended on the Peelite contingent which as in 1852 would have given him fair play. His opponents were discredited by apparent failure: the existence of the war *with* their failure would have compelled their forebearance. I have since understood that Mr. Disraeli also held the opinion, which I have now expressed.

Let me make one brief addition. I had a warm and grateful affection for Lord Aberdeen: I thought he had been ill used, and had no great desire probably to assist any one in mounting to the position from which he had been rudely cast down. And undeservedly: for on any showing it was impossible to associate him in any special manner with the sufferings of the army.

At the outset of the Palmerston Government I was in no way unfriendly. I used every effort to smooth the way for the succession to my own office: and Sir George Lewis on agreeing to take it very frankly said to me that in all probability he would have declined had it not been for my efforts to place him in command of all the circumstances of the situation. Notwithstanding this, after a time I found myself in sharp opposition to him. Our financial ideas and tendencies were radically at variance: as I found when in the second Palmerston Cabinet I found him usually an opponent.

During the American Civil War I committed another palpable error which was of a very grave description; and which illustrates vividly that incapacity of viewing subjects all round, in their extraneous as well as their internal properties and thereby of knowing when to be silent and when to speak.

In the year 1862 I had emerged from the very grave financial difficulties which in 1860 and 1861 went near to breaking me down. Some compassionate references to my woebegone condition will be found in Charles Greville's memoirs of the period.[1] A blue sky was now over me

---

[1] See Greville's Journal for 12 May and 17 July 1860.

and some of the Northern Liberals devised for me a triumphant visit to the Tyne, which of course entailed as one of its incidents a public dinner.

I was not one of those who on the ground of British interests desired a division of the American Union. My view was distinctly opposite. I thought that while the Union continued it never could exercise any dangerous pressure upon Canada to estrange it from the Empire: our honour as I thought rather than our interest forbidding its surrender. But, were the Union split, the North no longer checked by the jealousies of slave-power, would seek a partial compensation for its loss in annexing or trying to annex British North America. Lord Palmerston desired the severance as a diminution of a dangerous power but prudently held his tongue.

It was the moment when the South was at the climax of its military success, and the friends of the North in England were beginning to advise that it should give way for the avoidance of further bloodshed and great calamity. I weakly supposed that the time had come when respectful suggestions of this kind, founded on the necessity of the case, were required by a spirit of true friendship: which in so many contingencies of life has to offer sound recommendations with a knowledge that they will not be popular. And so at the Newcastle public dinner I said that Jefferson Davis had made an army, and what was more he had made a nation: expressing the hope that nothing would be said or done in England to aggravate the pain with which patriotic Northerners would regard the transition through which they had to pass.

That this opinion was founded upon a false estimate of the facts was the very least part of my fault. I did not perceive the gross impropriety of such an utterance from a Cabinet Minister of a power, allied in blood and language and bound to loyal neutrality; the case being further aggravated by the fact that we were already so to speak under indictment before the world for not (as was alleged) having strictly enforced the laws of neutrality in the matter of the cruisers.

My offence was indeed only a mistake but one of incredible grossness, and with such consequences of offence and alarm attached to it that my failing to perceive them justly exposed me to very severe blame.

When we came to the arbitration at Geneva my words were cited as part of the proof of hostile *animus*. Meantime I had prepared a lengthened statement to show from my abundant declarations on other occasions that there was and could be on my part no such *animus*. I was desirous to present this statement to the arbitrators. My colleagues objected so largely to the proceeding that I desisted. In this I think they probably were wrong. I addressed my paper to the American Minister for the information of his Government: and Mr. Secretary Fish gave me, so far as intention was concerned, a very handsome acquittal. The paper was then published in *Harper's* or some other American review.

And strange to say, *post hoc* though perhaps not *propter hoc*, the United States have been that country of the world in which the most signal marks of public honour have been paid me and in which my name has been the most popular, the only parallels being Italy, Greece, and the Balkan Peninsula.

7 November 1896

Appointments of 1892.

I do not think in forming the Cabinets of 1868 and 1880, I had to introduce any member into them apart from or against my own judgment. In 1880 two names were pressed upon me, those of Chamberlain and Dilke. But these were both men of Cabinet *calibre*. I remember too that Chamberlain behaved extremely well. For after I had laid upon him a general exposition of the situation, he said, 'I am perfectly ready to serve, if you think proper, without entering the Cabinet.' But I did not hesitate to offer him the rank of a Minister of the Crown, and Dilke whose capacity was also undeniable was introduced at a later period. In 1886 I think my hands were very free but that Government was formed without much prospect of solid endurance. In 1892 I was beset right and left. I agreed to go up to the outrageous number of seventeen, and in doing this consented to include more than one man insufficient in experience or in force. But the more important mistakes were in the persons of men whose title to Cabinet office was indisputable, and whom by my very own fault I misplaced. Lord Spencer was with his whole soul desirous to take the Admiralty; and though I did not suggest it and probably should not have made that choice but for his desire, I thought that the firmness he had shown in Ireland would enable him to hold his ground as against the professional element. In this I was sadly disappointed for he both proposed to the Cabinet the outrageous estimates of 1894–5 and clung to them with a desperate and successful tenacity and with the fatal aid of Harcourt. True, he had fought a battle in his department, for although it seems almost incredible the plans and demands of his Admirals had been yet more outrageous and beyond all precedent, and he had insisted upon their being reduced. But they were still in my judgment only to be accepted by men 'drunk and mad' and thus it was he, who excellent as he always is, stabbed me under the fifth rib.

Another and perhaps even worse error was the appointment of Rosebery to the Foreign Office. And here I had none of the excuse which I was able to plead up to a certain point in the case of Spencer. Rosebery had a sort of presumptive title to the Foreign Office, from a former tenure of it, although a very brief one, in 1886. But instead of founding a claim upon this tenure, he did everything in his power to avoid the resumption of it. Again and again he resisted my overtures. It was only by a telegram received at Osborne on the morning of the day when I had to settle the principal appointments with the Queen, at Osborne, an hour or two later, that I received from him a telegram which authorised me to put him there if I thought proper. Considering what followed I have great satisfaction in recording on his behalf his rather determined resistance. The only palliations of my great error are these two. First, though he had never spoken directly to me on the Egyptian [question], yet I had through J. Morley an account of his opinions about evacuation, which appeared to guarantee them as perfectly satisfactory. Secondly, he had not in 1886 developed any of the ideas as to the position and discretion of the Foreign Secretary which very soon made themselves manifest in 1892. Besides these he showed himself in the Uganda business to be rather seriously imbued with that territorial greed, which constitutes for us one of the grave dangers of the time. As to Egypt I am bound to say that, although his views were not quite what I had wished and expected, yet I think that, if the French Government had duly followed up the notice at a very early date through Waddington their Ambassador, we might, as far as the merits of the case were concerned, have been able to arrive at a conclusion substantially right.

But the fatal element in this appointment was his total gross misconception of the relative position of the two offices we respectively held and secondly his really outrageous assumption of power apart both from the First Minister and from the Cabinet.

I shall illustrate the first point by reciting what took place in 1880 [sic] with relation to Egypt.

Waddington addressed himself to me in a grave manner on the part of the French Government, and said that the question might or would soon become a burning one. France wished to know from us whether, if she addressed to us a friendly representation on the subject of the occupation, it would be received by us in a friendly or corresponding manner. Of course I felt that I had no title to reply on behalf of the Government to such an inquiry and I promised accordingly to communicate with the Foreign Minister and the Cabinet.

But when I named this subject to Rosebery, he was up in arms, and full of indignation against Waddington. No Ambassador had any title to introduce a foreign matter except through him. He was the doyen of the diplomatic body (?) and was in a position unlike that of any other Minister. I pointed out the position in which I stood and the absolute duty of returning an official answer to the French, but I could not obtain from him a single word of aid. Of course he saw that I must introduce it at a Cabinet. But when I did this he remained sulky and [*unfinished*].

GENERAL RETROSPECT

ADD.MS 44791, f. 51

I am by no means sure, upon a calm review, that Providence has endowed me with anything which can be called a striking gift. But if there be such a thing entrusted to me, it has been shown, at certain political junctures, in what may be termed appreciation of the general situation and its result. To make good the idea, this must not be considered as the simple acceptance of public opinion, founded upon the discernment that it has risen to a certain height needful for a given work, like a tide. It is an insight into the facts of particular eras, and their relations one to another, which generates in the mind a conviction that the materials exist for forming a public opinion, and for directing it to a particular end.

There are four occasions of my life with respect to which I think these considerations may be applicable. They were these:

1. The renewal of the income tax in 1853.
2. The proposal of religious equality for Ireland in 1868.
3. The proposal of Home Rule for Ireland in 1886.
4. The desire for a dissolution of Parliament in the beginning of 1894, and the immediate determination of the issue then raised between the two Houses of Parliament.

I will consider these four junctures severally.

Unfinished

CHIEF HEADS OF LEGISLATIVE WORK[1]

ADD.MS 44791, ff. 49–50

1842 The Tariff (as contradistinguished from the Budget).
1843 Joint Stock Companies Act (first).
       Coal Whippers Act. Small but of much interest and consequence.
1844 Railways Act (paralysed by subsequent proceedings).
1845 Tariff. Prepared by me before resignation in January 1845.
1852 Colonial Church Bill (was never passed: but its designs are
       accomplished by tacit consent).
1853 Budget and Tariff.
1854 Succession Duty Act.
1854 Oxford University Act.
1860 Tariff (French treaty). Wine duties.
1861 Paper Duties Act (Lords crippled in finance).
1862 Bank Notes Bill. Failed on 3rd reading.
1862 Post Office Savings Bank.
1866 Reform Bill.
1868,9 Irish Church Disestablishment.
       Abolition of church rates.
       Abolition of university tests.
1870 Irish Land Act.
       There were four other important measures of this Government,
       two of which passed: 1. Education, 2. Ballot; two did not:
       1. Public house licences, 2. Army purchase (done by Royal
       warrant). They were not under my personal charge.
1873 Irish University Bill (failed on 2nd reading).
1881 Irish Land Act.
       Abolition of malt tax.
1882 Arrears Act.
1884,5 Franchise and Redistribution Acts. Redistribution Bill: worked
       through House of Commons by Sir C. Dilke. Corrupt Prac-
       tices ditto by Lord James.
1886 Government of Ireland Bill (lost on 2nd reading).
1893 Government of Ireland Bill.
N.B. New Lectionary Bill.

January 1896

---

[1] This document contains a number of later additions which have been
incorporated into the text in their correct chronological order.

Including the larger measures and looking solely on achieved results, I should take the following heads.

1. The Tariffs, 1842–60.
2. Oxford University Act.
3. Post Office Savings Banks (see comment).
4. Irish Church Disestablishment.
5. Irish Land Acts.
6. Franchise Act.

Although this excludes the last of all the efforts, viz. the Irish Government Bill.

Post Office Savings Banks. The points to be noted are three:

1. The whole of my action in 1859–65 was viewed with the utmost jealousy by a large minority and a section of the very limited majority. It was an object to get this bill passed *sub silentio*. A full statement of my expectations from it would have been absolutely fatal. Indeed they have been more than realised.

2. The Trustee Savings Banks were doubly[1] defective. (1) Their principle was left in doubt. Were the funds, funds in trust, or cash at a banker's? This was vital. (2) They never got or could get within the doors of the masses for they smelt of class. It was necessary to provide for the savings of the people with (a) safety, (b) cheapness, (c) convenience. The banks *cost* money to the State. The Post Office Savings Banks bring in a revenue.

3. Behind all this I had one object of first-rate importance which has been attained: to provide the Minister of Finance with a strong financial arm, and to secure his independence of the City by giving him a large and certain amount of money.

ADD.MS 44791, f. 20

9 November 1894

That political life considered as a profession has great dangers for the inner and true life of the human being, is too obvious. It has, however, some redeeming qualities.

In the first place I have never known, and can hardly conceive, a finer school of temper than the House of Commons. A lapse in this respect is on the instant an offence and a jar, a wound, to every member

---

[1] Nay trebly: for they sometimes broke [WEG].

of the assembly; and it brings its own punishment on the instant, like the sins of the Jews under the old dispensation.

Again I think that the imperious nature of the subjects, their weight and force demanding the entire strength of a man and all his faculties, leave him no residue, at least for the time, to apply to self-regard: no more than there is for a swimmer swimming for his life.

He must too in retrospect feel himself to be so very small in comparison with the themes, and the interests of which he has to treat.

It is a further advantage if his occupation be not mere debate but debate ending in work. For in this way, whether the work be legislative or administrative, it is continually tested by results, and he is enabled to strip away his extravagant anticipations, his fallacious conception, to perceive his mistakes, and to reduce his estimates to the reality. No politician has any excuse for being vain.

RELIGION

EARLY RELIGIOUS OPINIONS

ADD.MS 44791, ff. 1–19

Drawing a clear distinction between religious opinions and religious character, although I admit they are related the one to the other, I proceed to give some account of the formation of my opinions in the matter of religion.

In childhood I accepted those current in the domestic atmosphere without question and without interest: and I think I had better proceed at once to the time and the manner in which breaches came to be made in them.

This was I think in the year 1828. I had left Eton at Christmas 1827. During 1828 I had much of the society of my elder sister, deeply beloved by all. Her mental gifts were considerable, her character most devout and fervent: her religious rearing had been in the Evangelical tenets but her mind was too pure for prejudice. She must have infused into me some little warmth, and I think she started me on some not very devious bypaths of opinion. At any rate I remember these two things. Whereas baptismal regeneration had of course been registered as a heresy in my mind, I fell upon an article in the *Quarterly Review* which appeared to deduce all manner of patristic testimonies in its favour. I was not at all prepared to stand fire of this description: in the question what was true Christianity I could not but suppose that these Fathers must have known something about it. But what struck me most was that St. Augustine was included among the witnesses: for I had always heard of him as a truly Evangelical Christian, and possibly I knew that in Milner's *Church History*, the only one on the domestic shelves, he filled a very considerable space. I was thus lifted up to the level of baptismal regeneration: and so I think must have been my dear sister. This probably set me upon reading Hooker's works which I found in my father's library.

I went to reside at Christ Church in October 1828, and remained until December 1831. Ecclesiastically, I was fed upon Bishop Burnet's book on the Thirty-Nine Articles, not then superseded by higher teaching. The divinity lectures for undergraduates moved I think much on the same lines. The religious atmosphere of Oxford generally was calm, and indeed stagnant. Happily for her sons the study of Butler had come into vogue. In due time I read him as closely and intensely as Aristotle. But, with a great general admiration, I was ignorantly shocked at his doctrine of human nature. Nor did I recover entirely from this shock until some six or seven years later or thereabouts, I became an interested reader of St. Augustine (many of whose works I have in summaries) and found him in accordance with Butler so that I was profoundly satisfied.

A brief residence as private pupil with Dr. Turner, made Bishop of Calcutta under the Duke of Wellington, had led to my bringing introductions to Oxford, which threw me into partial relations with the small Evangelical group at Oxford, which was for the most part sharply Calvinistic, and was concentrated at two points, one in St. Edmund Hall under its Vice-Principal Mr. Hill, the other at St. Ebbe's Church under the curate in charge Mr. Bulteel. This partly held and partly repelled me. One Sunday a Mr. Blackstone preached what I thought a very Christian sermon in the University pulpit, I was scandalised by hearing Henry Wilberforce (already a High Churchman and very sarcastic as well as acute) treat it contemptuously. I was also scandalised when Mr. Vaughan Thomas in that pulpit spoke of 'Calvin and Socinus, and other like aliens from the Gospel truth'. I knew and respected both Bishop Lloyd and Dr. Pusey, but neither of them attempted to exercise the smallest influence over my religious opinions. I also knew Mr. Churton of B.N.C., almost the only pure Evangelical in the university (unless Newman, 1829) which was all high, mostly moreover dry, except this irreducible knot of Calvinists. Amidst these diverse surroundings, and undoubtedly with a large increase of religious interest testified by observances and otherwise, I continued to hold in the main mildly Evangelical opinions, without any real ideas of the Church, but also without any factious energy of private judgment: I have memoranda of this period which on examining them for the purposes of these notes I find testify to[1]

I knew Maurice well, had heard superlative accounts of him from Cambridge, and really strove to make them all realities to myself. One Sunday morning we walked to Marsh Baldon to hear Mr. Porter the incumbent, a Calvinist independent of the *clique* and a man of remarkable power as we both thought. I think he and other friends did me good, but I got little solid meat from him as I found him difficult to catch and

---

[1] This sentence was left incomplete.

more difficult still to hold. The upshot is that I am unable to[1] trace, down to this date, any appreciable influence of any individual or individuals whatever upon the formation of my religious opinions.

Their general colour is clearly established by a fact of a little later date. In March 1832, on my first Continental journey in company with my brother John, I pressed him and he kindly consented to travel from Turin up to Pinerol and see one of the Vaudois valleys. I had framed a lofty conception of the people as ideal Christians. I certainly underwent a chill of disappointment at finding them much like other men. In a cottage when I inquired of an oldish woman about their public services I found the measure of them was one service on Sunday and one on Thursday evening. I must have made some observation probably about their private devotions, when as I remember she replied to me 'Et les Catholiques ils font leurs dévotions aussi.' I went on to call on the Pastor (M. Bert) and found him quiet and inoffensive in manner without the smallest sign of energy or what would then have been called in England vital religion. I left with him a little money, what I thought I could afford, the small packet bearing on it what was meant for a pious inscription. I strove on the whole to make the best of it, their case seeming absolutely negative, though without anything to disgust or repel. So I wrote verses on some violets that I found in the valley to which I may here give a place if I find on referring to them that they are passable, as they certainly form a kind of landmark.[2] Soon came, for the first time, something like a new point of departure.

In May of the same year we had got to Naples: and one Sunday something I know not what set me on examining the occasional offices of the Church in the Prayer Book. I do not recollect that I had ever before this time been present at a baptism: and I fear that I was practically in complete ignorance of the whole of this portion of the work. But they made a strong impression upon me on that very day, and the impression never has been effaced. I had previously taken a great deal of teaching direct from the Bible, as best I could: but now the figure of the Church arose before me as a teacher too, and I gradually found in how incomplete and fragmentary a manner I had drawn down truth from the sacred volume, as indeed I had also missed in the Thirty-nine Articles some things which ought to have taught me better. Such, for I

---

[1] The words 'I am unable to' were added in pencil.
[2] See Appendix 4.

believe I have given the fact as it occurred, in its silence and its solitude, was my first introduction to the august conception of the Church of Christ. It presented to me Christianity under an aspect in which I had not yet known it: its ministry of symbols, its channels of grace, its unending line of teachers joining from the head: a sublime construction, based throughout upon historic fact, uplifting the ideas of the community in which we live, and of the access which it enjoys through the new and living way, to the presence of the most high.

From this time I began to feel my way by degrees into or towards a true notion of the Church. It became a definite and organised idea when at the suggestion of James Hope I read the just-published and re-markable work of Palmer. But the charm of freshness lay upon that first disclosure in 1832. It was not one passage in particular though many are remarkable but it was the *ensemble* and its effect. And of the new prospect thus opened to me I would in my very small measure and in feeble and remote imitation base the words of the great St. Augustine: *quam sero te amavi, O pulchritudo, tam antiqua et tam nova.* It follows from this disclosure to the mind that Protestantism takes its stand and is estimated from an altered point of view. It ceases to present the idea of a republication of the Gospel under which it has been so largely con-ceived. It becomes a great incident in a continuous history, into which it is imbedded: a great incident, necessarily like other great incidents marked with agony, of a mixed character. In writing an article years afterwards (1844) for the *Quarterly Review* on Ward's *Ideal of the Christian Church*, I endeavoured to represent that the Reformation stood upon the pages of Church history like a great statute in the volume of the laws, something as the Reform Act of 1832 stood in reference to the British constitution. It settles down into its place, to be judged upon its merits, but also in connection with, and in possible subordination to yet higher and deeper laws. A new and separate element of difficulty is of course introduced in cases where the access of Protestantism severed its teaching system at once from the historic organisation of government in the Church. It will be understood that the Oxford movement was as outside my period of residence at Christ Church as the trial of Dr. Sacheverell. The stir in my mind at Naples came before it. When it had begun I was personally outside it. Once I met Newman at Clapham in the house of Mr. B. Harrison, after his return from the Continent, and I recollect propounding to him that the Roman Catholics used the word merit very mischievously to which he replied that no doubt they said many crude things about it. I did not see the Tracts, nor follow details. For the years 1833–6, I lived in The Albany, attending St. James's Church morning and afternoon with very little variation: when at Fasque going to the Presbyterian church in the forenoon, when at Edinburgh (where my father wintered) attending St. John's, of which Dean Ramsay was the incumbent.

It was after 1836 that I found James Hope (brought up in the school of the Low Church) had by careful study worked himself entirely out of it. We both took an interest in the Scottish Episcopal communion. It was a feeble plant. But there inhered in it a very striking Episcopal type. I came to know most of the bishops and greatly admired Bishop Moir (Brechin), Bishop Walker (Edinburgh), whom however I did not know personally: Bishop Skinner, firm as a rock: Bishop Torry, very like Archbishop Harcourt in face but with a wig like a doormat, whereas the Archbishop told me that keeping his wig or wigs in order was very nearly the work of one valet, and certainly one valet would absorb Bishop Torry's salary which I think only reached into the second £100 per annum. I must not however omit to mention an earlier incident which without making me a Churchman repelled me from the party men of the other camp. There was a Mr. Craig, Minister of St. James's Episcopal Chapel in Edinburgh to whom I think that I was introduced by Dr.Turner. He showed me active kindness and gave me a letter to Dr. Macbride at Oxford. But he shocked me much as a youth of eighteen, by coolly asking me one day, 'Is your father a Christian?'

Between Hope and me grew up about 1833[1] the idea of Trinity College, Glenalmond. We worked very hard to obtain for it support but with very partial success, though we drew in Dean Ramsay, most delightful of men, who had many friends among the aristocracy. About four or five peers supported it. My father went into it warmly. It helped on my churchmanship: but James Hope was much above me. So did the writing my work on Church and State, which he carried through the press while I went abroad in 1838 on account of my eyesight. So without doubt did my intercourse (mostly by letter) with Archdeacon Manning, who however did not acquire the power over me which seemed as of right to fall to Hope. I had not however yet learned to regard the Reformation with a fair historic freedom. The young of today can hardly conceive the servility in which we were held or rather

---

[1] The date was added in pencil.

born and bred on this great topic. The reaction from this servitude has without doubt engendered much licence and injustice: of which Dr. W. G. Ward was nearly the first and certainly an egregious example.

After the publication of my book on Church and State O'Connell passing me behind the Speaker's Chair said good naturedly, 'We claim the half of you.' It was followed in 1840 by *Church Principles considered in their results*; a work of very sanguine Anglicanism, of which however the composition had led me over important fields of thought. When in 1841 [1] the storm broke upon Tract 90, I thought there were one or two glaring sophisms in the Tract, but I became indignant at the spirit of persecution which now began to hunt down every person marked for his sympathy with the movement. On this account I worked in conjunction with B. Harrison, afterwards Archdeacon, to get Mr. Isaac Williams out of the strife about the Poetry Professorship; but we were not strong enough. It was not far from this point of time when the Benchers of Lincoln's Inn absolutely rejected Manning, a man admirably adapted for their Preachership (by one vote only) and appointed to the office the Rev. James Anderson, a poor creature and totally unfit.

I suppose that these and other like incidents and influences made me feel that the time was come to test my position all round by bringing my theological ideas into shape: and I wrote accordingly in 1842 [2] with care a paper for the purpose which may properly be inserted in this narrative. But before I give it I must dwell rather more fully upon the growth of my religious interests and studies.

The change in the professional direction of my life which took place in deference to my father's wish did not imply a transfer of my governing interest to the field of politics. In December 1832 when I entered Parliament politics did not offer a very exciting field to a youth associated with the Conservative party, for that party had all the appearance of being in a state of hopeless defeat and discomfiture. But in my imagination I cast over that party a prophetic mantle and assigned to it a mission distinctly religious as the champion in the state field of that divine truth which it was the office of the Christian ministry to uphold in the Church. Nor was this mental attitude however strange it may now appear altogether unaccountable. For it must be remembered that the Grey Ministry was split in 1834 and the Peel Ministry ejected in

---

[1] The date was added in pencil.
[2] The date was added in pencil.

1835 on the ground of the absolute inviolability of the Irish Church. Neither then did I nor now can I see on what ground this inviolability could for a moment be maintained, except that the State had such a mission.

The friendships I had formed at college with Hamilton, afterwards Bishop of Salisbury, and with Anstice, a youth of the highest promise, who became Professor of Classics at King's College (and entered into his rest a very few years after), together with the stir at Oxford, tended to concentrate and enhance my religious interests. The study of Dante to which I took heartily and even intensely (though with no learning to give it depth) worked in the same direction. I passed usually a good deal of the parliamentary recess at Fasque and became a fond and constant reader of St. Augustine in particular. Of the earliest Fathers I read much, and I went through the works of St. Bernard. Thus in an irregular way I gave much time to theology. Not wholly the most orthodox: I read not only Locke and Edwards but Strauss's *Leben Jesu* soon after its appearance. Here was a sort of *apparatus criticus* for my books; but my Anglicanism was brought into order and system almost entirely by Palmer's remarkable book although I did not altogether follow the severe judgments which it passed upon all who were in schism or willing domestic separation from the English Church. As to my own practice, in 1832 I attended at Lyons and Turin, there being no Anglican church, worship conducted by a Protestant pastor. In 1838, which was the date of my second visit to the Continent, I did not. At both periods I attended sermons in the Roman Catholic churches but had little of the idea of community of worship there, which indeed the nature of the services tends somewhat to obstruct. In the long years which have since elapsed there has been a gradual change not in my principles but in the mode of applying them to action, on which I need not now enter. I did not then see as I now see the difference between the founders of schism—*seminator di scandali e di scismo*, and its inheritors, to whom it comes with presumptive authority of a traditionary system. It was Mrs. Milnes Gaskell (née Brandreth) who when I was visiting about 1827 or 1828 at Thornes encountered some piece of Evangelical intolerance (I know not what) which I had been venting, with an invaluable piece of instruction then quite new to me. 'Where there is union with Christ by faith and love', she said, there we might recognise the essence of the one thing needful. Probably she would have gone even further and admitted that where Christ is not known at all there may nevertheless be union with God under a thousand forms available in their various methods and degrees for the suppression or repression of the selfish life, and the evocation of a life divine.

And now I will give the paper I refer to.[1]

From 1841 and from the date of this paper till the beginning of 1845 I continued upon the same lines; a hardworking official man but with a decided predominance of religious over secular interests. Although I had little of direct connection with Oxford and its teachers I was regarded in common fame as tarred with their brush; and I was not so blind as to be unaware that for the clergy this meant not yet indeed prosecution but proscription and exclusion from advancement by either party in the State, for laymen a vague and indiscriminate prejudice with serious doubts how far persons infected in this particular manner could have any real capacity for affairs. Sir Robert Peel must I think have exercised much self denial when he put me forward into his Cabinet in 1843.

In that year I joined in protesting against the suppression of Dr. Pusey for his sermon on the Real Presence: and early in 1845 I voted at Oxford against depriving Ward of his degree and against the censure on him (while vehemently differing from him) on the ground that the decree accused him of bad faith. I also voted against the censure on Dr. Newman which was vetoed by Mr. (afterwards Dean) Church and his brother proctor by actively promoting the address of thanks to them for the act which they had I think wisely as well as courageously performed. Neither my refusal to support Peel about Maynooth as a colleague, nor my full support of him as an independent Member, were the fruit of religious opinion. The first I thought due to honour, the second meant a radical change in the basis of my views as to Church and State.

As 1845 drew onwards, it became requisite that I should proceed for a family purpose to the Continent, and this purpose carried me first to Munich, and to the door of Dr. Döllinger, in what is I think now von der Turn Street, which was opened by himself. When I gave my name he surprised me by inquiring (with a complimentary expression) whether I was the Minister or late Minister Gladstone: for I could not conceive how my name could have reached him, being unaware of the minuteness and comprehensiveness of his knowledge as to England, and things English. I passed nearly a week in Munich and this principally

---

[1] See Appendix 6.

in his society. He entered freely with me into deep matters of religion and he alike enlarged, uplifted, and studied my belief. Although already in the first rank of living Roman theologians, he did nothing to disturb me, did not in any way attack but sought only to assist my religious convictions, and led me in that short term to reckon him first among my religious teachers. At the same time I perused his book on Church history, and his account of the fourth century and the great Arian controversy most strongly confirmed me in my allegiance to the Church of England by the light it threw on the nature and condition of the provision which the Almighty has been pleased to make for the maintenance and establishment even of the most central of all dogmas.

> There is a Providence that shapes our ends
> Rough-hew them how we may.

I think that no one can be more deeply penetrated with these words than I am or ought to be.

The whole of my public and exoteric life had been shaped as to its ends for me, scarcely rough-hewn by me.

In its beginnings it was exceedingly narrow: I think that at this time its most marked characteristic may be its breadth of field, in respect to the number and greatness of the national masses with which it has placed me in contact, and in sympathetic contact.

How has this come about? I will endeavour to enumerate some of the leading landmarks.

The desire of my youth was to be a clergyman. My mental life (ill represented in the moral being) was concentrated in the Church: in the Church understood after the narrowest fashion, that of the Evangelical school, whose bigotry I shared but whose fervour if it possessed me at all possessed me only by fits and starts.

Apparently unfinished
26 July 1894[1]

1828–41

ADD.MS 44790, ff. 156–165

I can give a tolerably clear account of the steps by which I was theoretically by a very gradual process built up into a Churchman. Of the relation between this process which had its seat in my understanding and

---

[1] This section incorporates additions and alterations made 7 February 1897.

any true conversion of the heart to God I do not dare and indeed I am not competent to speak.

I had been brought up with no notion of the Church as the church or body of Christ. Not only was there no visibility, but there was not even any collectivity in my conception of outward religion and religious observances.

It once happened to me, on the top of a coach between London and Eton, to hear a conversation in which the interlocutors were a 'converted' private soldier and an unconverted comrade of the Foot and Life Guards respectively. There came a turn in it, at which the first named of the two put the question, 'Come now, what is the Church of England?' To which the other replied, 'It is a d---d large building with an organ in it.' I think this expressed the ideas of my childhood. My environment was strictly Evangelical. My dear and noble mother was a woman of warm piety but broken health and I was not directly instructed by her. But I was brought up to believe that D'Oyly and Mant's Bible (then a standard book of the colour ruling in the Church) was heretical and that every Unitarian (I suppose also every heathen) must as matter of course be lost for ever.

This deplorable servitude of mind oppressed me in a great or less degree for a number of years. As late as in the year I think [1836[1]] one of my brothers married a beautiful and in every way charming person who had been brought [up] in a family of the Unitarian profession yet under a mother very sincerely religious: the family of Mr. Jones, the banker, of Liverpool. I went through much mental difficulty and distress at the time as there had been no express renunciation of the ancestral creed, and absurdly busied myself with devising this or that religious test as what if accepted might suffice.

So, as will be seen, the first access of churchlike ideas to my mind by no means sufficed to expel my inherited and bigoted misconception, though in the event they did it as I hope effectively. But I long retained in my recollection an observation made to me in (I think) the year 1829 by Mrs. Benjamin Gaskell of Thornes near Wakefield, a seed which was destined long to remain in my mind without germinating. I fell into religious conversation with this excellent woman, the mother of my Eton friend Milnes Gaskell, and herself the wife[2] of an Unitarian. She

---

[1] Paper torn.
[2] MS: husband.

said to me, 'Surely we cannot entertain a doubt as to the future condition of any person truly united to Christ by faith and love, whatever may be the faults of his opinions.' Here she supplied me with the key to the whole question. To this hour I feel grateful to her accordingly, for the scope of her remark is very wide: and it is now my rule to remember her in prayer before the altar.[1]

There was nothing at Eton to subvert this frame of mind: for nothing was taught us either for it or against it. But in the spring and summer of 1828 I set to work on Hooker's *Ecclesiastical Polity* and read it straight through. Intercourse with my saintly elder sister Anne had increased my mental interest in religion and she though generally of Evangelical sentiments had an opinion that the standard divines of the English Church were of great value. Hooker's exposition of the claims of the Church of England came to me as a mere abstraction: but I think that I found the doctrine of baptismal regeneration, theretofore abhorred, impossible to reject and the way was thus opened for further changes.

In like manner at Oxford I do not doubt that in 1830 and 1831 the study of Bishop Butler laid the ground for new modes of thought in religion, but his teaching in the sermons on our moral nature was not integrated so to speak until several years later by large perusal of the works of St. Augustine. I may however say that I was not of a mind ill disposed to submit to authority.

In January 1832 I went with my brother John to the Continent, equipped as it were in a full suit of Protestantism. He most kindly as was his way agreed at my urgent instance to a trip from Turin into one of the Vaudois valleys which I undertook more in the spirit of a pilgrimage than any other journey I have ever made. The general effect, however, of what I saw was chilling: and I thought it strange that these saints of God should be content with their one Sunday service and a Thursday evening lecture. I wrote verses to glorify them [2] but our visit to them distinctly lowered my temperature as to Protestantism.

In May of that year we were at Naples, and some circumstances, I do not remember what, led me to make for the first time an examination of the Prayer Book and especially of the occasional services. It was, I have no doubt, partial and superficial enough: but it imparted to the framework of my Evangelical ideas a shock from which they never thoroughly

---

[1] The last two paragraphs are an insertion made on 7 February 1897.
[2] See Appendix 4.

recovered. I found that in regard to the priesthood and to sacramental doctrine in its highest essence we remained upon the ground of the pre-Reformation period, and stood wholly apart from the general mass of Protestantism. And I think that the discovery was to me a matter of satisfaction. I remember that the impression was deep: I felt that an event had happened in my life.

I did not proceed so far as to attain a distinct conception of the Church. But I had some correspondence a little later with an Oxford friend, afterwards Archdeacon Harrison, where the notion of succession in the sacred ministry and of the historic chain thus found to connect us with the authority and teaching of our Lord, dawned upon my mind.

The Oxford movement properly so called began in the next year but it had no direct effect upon me. I did not see the Tracts and to this hour I have read but few of them. Indeed my first impressions and emotions in connection with it were those of indignation at what I thought the rash intemperate censures pronounced by Mr. Hurrell Froude upon the Reformers.

My chief tie with Oxford was the close friendship I had formed in 1830 with Walter Hamilton. His character, always loving and loved, not very greatly later became deeply devout. But I do not think he at this time sympathised with Newman and his friends: and he had the good sense in conjunction with Mr. Denison, afterwards Bishop, to oppose the censure upon Dr. Hampden, to which I foolishly and ignorantly gave in, without, however, being an active or important participator.

But the blow struck by the Prayer Book in 1832 set my mind in motion, and that motion was never arrested. I found food for the new ideas and tendencies in various quarters, not least in the religious writings of Alexander Knox, all of which I perused. Moreover I had an inclination to ecclesiastical conformity and obedience as such which led me to concur with some zeal in the plans of Bishop Blomfield. In the course of two or three years, Manning turned from a strongly Evangelical attitude to one as strongly Anglican, and about the same time converted his acquaintance with me into a close friendship. In the same manner James Hope whom I had known but slightly at Eton or Oxford made a carefully considered change of the same kind: which also became the occasion of a fast friendship. Both these intimacies led me forward: Hope especially had influence over me more than I think any other person at any period of my life.

When I was preparing in 1837–8 *The State in its relations with the*

Church, he took a warm interest in the work, which, during my absence on the Continent, he corrected for the press. His attitude towards the work, however, included a desire that its propositions should be carried further. The temper of the times among young educated men worked in the same direction. I had no low Churchman among my near friends except Walter Farquhar. Anstice, a great loss, died very early in his beautiful married life.

While I was busy about my book, Hope made known to me Palmer's work on the Church, which had just appeared. I read it with care and great interest. It took hold upon me: and gave me at once the clear, definite and strong conception of the Church which through all the storm and strain of a most critical period has proved for me entirely adequate to every emergency and saved me from all vacillation. I did not however love the extreme rigour of the book in its treatment of non-episcopal communions.

It was not very long after this, I think in 1842, that I reduced to form my convictions on the large and important range of subjects which recent controversy had brought into preeminence.

I conceive that in the main Palmer completed for me the work which inspection of the Prayer Book had begun.

Before referring further to my *redaction* of opinions, which will be subjoined, I desire to say at this moment I am as closely an adherent to the doctrines of grace generally and to the general sense of St. Augustine as at the date from which this narrative set out. I hope that my mind has dropped nothing affirmative. But I hope also that there has been dropped from it all the damnatory part of the opinions taught by the Evangelical school; not only as respects the Roman Catholic religion, but also as to heretics and heathens: Nonconformists and Presbyterians I think that I always let off pretty easily. But I may record here one precious saying which was spoken to me I think in 1828 by Mrs. Milnes Gaskell (née Brandreth). It sank into my mind and had a gradual and silent but lasting influence over me. She said that assuredly the real question was whether a soul was 'united by faith and love to Christ': this was the essence and decided the matter. I remember, when she said it, how new it seemed to me. Doubtless it took some time for its full apprehension: but I did not in any way repel it.

I subjoin the document to which I lately referred[1].

---

[1] See Appendix 6.

CARDINAL MANNING

ADD.MS 44790, ff. 177–181

I habitually considered Manning's faculties of action, I mean in the management and government of men, to be far in advance of his faculties of thought. In polemical matters he was narrow and positive: he had not the power of looking all round a great subject: accordingly he was intensely satisfied[1] with all his conclusions. And I need not say that in the course of a progress from Low Churchism to high Ultramontanism these conclusions varied very greatly and traversed a wide region. But there was one feature in which they were uniform from first to last. They always excluded doubt: there was not a cranny at which it could find entrance: every one of them was held successively in perfect and absolute repose. I speak of course of the aspects of his mind as they were presented to me in his conversation and correspondence. But it must be remembered that our intercourse though for many years intimate was always intermittent. I do not think we ever slept in the same house (unless perhaps once at Coleridge's in Eton): we never lived in the same place, except as undergraduates at Oxford, where we were mere acquaintances, and when perhaps character had not altogether taken its form. I think in short that his mind was not philosophical: that he viewed humanity on its active side: he arrived with extraordinary facility at broad conclusions: and held to them with a tenacity not less remarkable. He was not subtle, but was always intensely clear: if he deceived anybody, the person taken in was alone responsible.

With all this I valued his letters very highly during the time of our close correspondence, some twelve to fifteen years: upon his secession he proposed an exchange: and I was very sensible of the marked and clear superiority of what I parted with to what I received in return. Moreover there were certain things said by him to me which deeply as well as justly impressed me: and which I shall gladly record if and when they revert to my mind.

Very early in the days of his Churchmanship, I think when I was meditating the book entitled *The Church in its relations with the State*, he said to me, 'The Church is going back into the condition in which it stood before the days of Constantine.' Of course this will not hold water as a formula: but it is widely, profoundly and multifariously true. And

---

[1] 'self' crossed out in MS.

the date of the saying adds to its importance. The Church came into contact with human nature at every one of the thousand points upon its face. She took possession of each and all of them in succession, and brought the thinking faculty of men very near to God. And this was true not of individuals only, but of man in a community. There was created an atmosphere of faith, which every one traditionally, it might be unconsciously inhaled. The atmosphere is now in a state of progressive dilution. That grasp of the Church, and with the Church of the Faith, and with the Faith of the tradition, upon the individual human creature has been, and is being continually relaxed. The Gospel is become for us at once more external, and less objective.

I say this of the Christian community, and of individuals in so far as they are shaped or affected by the community: I nevertheless believe that there is a counter process at work in individuals: but in conflict with, and in emancipation from, the influence of the community in which they live.

Again: the argument against transubstantiation as a dogma is (as I apprehend it) most conclusively founded upon this, that it asserts the change, annihilation, disappearance, of a *substantia* about which we know and can know nothing in the way of faith and nothing in the way of sense. We have nothing but an hypothesis: a philosophical analysis of the composition of material things by which it is supplied. This is nowhere transplanted by divine authority into revelation. Unless and until it has been so transplanted, how can it possibly be raised from the level of philosophical speculation up to the level of faith? But then there is the word substance in the Nicene Creed—Is the use of the term in that Creed open in the same, or in any, degree to the same objection?

It was Manning who pointed out to me that it was not. It depends on no philosophical analysis. It aims at no definition. It attempts no analysis. It is a mode of expression analogous to the 'I am that I am' of the Bible. It indicates the *natura naturam* of God, that whereby he is God without in the least degree attempting to define what it is, or drawing any distinction between parts of the Divine Nature, such as we draw in regard to matter when we say that it is made up of substance, nothing of accidents, in the Divine Nature. The Son is of one substance with the Father, ὅτι πότ ἐστιν[1], be that substance what it may. Here we have a strong example of the reverent wisdom of the early Church, of the final efficacy of the Divine guidance over her. During all those years of our

---

[1] 'Whatever that may be'.

intimacy Manning displayed none of that morbid tenderness towards the Roman Church, which began at a rather early date to appear among the Oxford party.

ADD.MS 44790, ff. 170–174   *17 October 1894*

Although I have not been accustomed to consider Cardinal Manning as either a great or a highly accomplished man, outside the world of ecclesiastical action, in which he was a master, yet he said to me from time to time things which as I may remember them one by one I should wish to note down.

And first, the very latest of them. It was I think on the last occasion of my seeing him that he expressed to me his great desire to die without property, and without debts.

Very soon after our acquaintance had ripened into friendship he announced to me with a sly smile that the *Record* newspaper had proclaimed his fall from the Gospel: on the occasion I think of his sermon on the consent of the Church.

A few years earlier, say in 1834 or 1835 (but I cannot be sure of the date) there was a contest in the S.P.C.K.—I do not remember the point in dispute but the bishops made a formal muster, as did their friends, and their foes. So mild, however, was the contention on their side, that Lord Cholmondeley, an amiable and excellent man of the strict Beaufort connection, went to Lincolns Inn Fields to support them, and I, who had made little way into ecclesiastical studies, walked there and away with him. We had I think a very large majority. But in coming away we stumbled upon Manning. I said to him, 'Ha! Manning, are you here, did you come up for this?' 'Yes', he said, 'I would have come any distance for it!' And I found his vote had been against the bishops. He was not excited: I never saw him excited. But he was positive, and I never saw him when he was not. In no one of his phases did he ever seem to be troubled with a doubt.

After his secession, and during the interval when Henry Wilberforce, an old High Churchman, found himself as yet unable to follow, he told me this curious story. 'When the time for my ordination approached, my family, knowing me to be a High Churchman, were in great grief, for they thought the name of Wilberforce would be dishonoured by my opinions. They spoke to Manning who was already in orders, and he said, "Oh never mind, never mind. Let him once come to stand by the

L

bedsides of the sick and the dying, and all this nonsense will melt away like the morning dew."'

I do not think there was any record in correspondence between us of this period of his life. He had, however, made an impression, still sooner, upon James Stephen of the Colonial Office: who said to me in 1835, 'I think Manning the wisest man I have ever seen in my life.' Speaking no doubt of his brief sojourn in the office. His retirement did him honour, especially as he was poor.

Es machte mir zu lug: ich musste fort.

Ah, that correspondence! When he seceded he astutely proposed, and I like a donkey accepted, an exchange of letters. I gave him χρύσεα χαλκείων[1]. Lately I heard with extreme vexation that he had destroyed his Anglican letters to me. They were of real value: covering *about* 1836–51. And they were Anglican indeed: to the very fingers' ends. The sun of his Anglicanism set like the sun of the tropics, without a premonitory decline.

For example. In 1840 I published a book entitled *Church principles considered in their results*. He spoke to me about it. 'The Romanists,' he said, 'will not notice it: they know full well they cannot meet the argument (or arguments) it contains.'

About 1838, or soon after the opening of St. Mark's, Chelsea, we walked down there to the morning service. He spoke of the great need of a preaching Order in the Church of England: and said he thought it perfectly practicable to establish one. And things he would have done for the Church of England both good and great, had he not been stifled and suffocated through faithless fears.

It was I think about the time when I published my first book, *The Church in its relations with the State* that he said to me, 'The Church of Christ is visibly moving back into the position which it occupied before Constantine.' This I think was a really great generalisation; profoundly true: harder to see half a century and more ago, than now.

A great rallying address was presented, about that time I think, to Archbishop Howley. The Archbishop was declared 'supreme spiritual head of the Church of England': and Manning contended that this was the proper title.

After Newman published his book on *Romanism and popular Protestantism* Manning observed to me it was the book of a man in difficulty

---

[1] 'Gold in return for bronze'.

struggling to maintain his foothold. The fact I think is that Newman passed from Evangelicalism into ulterior phases and never had a true conception of the historic Church, such as that on which the Eastern Church rests, and on which Palmer's great book is founded.

Later in the day, I mean long after his secession and after intercourse between us had been resumed, Manning expressed an apprehension that I had sincerely changed in the direction of rationalism; and was much comforted when I told him that the idea was without foundation.

Later still he referred to the cessation of intercourse (I think for ten or more years) and said in relation to it that we never had had a quarrel before. My reply to him was, that it was not a quarrel: it was a death.

There are two remarkable sayings of his, out of which polemical advantage (for us) might have been extracted: for this reason I thought it right to keep them back when Mr. Purcell with a view to his *Life* invited communications from me.

About the year 1848 or 1849 (I fix my date by the *locale*) Manning was standing in my room at No. 6 Carlton Gardens. I was sorely distressed by the secessions, then raining so thick upon us, and did not know what was to come of it. I said to him, 'Now Manning, you have kept up relations with Oxford so as to know all these men which I do not. Viewing the strange error into which they have fallen, I am tempted to ask whether there is any point of character, common to them in general, which goes to account for it?' Looking very grave indeed he answered, 'Yes I do know them: and there is.' 'What is it?', I enquired. 'Want of truth,' was his reply. A singular declaration when one remembers all that happened.

ADD.MS 44790, ff. 175–6

In justice to Cardinal Manning, I feel that I ought to put together as memory serves the most remarkable of the things he said to me: apart from such as had any controversial character three in number.

1. The most remarkable of them was a very distinct announcement (but then it must be admitted that all his announcements of opinion were distinct and positive, and I am not sure that I ever heard him express a *doubt*) that under modern circumstances the Church was about to resume gradually the position it had held before Constantine.

This was of the Anglican period, and early in it. The others are also of that period, unless I specify to the contrary.

2.   In walking to service at the Chelsea College, he said there was no conceivable reason why the Church of England should not recognise and train an Order of preachers; on a footing resembling those in the Church of Rome.

3.   Some time after I had published (1840?) *Church principles considered in their results*, I remarked to him that I had never seen it noticed in any Roman Catholic quarter. He replied: 'No: they will say nothing about it, for they know that they cannot answer it.'

4.   Referring to Newman's *Romanism and popular Protestantism*, he said it had always appeared to him to be the work of a man who felt the ground slippery under his feet, and who was struggling hard to maintain his position.

ON CONFESSION-REFLEXIONS[1]

ADD.MS 44790, ff. 89–95   *17 December 1893*

In the year 1841 or 2, under a variety of combined influences my mind had attained a certain fixity of state in a new development. I had been gradually carried away from the moorings of an education Evangelical in the party sense to what I believe history would warrant me in calling a Catholic position in the acceptance of the visible historical Church and the commission it received from our Saviour to take charge in a visible form of this work upon earth. I do not mean here to touch upon the varied stages of this long journey: and I shall only at present say that the Oxford Tracts had little to do with it: nothing to do with it at all I should be inclined to say, except in so far as it was partly and very considerably due to them that Catholicism so to speak was in the air, and was exercising an influence on the religious frame of men without their knowing it: just as I have very long suspected, perhaps I ought to say believed, that Seneca, Aurelius, and Epictetus, were largely influenced in the soul of their works by Christianity in the air, to which they probably would have denied, and did not indeed know, that they were in any way indebted.

Let me say, however, that I am now speaking all through not of spiritual life, a very interior subject, but of convictions and opinions in

---

[1] The first part of this section contains additions and corrections made by Gladstone in 1897. These have been incorporated into the text.

theology, a much lower and less inward matter: not that I am ignorant how these things are connected, but I am not entitled to assume that in my case the connection was a vital one. However, the points of the 'movement' as it is called, and very deservedly, have been for the most part brought before my mind and a good deal considered from time to time.

Among the most 'burning' of the questions which it raised was that of auricular confession, confession to the private ear of a priest, a thing widely apart on the one hand from the public confessions of our daily and Eucharistic worship, and on the other from the system of direction as it is largely practised in the Roman but not as I imagine in any other Church.

I could not fail to observe several matters in connection with the subject which gave it a rather special title to consideration. Confession to a priest with absolution as its sequel, had an incontestable place in our formularies. It was known to have been practised by men who were unquestionable adherents and powerful champions of the Reformation. It was spoken of by [those] who adopted the practice with a modest but warm enthusiasm. On the other hand, who could fail to see that confessions made in common with a promiscuous congregation, and wholly general in their character might easily, as before God, degenerate into an ineffectual feebleness and indeed a mockery of God? Confession, however, was not one of the questions most agitated during the early stages of the movement. If my memory serves me right, this subject reached an acute stage after the bulk of the more important secessions to the Roman Communion had taken place. Still there are several questions to be considered in this matter: independently of the practical difficulty arising from the fact that the English clergy as a body had for generations passed out of practice of hearing confessions. With the practice, they had lost what cannot be recovered by the mere goodwill and intelligence of the individual, namely the tradition of the practice, and the transmitted habit and surely arduous act of management associated with that tradition.

I find it necessary for the present purpose to sever the question of confession from that of absolution.

With regard to confession personal, particular, and confidential, who can fail to see that such an act (I do not now speak of habitual repetition) ought to have a powerful effect in bracing, so to speak, the mental process of repentance. A man is brought face to face with his greater sins one by one. Many a flimsy extenuation will explode under the very act of bringing it into the light, or by force of fair and legitimate questioning upon it. Wherever restitution is in any way involved, it can hardly fail to be extricated and to become practical. The terrible character and consequences of sin must be more deeply felt in proportion as confession whether private or public is effective. The salutary pains of shame ought to be of a high value. The arduous nature of that work of transformation, through which in very searching forms many of us have to pass, is likely to open out upon our view, and in the natural course of things to be prosecuted, with an increase of vigour or shall I say a diminution of languor. How grave, how terrible it is, even to pen these sentences on the subject of that havock which the enemy has wrought within us, and around us.

But, so far, the subject is merely subjective, and confession is taken into view as a spiritual exercise like other spiritual exercises, such as prayer, meditation, reading of Holy Scripture, with the study or digestion of the same.

This, however, is not the point of view from which the subject has been commonly regarded or examined, and will appear to many but an inferior presentation of one of its minor parts. It is not a question they will say of the healthful reaction of an humble and earnest confession on the soul of him who makes it, resembling the healthful reaction of vigorous exercise upon the body. It is a question of removing from that soul the burden of sin, and carrying it away, afar off into the wilderness.

And here I may say that of any works which I have read upon confession with regard to modern wants and conditions, I think the work going nearest to the point was a pair of sermons by Bishop Wilkinson when a parish priest. The essential and pervading idea which he brought into view was that confession to a priest is a practice properly belonging not to a condition of spiritual health, but to one of disease. The healthy soul ought to be able to discharge its burdens at the foot of the great throne without the assistance of an intermediate person.

There are then not less than four forms, in which the question presents itself:

1. Personal confession to God.
2. Public or general confession.
3. Confession of mortal or grave offences to a priest.
4. Confession made a part of direction.

And further: there are a variety of points bearing upon the subject and imparting to it a widely different character for different classes of cases.

1.   Complexity, intensity, and unremitted activity of life as compared with simplicity, and with moderation and intermission of pressure.

2.   The varying ideas which may be formed of the nature and force of absolution. My own ideas upon this head are more or less indicated in a paper on the Atonement of 1894. (*Gleanings*, Vol. VIII).

3.   The virtue of true and strict confession, as a bracing and searching exercise of humiliation, apart from absolution as well as from any sacramental idea.

There is much to be said on these heads. What is strictly personal to myself I shall probably reserve for a more confidential chapter.

9 February 1897

LAST YEARS

ADD.MS 44790, ff. 166–168   *13 September 1894*

The appearance of cataract in my eyes, announced to me in the middle of 1892, by the Chester oculist, bore witness to the progressive exhaustion of nature in one great organ, after hard labour had been faithfully performed by it during more than fourscore years. It furnished a premonition that the like exhaustion must arrive in other organs, and preparation so be made for the fatal change.

The untouched eye served me with its expiring force to the best of its ability, through the time when it appeared doubtful whether the operated eye would be able through proper spectacles to supply me with such vision as science can provide for nature. The last book I read with the natural eye was Sir W. Scott's *Pirate*: and I got through with difficulty. The first reading with the operated eye was Wilkinson's Tract on Disestablishment, and then *The Vicar of Langthwaite*, Grote on Socrates, and Hoffmann (U.S.) on the office of the State.[1]

By the resignation of office, which the superintendence of the Almighty so notably and quietly enabled me to bring about, I have passed into a new state of existence. I am not yet thoroughly accustomed to it in part because the remains of my influenza have not yet allowed me wholly to resume the habits of health. But I am thoroughly content with my retirement: and I cast no longing lingering look behind. I pass onward from it *oculo irretorto*.

There is plenty of work before me, peaceful work, and work directed to the supreme, i.e. the spiritual, cultivation of mankind, if it please God to give me time and vision to perform it.

17 October 1894

As far as I can at present judge, all the signs of the eye being favourable, the new form of vision will enable me to get through in a given time about half the amount of work which would have been practicable under the old. I speak of reading and writing work, which have been principal with me when I had the option. In conversation there is no

---

[1] The initials are not clear, but Gladstone is referring to Frank Sarjent Hoffman, *The Sphere of the State* (1894).

difference, although there are various drawbacks in what we call society.

On the 20th ult, when I had gone through my series of trials, Mr. Nettleship at once declared that any further operation would be superfluous.

I am unable to continue attendance at the daily morning service, not [on] account of eyesight but because the condition of the bowel department does not allow me to rise before ten at the earliest. And so a Hawarden practice of over fifty years is interrupted: not without *some* degree of hope that it may be resumed: the evening services are at 5 p.m. (the other at 7) and these afford me a limited consolation.[1]

I drive almost every day: and thus grow to my dissatisfaction more burdensome. My walking powers are limited: once I have exceeded two miles by a little, but there is fear of disturbance. A large part of the day remains available at my table: daylight is especially precious: my correspondence is still a weary weight though I have admirable help from children.

Upon the whole the change is considerable. In early and mature life, a man walks to his daily work with a sense of the duty and capacity of self provision, a certain αὐτάρκεια[2] (which the Greeks carried into the moral world). Now, that sense is reversed: it seems as if I must, God knows how reluctantly, lay burdens upon others: and as if capacity were, so to speak, dealt out to me, mercifully, oh how mercifully, but yet by armfuls.

1894 1. PERSONAL LIBERATION
2. POLITICS OF THE YEAR

ADD.MS 44790, ff. 142–155   *25 July 1894*

For the first time in my life there has been awarded to me by the Providence of God a period of compulsory leisure, reaching at the present date to four and a half months. Such a period drives the mind in upon itself, and invites, almost constrains, to recollection, and the rendering at least internally an account of life: further, it lays the basis of a habit of meditation, to the formation of which the course of my existence, packed and crammed with occupation outwards, never stagnant and ofttimes overdriven, has been extremely hostile. As there is no life which in its detail does not seem to afford intervals of brief leisure, or what is

---

[1] There is a pencil mark here as if Gladstone intended to make an insertion.
[2] 'Sufficiency in oneself'.

termed "waiting" for others, engaged with us in some common action, these are commonly spent in murmurs, and in petulant desires for their termination. But in reality they supply excellent opportunities for brief or ejaculatory prayers.

As this new period of my life has brought with it my retirement from active business in the world, it affords a good opportunity for breaking off the commonly dry daily journal, or ledger as it might almost be called, in which for seventy years I have recorded the chief details of my outward life. If life be continued, I propose to note in it henceforward only principal events or occupations. This first breach since the latter part of May in this year has been involuntary: when the operation on my eye for cataract came, it was necessary for a time to suspend all exercise of vision. Before that, from the beginning of March, it was only my out-of-door activity or intercourse which had been paralysed. In looking back over the period I think it may warrant a summary review inasmuch as it has constituted a new chapter of my life, in which my dealings with my fellow men have been contracted, and those with my great judge somewhat enlarged: at least I have seemed more nearly to have assigned to me the attitude of one who stands before the final bar.

There has been a certain amount of kindly personal intercourse with several among my colleagues. With two of them, Rosebery and Harcourt, it has not been properly speaking confidential. Rosebery has been under no obligation to give me his confidence, and he has entirely withheld it as to inner matters, while retaining unimpaired all his personal friendliness. He does not owe his present position in any way to me, and has had no sort of debt to pay. My bringing him to the Foreign Office was indeed an immense advancement, but was done with a belief, not sustained by subsequent experience, in his competency and wisdom.[1] Harcourt only held to me the language he held universally when he announced to me, without any invitation or suggestion, some two months ago, his fixed intention to resign his office after he should have passed his Budget of this year. It is now apparent from the tone of his conversation that he has entirely abandoned this intention: but, in more recent conversation with me, he has not breathed a syllable upon the subject. He will without doubt fret and wince in the future, as in the past, under the premiership of one who is his junior by a score of years

---

[1] This sentence was added later and is dated February 1897.

in age, and by nearly half that term in official life: who was moreover at no very recent date his own under-secretary. Whether he or whether Rosebery ought either of them to have come to the top, are different questions. My choice upon the whole would have fallen upon Spencer. Less brilliant than either he has far more experience, having entered the Queen's service over thirty years ago: he has also decidedly more of the very important quality termed weight, and his cast of character I think affords more guarantees of the moderation he would combine with zeal, and more possibility of forecasting the course he would pursue. He is not I think well placed at present, being more of a statesman than an administrator. But the opportunity has gone by: and gone by in all likelihood once for all.

When the occasional impediment offered by the state of my vision led me to resign, I had in view though not in actual touch the outrageous mischief as I estimated it of the Navy estimates for the year, to which it was absolutely impossible for me to be a party on any terms. Since they were produced the financial proposals of the year have been introduced and carried. They constitute by far the most Radical measure of my lifetime. I do not object to the principle of graduated taxation: for the just principle of ability to pay is not determined simply by the amount of income: and further, the reduction and abolition of taxes on the ground of their falling largely on the wealthy classes really involves the same principle as the graduated tax. But, so far as I understand the present measure of finance from the partial reports I have received, I find it too violent. It involves a great departure from the methods of political action established in this country, where reforms, and especially fiscal reforms, have always been considerate and even tender. In striking so heavily at the owners of realty, it rules very summarily a question which seems to me to involve much doubt, namely whether realty is absolutely devoid of claim on the ground that this description of property bears exclusively the heavy charge of the rates: a subject on which I for one could not decide without much more thorough investigation than I have ever had occasion to give it. I do not yet see the ground on which it can be justly held that any one description of *property* should be more heavily burdened than others, unless moral and social grounds can be shown first: but in this case the reasons drawn from those sources seem rather to verge in the opposite direction, for real property has more of presumptive connection with the discharge of duty that that which is ranked as personal. No doubt the ownership of land carries with it social and political advantages, for which men may be willing to pay: but there remains behind the question of amount, and amount may appertain to essential justice.[1]

Besides this large matter for inquiry, the aspect of the measure is not satisfactory to a man of my traditions (and these traditions lie near the roots of my being) in several respects.

A land or house owner having £100,000 a year, and now paying say £3000 a year for income tax, will have his estate valued at $2\frac{1}{2}$ millions, and will on succession to the fee simple be called upon to pay £200,000: a similar payment again becoming exigible from the next successor say thirty years hence. Even if we consider the 200,000 as spread over the thirty years (whereas it is all payable at the outset) it amounts to nearly three times the income tax, and is of course in reality much more. For the sudden introduction of such change there is I think no precedent in the history of this country. And the severity of the blow is greatly aggravated in moral effect by the fact that it is dealt only to a handful of individuals. I do not think there can be two hundred persons in the country owning land or land and houses to the value of a million sterling.

Further, as I understand the owner of land in settlement (and such are the great bulk of landowners) will have the power of attaching the tax to the *corpus* of the estate and charging himself only with the annual interest of the sum. This I am afraid many successors will do: their successors in turn following their example. Thus the incumbrances on the land will be progressively and heavily increased. But that the land of a country should be heavily incumbered is known to be a great public evil. This great public evil will be put under a process of involving its rapid increase. The ultimate result will be the forcing out of the old possessors and the introduction of new (perhaps after long struggles to retain a crippled and impotent ownership).[2] Some will reply; no: the result will be the breaking up of the estates. I am not sure that the substitution of small non-occupying landowners is necessarily or universally a good. But as it seems certain that the creation of new fortunes in personalty to a vast amount will continue, will not this class supply buyers for the estates in block? In this multiplication of the *neo-ploutoi* I can find nothing to give me satisfaction.

---

[1] This sentence was added later.

[2] The words in parentheses were added later.

And I fear that the operation of the Act may be to drive more and more land into settlement with a view to the mitigation of the present and immediate burdens. I am not certain, however, that in this point I understand the probable operation of the measure.

Another most grave objection remains. The great evil of the death duties is the enormous amount of incidental expenditure which they entail, in association with long delays and great uncertainties. It ought, in my judgment, to have been a primary object in any great change of those duties to operate a fundamental reform by sweeping away as much as possible of the necessity for this expenditure. And my opinion is that this advantage might have been gained. If so we might have had a large increase of revenue without any proportional increase of burden to the tax payer, perhaps, in numerous cases without any increase at all. But the present plan entirely passes by this great and primary object of policy: nay, tends if I understand it right in certain ways to create an enhanced necessity for the intervention of the lawyer.

All this is drawn from me by the importance of the case: but is no better than a digression with reference to the immediate object of this paper, which is to review briefly a morsel of my life not to arraign the politics or politicians of the day.

I have had very free communications with Tweedmouth and with J. Morley. From them I gather that we have a prospect of an anarchical Cabinet, abundant pledges, obstructive opposition, compulsory acquiescence in small achievement, and an apathy and languor in the general mind curiously combined with a decided appetite for novelties and for promises apart from the prospect of performance.

For my own part, the *suave mari magno* steals upon me: or, at any rate, an inexpressible sense of relief from an exhausting life of incessant contention. This is an immense blessing.

A great revolution has been operated in my correspondence, which had been for many years a serious burden, and at times one almost intolerable. During the last months of partial incapacity I have not written with my own hands probably as much as one letter *per day*. I have had most efficient aid in my family, especially from my daughter Helen: but I do not think the demand on her in connection with this matter has been very large. Few people have a smaller number of *otiose* conversations, probably, than I in the last fifty years; but I have of late seen more friends, and more freely though without practical objects in view. Many kind friends have read books to me; I must place Lady

Sarah Spencer at the head of the proficients in that difficult art: in distinctness of finished articulation, with low clear voice, she is supreme. Dearest C[atherine] has been my chaplain from morning to morning, my churchgoing has been almost confined to mid-day communions, which have not required my abandonment of the reclining posture for long periods of time. Authorship has not been quite in abeyance: I have been able to write what I was not allowed to read, and have composed two theological articles for the *Nineteenth Century* of August and September respectively. Independently of the days of blindness after the operation, the visits of doctors have become a noticeable item of demand upon time. Of physic I incline to believe that I have had as much in 1894 as in my whole previous life. I have learned for the first time the extraordinary comfort of the aid which the attendance of a nurse can give. The influenza which seized me early in March has not yet wholly withdrawn its hold: it began with the chest and then descended to the lower bowels. The eye process has been curiously intermixed with the controversy in a lower region. My wife has suffered from an attack of influenza for the most part curiously similar: but she thank God is well and this is the main matter. My health will now be matter of little interest except to myself. But I have not yet abandoned the hope that I may be permitted to grapple with that considerable armful of work, which has been long marked out for my old age; the question of my recovering sight being for the present in abeyance.[1]

INCIDENTAL TO RESIGNATION

ADD.MS 44791, f. 22   *2 January 1896*

We may sometimes, even if it be rarely, obtain a morsel of self knowledge through the medium of a dream.

Aware by signs perfectly unequivocal if partly negative [of] the state of the Queen's feelings towards me, I have regretted to be in such ill odour with one in whom there is so much to admire and respect; but, as I seem to myself conscious without mistrust of having invariably rendered to her the best service that I could, I have striven to keep down that regret, and set it, as it were, behind me, and to attain as nearly as I could to indifference in the matter.

---

[1] The last phrase was added later.

Since my retirement I have dreamt sometimes of Parliament and sometimes (both of them very rarely) of the Court, but without much meaning. Last night I dreamed that I was at Windsor. There had been a sort of breakfast, fugitive and early, at which several attended, and the Queen appeared, but without incident. However it was conveyed to me through one of the 'pages' (servants out of livery?) that *I* of all people in the world was to breakfast alone with the Queen at ten o'clock: a circumstance which was not accordant with what is known as to H.M.'s (very judicious) habits with reference to the early part of the day. Well, the time slid on, and the hour approached, and I was getting duly into what I may call a small perturbation as to the how and where of access. But the dream had lost its tail. The hour never came. And the sole force and effect of the incident is to show that the subject of my personal relation to the Queen, and all the unsatisfactory ending of my over half a century of service, had more hold upon me, down at the root, than I was aware.

I take the opportunity of recording another point. Granted that the absence of every act and word of regard, regret, and interest is absolutely deserved. But then I have a wife. Of her, H.M. in her concluding letter, wrote in terms (which conveyed some implication of reproach to me) of the warm[est] interest and praise. What a fine opportunity of conveying by language and by token to this wife herself some voluntary offering, which would have been so well merited and appropriate, and would have furnished a conclusive answer to any criticism which might have been suggested by the cold negations of her conduct to me. But there was nothing of the kind. For I cannot reckon as anything what appeared to be a twopenny-halfpenny scrap, photographic or other, sent during the forenoon of our departure, by the hand of a footman.

MARCH 1894 LATEST VISIT TO WINDSOR

ADD. MS 44791, ff. 53–54

During my latest visit to Windsor Castle, when I resigned my office, an incident happened of no great moment yet of a rather curious interest. *Apropos* of nothing in particular, I was told, I think by Sir Henry Ponsonby, that the Queen had never had any particular [?] attachment to Sir Robert Peel, though she looked upon him with respect and regard. I felt quite certain that this communication, though it grew out of nothing and ended in nothing, was made to me by command. And if by command, then why? Certainly for some reason? And this leads out into a curious field, of conjecture, I admit, but I think strongly supported conjecture.

In the first place the statement certainly did not correspond with the fact; and the Queen in making it was 'falsely true'. An opaque medium had risen up in her later experience between the present with its impressions, and the figure of Sir R. Peel.

In contradiction to the statement, there was not only my very strong general recollection, but also the fact of her presenting Sir R. Peel on his retirement in 1846 with portraits of herself and the Prince Consort, a gift which unquestionably indicated something of attachment or friendship, as distinct from mere respect and regard. I do not say that she loved him as she certainly and very justly loved Lord Aberdeen, but that she had towards him an unquestionable sentiment of attachment or friendship. But Mr. Brett in his recently published volume[1] has quoted from a letter of the Queen written soon after the resignation (or death?) of Peel words which are perfectly unequivocal in the sense I have described. So then her statement was 'falsely true': she believed it to be true, but it was not so. Her memory is not merely good but admirable, and could not have failed her in this way except under the action of some disturbing cause.

How, then, did the Queen's curious self-delusion come about? And why did she cause it to be made known to me?

I confess it to be my opinion that there are certain contrarieties of character such as preclude their both being the subject of admiring attachment from persons of intelligence accurately acquainted with them both. Such a contrariety in my opinion existed (but I may be no impartial witness) between Sir Robert Peel and Lord Beaconsfield. And the admiring attachment which the Queen formed to Lord Beaconsfield between 1874 and 1880, so darkened her older sentiment towards Sir Robert Peel that it became incapable of recognition.

But why was the statement made to me? I think out of compassion due to her general kindliness of nature. She was parting from a man well past eighty, whom she had known for half a century, who had served her much longer than either of those two remarkable men, and from

---

[1] Reginald Baliol Brett (later 2nd Viscount Esher), *The Yoke of Empire. Sketches of the Queen's Prime Ministers* (1896).

whom she was on the point of parting, and this not capriciously but without doubt for reasons which seemed to her conclusive, without any the slightest mark, to say nothing of the other and higher sentiments, of personal respect or regard. Still she might feel for me under the circumstances. She might say for herself, 'He could not suppose himself qualified to stand as Lord Beaconsfield stood in my estimation, but I will give him this comfort that that was a position to which Sir Robert Peel never attained, and which accordingly he may with less pain forego.'

I do not speak lightly when I state my conviction that the circumstances of my farewell, which I think were altogether without parallel, had serious causes, beyond the operation of political disagreements, which no doubt went for something, but which were insufficient to explain them. Statements, whether true or false must have been carried to her ears, which in her view required (and not merely allowed) the mode of proceeding which was actually adopted.

1 February 1897

CANNES IN 1897

ADD.MS 44791, ff. 57–63   *April 1897*
We left England in the end of January, direct for Cannes, and all made out the journey well. About eight weeks of our time were passed in the region of our destination. Of this one fortnight, shortened by medical necessity to twelve days, at the (excellent) Grand Hotel, Grasse: all the rest in two about equal sections, at the palazzetto of Lord Rendel, he himself being unfortunately though most honourably exiled from it for the principal part of the time.

Catherine's nights became excellent at Grasse, but with the aid of bromide. On rare occasions she became a little excitable, which raised a question as to the influence of that medicine, not admitted by our able physician, Dr. Frank, to have an effect of that kind upon the brain. Especially she broke down during the night journey on the way home, which appeared to be too much for her. All things considered it had become plain that Mr. Armitstead had acted most wisely in detaching himself from us, we had become much too great an armful even for his kindness: and also it seemed probable that this journey to the Riviera would be our last.

I got on very well there for the first ten days or a fortnight when I was taken nearly the last in the house, with what proved a sharp bronchial cough. It broke with rapidity, and ceased to trouble me in the day, but was very annoying at night. We could not get it under effectually at Cannes, but on the first night at Grasse, it unexpectedly and wholly disappeared. For some days I was entirely off the sick-list. Then came on rather sharp though harmless diarrhoea. To return under the constant care of Dr. Frank we went back to Cannes, where we effectually checked it by Batley's drops. And I became able to resume Sunday church going in which I had been sadly interrupted.

I had hoped during this excursion to make much way with my *Autobiographica*. But this was in a large degree frustrated, first by invalidism, next by the Eastern Question, on which I was finally obliged to write something.[1] Lastly and not least by a growing sense of decline in my daily amount of brain force available for serious work. Since my return to England this has become more and more sensible. My power to read (but to read very slowly indeed since the cataract came) for a considerable number of hours daily, thank God continues.[2] This is a great mercy. While on my outing I may have read, of one kind and another, twenty volumes. Novels enter into this list rather considerably. I have begun seriously to ask myself, shall I ever be able to face 'The Olympian Religion'?

I have made up a new volume of *Gleanings:* and in this a short original paper upon the fresh Papal aggression. But I have of course since my return been much entangled in the reading and correspondence entailed by arrears accumulated during my absence.

My meeting with the Duke of Cambridge was for a considerable time prevented by my invalidism. The first Royalty we saw at Cannes was Princess Louise. She at once developed a desire that we should see the Queen who had come to Cimiez. She said the Queen felt that being so near she ought to come down and see various persons who were here. No doubt Princess Louise had in view the batch of Hanoverian Royalties at the *Hotel du Parc:* and she had contrived to put us into the same category. I was quite able to conceive the Queen's desire to see my wife; but most sceptical as to any corresponding wish about myself. All however which I had to do was to resolve inwardly that I would do

---

[1] Letter to the Duke of Westminster, 1897 [WEG].

[2] Considerably curtailed at present, September 3, 1897 [WEG].

nothing which could possibly wear the appearance of an endeavour to lay myself in the Queen's way or to force myself upon her.

In passing I may observe that Princess Louise in our conversation referred to Greece and Crete. I said I felt a scruple about speaking to her on that subject because my opinions were so violent. She said she was aware of that, but, beginning to speak on it for herself, at once showed that her opinions were as strong as mine. Neither the Duke of Cambridge, nor the Prince of Wales, both of whom I saw afterwards, broached this subject at all.

However, it gradually became evident both that the Princess Louise had set her heart upon this meeting with the Queen, and also that the Prince of Wales shared her ideas. I had never in all my life known any sort of intervention, between Her Majesty and myself, from any member of the Royal Family: and I attached though very vaguely a serious character to the change.

Many notes flew backwards and forwards between the *Château Thorene* and the *Hotel du Parc*: the upshot of which was to show determination on that side that the thing should come about, and on my part the intention that nothing should be done tending to force it. At last it came to this point that we were invited to visit the *Princess* on the afternoon when the Queen was to come to the hotel. This I declined but agreed to take it in our drive, and go past it at the hour so that any specific message might not fail through ignorance of my whereabouts. Accordingly a message came down to us, inviting us to go in and have tea with the Princess. This obviously could not be declined, so we repaired at once to the hotel and had our tea with Miss Paget who was in attendance. The Princess soon came in and after a short delay we were summoned into the Queen's presence. No other English people were on the ground.

We were shown into a room tolerably but not brilliantly lighted, much of which was populated by a copious supply of Hanoverian Royalties including the Queen of Hanover, the Duke of Cumberland and others. *The* Queen was in the inner part of the room, and behind her stood or sat the Prince of Wales with the Duke of Cambridge. Notwithstanding my enfeebled sight, my vision is not much impaired for practical purposes in cases such as this where I am thoroughly familiar with the countenance and the whole contour of any person to be seen. I became at once conscious that there was a change in the Queen's appearance, not only as compared with what she used to be during my political life, but as compared with her appearance at the marriage in the summer of last year.

My wife preceded, and Mary followed me.

The Queen's manner did not show the old and usual vitality: it was still, but at the same time very decidedly kind, such as I had not seen it for a good while before my final resignation: and she gave me her hand, a thing which I apprehended rather rare with men, and which had never happened with me during all my life, though that life be it remembered had included some periods of rather decided favour. Catherine sat down near her, and I at a little distance. For a good many years she had habitually asked me to sit, knowing that a standing position did not suit me: this time it seemed to come as a matter of course.

My wife spoke freely and a good deal to the Queen but the answers appeared to me to be very slight. As to myself I expressed satisfaction at the favourable accounts which I had heard of the accommodation enjoyed by Her Majesty at Cimiez and perhaps a few more words of like nature. I think that she referred to Grasse of which and its hotel I spoke in honour; and I believe this was all. To speak frankly it appeared to me that the Queen's peculiar faculty and habit of conversation had disappeared. It was a faculty not so much the free offspring of a rich and powerful mind, as the fruit of assiduous care with long practice and much opportunity; but it was striking to observe its (as it seemed to me) total cessation. Along with this came back upon my mind the marked change which was exhibited in the intervention of the Heir Apparent and Princess Louise about our interview. After a period of about ten minutes it was signified to us that we had to be presented [to] all the other Royalties and so passed the remainder of this significant meeting.

Significant on many grounds. First on account of the change indicated in the Queen herself. Secondly of the change in the position of those around her. Even in the easy position of the Duke of Cambridge sitting quietly all the time behind her head, there seemed to me something new. Still more I thought there was an indefinable but important change in the attitude of the Prince of Wales. He had become a more substantive personage, so to speak, in the Queen's presence.

Princess Beatrice was not present and perhaps had not come from Nice: either from her having plenty to do there as manageress general, or from her not wishing to forward a rectifying operation between the Queen and me. I understand that she is omnipotent, at the same time rather obstinate, and narrow-minded. (She has always been very kind in manner.)

These things taken as a whole make a deep impression upon me apart from the pleasure of reflecting that my last interview with Her Majesty has been marked on her part by kindness. Not with conviction but as probable surmise, I incline to the belief (1) that the Queen considered as Sovereign is now more nearly a cypher: (2) that it will require much care and skill to carry her through the labour and anxiety of the crisis in June; (3) that all this may be and assuredly ought to be in forethought and preparation for an abdication when the crisis is well over, and for the beginning of the reign of Edward VII.

28 April 1897

(My anticipation of a probable abdication has now been entirely quashed. The Queen has with obvious spontaneity and perhaps purpose declared that she intends to perform her duties as long as life lasts. A large order! were it only [on] account of her cataract, certain though rather secret. WEG, September 3, 1897.)

ADD.MS 44791, f. 69   *18 November 1897*

Until the month of August last, old age had not brought about either permanently or for a time any fundamental or grave change in the condition of my physical existence. There was a mild need for special care of the bowels but it entailed no serious charge. My ordinary life from day to day, though of diminished power, had suffered no interruption and consequently I was able to continue my Homeric work.

With respect to the other world, my only special call to it was that of my age. The attitude therefore in which I endeavoured to fix myself was as follows. I desired to consider myself as a soldier on parade, in a line of men drawn up, ready to march, and waiting for the word of command. Only it was not to be 'march' but 'die' and I sought to be in preparation for prompt obedience, feeling no desire to go until the work I had in hand was completed, but on the other hand without reluctance because firmly convinced that whatever He ordains for us is best for us and for all.

APPENDICES

APPENDIX 1

GLADSTONE'S LETTERS TO WILLIAM WINDHAM FARR, 1826–1832

Gladstone's letters to Farr are in the John Rylands Library, Manchester (English MS 339). Farr's letters to Gladstone (not printed here) are among the Gladstone Papers in the British Museum.

Eton College, Tuesday evening, October 17th 1826 I write to you more for the purpose of reminding you of your promise to write to me when you got to the 'Grunting University', than from thinking that my letter will contain much that may be acceptable to you; especially when you are so well provided with better and more welcome correspondents.

I hope you are now tolerably well settled: I do not know whether the fate of new comers is the same at Cambridge as it is at Oxford—but at the latter place it is indeed wretched: continual change of rooms with very short intervals, etc. But as I believe you are allowed at Cambridge to have lodgings in the town, perhaps you are better off.

Pickering is 'as pleased as punch': was put into the sixth form on Saturday last, with Handley: they dealt about their almonds and raisins very liberally and extensively in five o'clock school yesterday. Pickering speaks next week. Hallam has been unwell for a few days: made a very brilliant speech of an enormous length, on Saturday last, in favour of the political conduct of Milton. Gaskell spoke very well on the other side: Doyle and Wentworth supported Hallam. The latter's was a maiden speech: he was very courageous, and wrote down nothing but heads; but he made it out very well: and sat down, to borrow Hallam's expression, 'amidst the most encouraging applause'. I have had the pleasure of reporting the debate, which covered *forty-four* pages. Hallam's speech covered twelve, written rather small. If, as has been asserted, I had any fondness for that sort of labour, sure I am that the unconscionable length of this debate has driven it away. We did not get out till twenty minutes before six. Selwyn and the Clerks amazingly sick of it, if we may judge by coughing and other external signs. Law was proposed, and elected, with one black ball. Shadwell major has expressed his readiness to stand at the end of this term; and hopes are entertained of Durnford. And we hope that Lord A. Hervey will return; in the event of all these surmises turning out well, our numbers will be

respectable. But the three members whom we have got in this half—I beg
your pardon—I mean this term, are *staunch Whigs*; Wilder, Law, and
Wentworth. We carried it on Saturday last against Milton by only one
vote. Pickering is Chairman in the absence of Hervey.

Will you be so good as to give me your opinion in a case which I will
now state to you without mentioning names? I trouble you with it,
because there has been much difference of opinion in the Society respecting it. A question was put down at the beginning of this term to
this effect: 'Was the conduct of Warren Hastings to the Rohillas deserving of censure?' This question was marked for discussion on Saturday the 7th ult. On Wednesday the 11th the House was summoned to
discuss the legality of it! We deserve to be laughed at for marking a
question and then discussing its legality. Then, ἐν ὁδοίῃ μάλα θυμὸς ἐμοί[1].
Some members declared the question illegal (the action *referred to* took
place in 1774) on the ground of the trial's having taken place within
the fifty years; and moved that it should be expunged on that ground
. . . asserted its legality; allowed it would be confined and cramped;
. . . to have it expunged on the ground of Pickering . . . having omitted
to mark a question, the rule ordaining . . . shall mark one.[2] The motion
for expunging it as illegal was carried by a casting vote: and the author
of the question fined half a crown on Saturday last. Please say whether
you think the question illegal: and on which side you would have voted.
I have stated, I believe, all the facts; and I shall be able to judge whether
I have stated them impartially, if you tell me, from my statement, on
what side I appear to be.

Hervey, if he returns, and if Keate fills the sixth form, will be lag this
term. If he does not, perhaps Keate may put me in. My tutor has been
staying out, confined with a bad cold: he is now, I believe, better. I was
glad to hear that you were sent up before you left. Your old friend
Wright was flogged today for going to the circus. Last night he had left
a bolster in his bed, and a certain utensil *with his night cap on it*, in his bed,
to pass for a bona fide son of Adam. Keate came; in came the servant
to his room: 'Oh, Mr Wright,' quoth she, 'I am glad you are there; get
up, sir, for here is Doctor Keate come.' Poor Wright's bolster could not
keep up the farce any longer; accordingly he suffered. You will have

---

[1] Possibly a reference to Callimachus, Hymn 1, line 5 ('My mind is in
  much doubt since . . . .')

[2] Paper torn.

seen by the papers the large defalcation in the revenue; and are, I suppose, looking forward with pleasure to the row which must be kicked up next session. I suspect you will win your bet, made last May, that either Canning, Huskisson, or Robinson, would be out of office by next May. I do not see your name cut out in school. Would you like me to give any directions about it, or remind Webber, if you have already instructed him. In any thing else I shall be very happy to serve you.

Hoping that you will repay this prosy epistle with a far worthier one, I remain *etc.*

Eton, Tuesday, October 31, 1826 I sit down to reply to your very welcome letter which deserved an earlier answer, had I had the means of giving one suitable to it—not that I pretend to give as animated and interesting a disquisition on politics as you have done. I am an humble retailer of commonplace: so you cannot accuse me of too great pretensions. The question about Warren Hastings (Dii immortales!) was mine! mine! Pickering and Gaskell the chief expungers. Hallam my ally in supporting it. It was thrown out by the double vote (i.e. single and a casting) which Pickering, as pro-Chairman, possessed. Selwyn, Doyle, Hallam, and I voted for it. Pickering, Gaskell, Wilder, and Wentworth, against it. I was fined the sum for putting it down, on the motion of Selwyn. Since that Hervey has returned, Law and Durnford have come into the Society. What Durnford would say about it, I do not know, but Hervey and Law say they would have voted with us. I think no blame attaches to Warren Hastings for his conduct to the Rohillas: however guilty he may have been in other points. But indeed the evidence, when it was produced, by no means justified or substantiated the twenty-two charges. For some there was no evidence and for others very little. India was indeed disgracefully [*word omitted*] by England: and our 'Fides Britannica' might have been as notorious there as Livy says 'Poena fides' was in his age and country. On Saturday last our question was, Epaminondas or Hannibal, which the greatest character? It was carried in favour of Epaminondas by seven to three. Blackwood and the New Monthly were proposed, but rejected. I would rather have the former of the two but think that we can do well enough without either. Law made his maiden speech on Saturday: very fair. Next Saturday the queston is, 'Whether the proceedings of the Commons against Earl Strafford were deserving of censure?' Six speakers are what you used to call 'libratis' three and three. Wilder, Doyle and Law in their favour; Gaskell,

Wentworth (remember the descent) and I against them. Law is a regular Radical. I am to open. 'Lord help us! you to open!', you will say. Such, however, is the lamentable fact. The nice *Edinburgh Review* proposes, in the last number, in the most modest manner, to deprive bishops of their votes, and separate the Church from the State. It has been lately, I think, more violent than ever.

Thanks for the Chameleon etc. I am sorry that I cannot agree with you in the major part of your speculations, eloquent as they are in form, but (pardon me if I say) extravagant in sentiment. I shall be as glad as you can be to see the day when England again shall raise her drooping head, and recover from the enormous load of debt, taxes, and misfortunes which now chains her down. Entirely dissenting, as I do, from your opinion that the present distress is owing to the measures of Ministers, I own that I do not at all like the reciprocity treaties; after reading Huskisson's very able speech and some things written in answer to it, I do not agree with him. Neither do I, though in this I am even less competent to form an opinion than in the other, see that a free trade in corn would benefit the country. But I should not deal fairly if I went with you thus far without telling you that I am far from liking the Corn Laws as they at present stand. I think we agree on one important subject; that of tithes; I do not like the present system, calculated as it is to sow . . . and ill will where of all other places one would think none ought to exist.[1] I have been talking with my tutor about you. He seemed to speak of you both with regard and with regret. He said you *never* used to show him an exercise without pretty lines in it; but that he found it difficult to choose one for sending up because there was a want of the 'series juncturaque' and the 'lucidus ordo' in your compositions. He said (though I told him you did not like rhomboids and triangles) he thought mathematics would suit you very well. I amused him much by telling him that you used to say in jest, that you allowed twenty verses for a beginning, twenty for an ending; and four or six to the purpose.

An investigation has taken place into the state of the library. It has been much benefited thereby: books recovered; new rules instituted; and additional securities provided for future good conduct. Warner is now Treasurer of it. Fines come in pretty thick, I believe. Poor Barnard! A few days ago my tutor told me he had been obliged to have one of his boys flogged for bullying the unfortunate captain. He says that now,

---

[1] Paper torn

whenever there is a noise, he is obliged to go and stop it himself, which was not the case last term. Your seal usurped the conclusion of the sentence about Webber's cutting out your name. Perhaps you will repeat it. Do not suppose I was offended at any thing you said about Huskisson. I am far, very far, from agreeing with you: but I hope we can agree to differ. Peel, Canning, Huskisson and Robinson are in my humble opinion most excellent Ministers. I rejoice at what you fear, namely, that the Catholics would now gain the day in the Society. I hope to see the time when we shall win the day in Parliament, believing as I do that justice and expediency united their powers to demand at our hands reparation to an injured people. The claim of justice may be evaded; that of expediency will force as a tribute what would now, or would have been lately, accepted as a gift. Every day of delay adds to the evil and both increases our guilt, and exasperates their spirits. Then shall our state derive its greatest lustre from its generosity. Then shall our Church give a noble instance of the first and greatest Christian virtue, charity.

Eton College, November 22, 1826 Apologies we have already had enough of: a long letter, albeit stupid, will be the best I can make to you for not having sooner answered your last letter to me. You provoke me on the subject of Catholics to a reply, which I am persuaded to make only by the hope that the goodness of the cause itself will compensate, and even counter-balance the inability of its advocate. Otherwise I should be far from entering into argument with so able and so ingenious an adversary as you are. But I must not let your questions go unanswered: or at least, unattempted to be answered. I am to show you any one country where the Catholic religion when predominant has been tolerant. To gratify you in that respect will not give me much trouble. I turn to France; there I see Catholics and Protestants sitting indiscriminately in the Chamber of Deputies; and Protestant clergy provided for by a Catholic government; nay, I even see an additional allowance granted to them, on account of their families. I am to show you any one instance when the Pope has disavowed persecuting dogmas ex cathedra. When Pope Pius the Sixth did so, I reply, fully and clearly; in or somewhere about the year 1796. Now I am to show you any one country where the Catholic priesthood have espoused the cause of civil and religious liberty. Alas! were I to put that question to a Catholic, might he not reply, 'Look at home; do your priesthood espouse that cause? No, they do not.

They deny us our political rights: granting therefore that our's as a
body do not espouse that cause, we are on a par with them: why then
are they admitted, and we excluded? Why are the pulpits which were
erected for the edification of Protestants, turned into vehicles for inveigh-
ing against, nay sometimes for *slandering*, Catholics? Why do they in full
blown dignity and luxurious ease, preach lessons to us which they have
not learned themselves? They tell us coolly and indifferently, when our
necks have been galled by the English yoke for years, aye for centuries,
they tell us forsooth that we ought to be patient and all that; and an
intemperate word from an Irish priest (who *is* oppressed) is considered
a more heinous crime than an intemperate action from an English one
(who *is not*).' Such I believe, might be the answer of a Catholic, not
without some plausibility. I am far, very far, from imputing such motives to the English clergy, that venerable and learned body. I lament
most sincerely their opposition to the Catholic claims; but I am far
from imputing bad motives, though I think their reasons are quite as
unsound as those which the laity in general make use of. But if you
accuse the Irish Catholic priesthood, by telling them they are not
friends to civil and religious liberty, may they not retaliate? When you
impute motives, may not they do the same? and is it not more excusable
in them to be intemperate in their method of recovering their rights,
than in you to be intemperate in withholding and refusing them?
Many Catholic priests are bigoted and superstitious: many perhaps
violently adverse to our Church. Many I hope are not so: many I fear
are. They have doubtless great influence over the people; and the more
so, because they now occupy the share which the gentry would occupy,
if the claims were granted. They have now every thing aiding to increase
their power over the poor and ignorant Irish: and they have you will
allow a specious theme whereby to excite discontent. They are entirely
free from the controul of Government. Such is their will and such their
power: the one we will suppose decidedly adverse to us, and of their
other over the feelings of the Irish, with such a grievance to complain of,
such means of exaggerating it, such additional weight as the reverence
paid them and the character their religion affords and no check on
them you can easily judge. A dreadful state of things, no doubt: grant
Catholic emancipation, and pay the Catholic clergy: you place a check
on the priesthood; you remove the grievance of which they complain,
and deprive them of their arbitrary and unregulated power. Disfranchise the forty shilling freeholders—but it may be long before such

another opportunity of doing that offers itself; such a one as the anti-Catholics voluntarily rejected when the matter was last brought before Parliament. In addition to this, remember that granting Catholic emancipation would throw a good deal of influence over the people into the hands of the gentry. Now it seems probable that a people like the Irish, and under all their peculiar circumstances, must be disposed and eager to confide in some class or other: in short, in the general order of things, the lower classes of a nation look up to and reverence the higher. Surely too when the Irish Catholic gentry had some political power, strength, and respectability, the peasantry would be disposed to place confidence in them far more than they can be at present—when a labourer that works on my Lord Fingal's estate may go and vote for a representative in Parliament, but my Lord himself remains unrepresented! A trifling anomaly. Would not this remove what is dangerous in the power of the priests? But suppose the Pope had never disavowed ex cathedra the persecuting dogmas—are we to take them up because he has not disavowed them? I deny the influence of the Pope over Ireland to be such as to be dangerous. I deny that, because no man, I think, who believes their evidence respecting the power of the Popes can do otherwise. And I do believe it; it was given upon oath; do you not believe it? if not, why do you swear to and ratify and confide in treaties with Catholic potentates? Why do you allow a Catholic jury to decide on the life and death of a Protestant culprit? Why do you allow a Catholic soldier to shed his life's blood for that country, that ungrateful country, from a share in whose government he is for ever excluded? A Catholic may command our armies and our navies—but within the walls of St. Stephen's he may not enter! A Catholic may decide on life and death—but in enacting a statute he may not give his voice. We may levy an army of sixty thousand Catholics, with Catholic officers, and a Catholic general! But twenty Catholic gentlemen in Parliament would ruin the constitution. I have endeavoured to answer your questions, but then in comes your saving clause, about Protestant ascendancy and British constitution, under which you can still continue your opposition. God grant that emancipation may be given, before it be extorted: and that English injustice may be removed and forgotten that we may not expiate it by the blood of poor England. Three things appear to me to require Catholic emancipation: justice, eternal justice; expediency, a strong and cogent collateral argument; and consistency. Do then as quickly as possible this action, expedient, as politicians;

consistent, as wise men; and just, as brothers and Christians. Be Popery what it may, we would not make it the predominant religion, notwithstanding what the Vice-Provost wishes to make us believe. You argue the question generally and vaguely; appeal to other countries; to the Pope and the fountain head of Catholicism. We would look to Ireland alone. Catholic emancipation must be yielded, if it be not given; remember former claims, former concessions; consider present claims and present circumstances; and then make up your mind.

I congratulate you on getting through if you have managed it.

Eton, Thursday evening, March 15th 1827 I received your letter of the 11th two days ago, and will give you in return such news as I have—though perhaps neither very plentiful nor very interesting. I must resort to the old topics—the society and its members. Poor Hallam has been laid up with an earache since Sunday last; he is now better, and desires me to say that he will answer your letter as soon as he is tolerably convalescent. Last Saturday we had a very amusing debate on Wat Tyler's opposition to the poll tax. Law opened, and said he trusted Englishmen would never forget, under such circumstances, the sacred duty of insurrection; he saw nothing sacred in the person of a king, and talked of the primitive equality of mankind, which no one could look back on without some degree of approbation. Gaskell got up next, and made a capital speech in answer to Law: cut him up right and left. Poor Law sat down amidst loud and long continued coughing. Pickering supported Gaskell, Hallam and Doyle spoke on the same side as Law, though not so violently. Selwyn made a very witty and amusing speech against poor Wat. On the division, the Tylerites were defeated. Gaskell has been, this term, a more useful member than ever, if possible; he has spoken well and frequently, and constantly writes out debates, thereby relieving Vice-Presidents, and benefiting the society: for none report half so well as he does. Hallam speaks extempore a great deal now, and very well as to fluency and arrangement; but he uses action, and bad action too. Wentworth speaks very fairly; he has lately been fined awfully for not writing out a debate, and they threaten a vote of censure next Saturday. Doyle astonished the house the Saturday before last by making a very good speech in favour of Mahomet's character, bringing forward all that his case would admit of. Coughing has now in great measure superseded the ironical cheering which I think used to be 'the go' in your time. We have only eleven—but the debates are, allowing for the wretched deficiency in numbers, very good. I have mercifully spared the house ever since the holidays, and have not inflicted on them a single speech. They made me chairman when Hervey left, but I do not suppose I shall be re-elected. Sandford is not in the sixth form yet. I found speaking in school by no means a bore; it is made a bugbear of, but there is nothing alarming in it, and something pleasing—namely, the skipping two exercises on the strength of it. Selwyn speaks well. He has been sent up twice this term, which I am glad of, as when in the fifth form he hardly (till latterly) got his deserts in that way. He is a great favourite with Keate. The said doctor improves decidedly on a more intimate acquaintance with him. Pickering holds forth on Saturday. I hope you were one of the sixty-five who voted against Elizabeth about the execution of Mary? If so, I should have agreed; as also in favour of hereditary aristocracy: on radical reform I believe we should be together again. On the character of George the Third—as a king—I think it is painful to decide. Disapproving as I do (as you ask me for my opinion) of many of his public measures and of his decided *opiniâtreté*, I still find it hard to say anything against a man so extremely amiable and so thoroughly good. Do you disapprove of the American war? That is one important point, as I think it was originally and fundamentally a King's measure. Again on the slave trade I do not think he was quite right in his opinions; nor do I approve of his views on the question of Catholic emancipation. But he supported Pitt from 1783 against the Coalition, which I think very much in his favour. This aided perhaps by my predilections for the man, will prevent my attempting to incline you either way in your opinion of the King. Buckridge I have not heard of lately. Have you? I hope Lofft will get the scholarship, for the honour of Eton. Many thanks for your offers of showing the lions, which I should be most happy etc to avail myself of if I had an opportunity of visiting Granta.

Eton College, Thursday, March 29th 1827 I sit down to thank you for, and to answer, your last letter. Imprimis: the sooner you trouble me again with what you call your nonsense the better: it is always most welcome and a very pleasant accompaniment to breakfast—whereby the mind and the body are benefited and pleased, both at once—and you know omne tulit punctum etc. It is rather insulting to couple you with rolls and butter—but they are not bad things in their way. I dare hardly ask you to write to me while you are in the country, where you must have a thousand more pleasant employments than either inditing epistles to, or wading through epistles from, me—and it is rather unmerciful to send you this one. But I do it in the hope of making you retaliate. If I direct wrong (as to spelling etc) correct me in your next—which be so good as to direct to Seaforth. Mentioning the directing to Seaforth reminds me of the Berwick business, and its bore; I say bore, because it has only one, but that is a most decided one—not having the advantage of franks, and making us not only waste our friends' time, but also attempt their purses. I see they are going to have a contest for the place. I envy neither candidate—nor is my opinion now anything changed from what it was at least six months ago. I am very glad to hear today, that Lofft has beaten Wordsworth, and got the scholarship: Etonians have done very great things within the last few years, and I hope you intend to win yourself some laurels, and your alma mater some credit. The Selwyns are the ornament and credit of my dame's. A very frequent and a very unacceptable guest has made his appearance here again—I mean Mr. Scarlet Fever: he has the singular property of being in several houses at once, and has put to flight a great many honester men than himself. Wentworth, a young rogue, has decamped without paying his subscription. I think the Society ought to issue an order to their serjeant at arms to go after him and take him into custody at his own expense. Next Saturday the question is to be whether the revolt of the Yorkists under Henry the Sixth was justifiable? I suppose you would say (what the majority of our august assembly say) that it was. Doyle and *Law* join with Gaskell and Pickering on this subject: but $\phi\epsilon\hat{v}$ $\phi\epsilon\hat{v}$[1] Gaskell has decamped too! And no one, I believe, intends to speak for the Yorkists, excepting Doyle and Law! Robert Wyndham Esq. and many other distinguished characters are coming up, in the expectation of hearing a good debate. So we are, on the whole, a failure. Three sixth form leave this time—Sivewright, Handley, and Antrobus. Poor John Sanford, in his zeal to adopt the classical doctrines of Homer and Horace with regard to wine, became, on Saturday last horresco referens, Qualis ab Ogygio concita Baccha deo—or, in plainer terms, bibulus liquidi Falerni. I use circumlocution, you see, to avoid the ill omened words. But the supreme Keate says he will not put him into the sixth form at all, and is incensed; which will be a bore not only for the guilty, but for the innocent, Hallam, Hanmer, and Divett—if Keate acts up to it: which it is not likely that he will do. It is intended, I believe, that a

---

[1] 'Alas!'

vote of thanks should be given to Gaskell on Saturday next. I go home on Saturday night. I am by no means tired of Eton as yet, and find the sixth form much more pleasant than any other part of the school. It certainly affords much greater opportunities for improvement in classics; Keate treats one with much more civility: and it is in all respects very pleasant. We have had no rows with lower boys lately: when they have occurred, as far as I recollect, they have always ended to the disadvantage of the latter. When Keate put me in, he gave me particular injunctions about strictness in performing my duty as a proposter. The other day my tutor took it into his head to set me some English verses to do, and I tipped him a divine effusion on Tuesday. Nicoll and Buller had the same to do. My paper is, and your patience must be exhausted.

Eton College, Tuesday, May 15th 1827 I have to thank you for your last too long unanswered letter, and to make a reply such as mine usually are. You accuse me of taking jokes to pieces; there is no fear of my attempting it in the case of your letter, for either there were none on which I could show my powers that way, or I was not bright enough to perceive them. There was in truth something about a fox and a butter-boat, but I presume you did not allude to this. By the bye though there was one decided jest, which I had almost forgotten. 'I suppose Lord Bathurst will be Premier'—I give you great κῦδος [1] for this. To tell you the truth, I do not like the present state of things. I rejoice to think that Catholic emancipation seems now more clearly in view, than it was a very short time ago: and so far, I think we are bettered by the change. But I do not like the abuse which has been so scandalously heaped on the ex-Ministers, particularly the old Earl of Eldon. I do not like the Marchioness of Conyngham's share in the business: I do not like Canning's accepting the premiership without the concession of the Catholic claims: and think it will be rather extraordinary to see His Majesty's Prime Minister, the actual head of the executive government, advocating so material a change in the formation of the constitution. That is not a situation (in my humble opinion) for an emancipationist to occupy while exclusion continues. I think Lord Grey has acted, in consistency with his opinions, a very manly and honourable part: and I do not think that the Whigs can be justified in forming, what so many of them have done, a thick and thin coalition with a man who differs so widely

---

[1] 'Glory'.

from them on reform, the Corporation and Test Acts, and the line of policy which ought to be pursued towards the West Indian colonial governments by the British. Peel has certainly acted a most manly, honourable, and dignified part, and one which will raise him even higher than he was before in the estimation of the country. A good deal of interest was excited here about your Cambridge election; principally, I think, in favour of Tindal. Are you pleased, or the contrary, with the result of the contest? *The St. James's Chronicle* and *Watchman* are violently in Banke's favour: principally it appears, on account of Sir Nicholas's unfortunate second name, Conyngham. We now take in at the Society the *Morning Chronicle, New Times,* and *St. James's Chronicle*—so as to please, as much as possible, all parties: though I confess I do not exactly like any of the three: but perhaps you will say I am of no party. Keate went into Norfolk last week, and we have heard since that his father-in-law is dead—therefore I suppose he will stay for the funeral. Mrs. Stansmore has taken her departure, and it is said that it is for the purpose of being united in . . . wedlock, as Matthew says, to William Oakley . . . to her as an admirer and intended spouse by the Eton public.[1] The change has not as yet made any difference to us beyond the mere name. I suppose the farewell supper will come soon. The Society gets on very well. We had an excellent debate on Saturday last, on the comparative merits of Clarendon and Hampden; and carried it in favour of the former by eight to four. Hallam, Doyle, Wentworth, and Law voting in the minority. Hallam opened; Law followed, and spoke a speech more seditious and levelling, if possible, than his Wat Tyler oration; Gaskell and I came next, and then Doyle. May we entertain any hope of seeing you here in the course of the summer? We hope to get up a few more good debates: one of them on the penal laws under Elizabeth. I expect on that to be in a minority, though a considerable one. Gaskell has three or four men under his thumb most completely, and they are disciplined for rounds of cheering and coughing in the most systematic manner. You would hardly, I think, recognise your Pickering's politics in those which he at present holds—I mean with regard to Canning and the Ministry of the day. Most singular schemes are afloat here but as I am not fully authorized, and believe Hallam intends to write and inform you fully of their nature and intentions, I will not meddle with them for the present. When you write—though indeed after my delays I have no right to expect

---

[1] Paper torn.

an early answer to this letter—give us Union news etc. Does Wellesley speak in it? We are to have a ballot or two on Saturday, I believe.

Eton College, Tuesday evening, May 22nd 1827 When I tell you that I received your very welcome letter this morning, you will see that I have not delayed for any length of time paying attention to the hint of my being a bad correspondent in the beginning, and the open admonition to write soon, at the conclusion. I cannot however promise to communicate any thing very substantial, or important, or entertaining, to you. I have not a very flattering account to give of our last Saturday's debate: I think it is now almost universally thought among us that Gaskell, on the whole, bears away the palm from Hallam in speaking. Last year, I thought Hallam decidedly superior: and though he still retains the same very great and extraordinary command of language, yet he has fallen into a bad style of action and delivery, while Gaskell's are so remarkably good, that Hallam's matter has not fair play in the comparison. Our last question was, 'Do the fine arts owe most to Leo the Tenth or Lorenzo de Medici?' I voted, in a majority, for Lorenzo, but Gaskell took off his Treasury men for Leo. He has two or three votes besides his own pretty much at his disposal: and his 'Treasury bench' men cheer what they like and cough what they dislike so vehemently, that opposition speakers are dreadfully browbeaten. Law however still continues to vent his principles, and talks about 'the jargon of the utility of kings and bishops'. He does not adopt the sentiment, yet would not say so, in consequence of which he was fined on Selwyn's motion. Next Saturday the question is to be, 'Did the Marquis of Montrose deserve well of his country?' Gaskell threatens to make a very violent speech. By the bye, his father is, he says, in great doubt with regard to choosing between the two universities: sometime ago, he had made up his mind for Cambridge, now however it appears he has unmade it, and is in the situation of the ass between the two bundles of hay. I do what I can to persuade him to come to Oxford. I should really have some difficulty in telling you what Pickering's present politics are; he says he still opposes the Catholics, but from reasons very different to those which he formerly made use of. I never hear [him] speak against Canning, or raise his voice in defending the principles of the anti-Catholic part of the late Cabinet. I believe none of us are quite so foolish as to join in the absurd and ungenerous calumnies which have been so plentifully heaped upon them. Do not suppose Pickering speaks against the seceders:

but he does not raise his voice as in days of yore. I really did not mean to give you the idea that I had any wonderful secrets in my keeping—indeed I should not have dropped a hint without proceeding further had I not thought Hallam was going to give you an immediate account of what had been projected. As he has not done so, I will tell you all which is at all certainly determined upon. A new publication is to be set on foot here; a successor . . . of Peregrine Courtenay and his comppeers, has appeared, under the name of Bartholomew Bouverie Esq.[1] I believe that it is his intention to publish . . . number of his work,[1] the said number containing forty-eight pages, every fortnight. He talks of getting out the first specimen of his abilities by Monday week. Neither a name nor a publisher are, however, as yet determined on. A general committee of twelve have the power of receiving or rejecting their own and other people's compositions, and from these four are selected to superintend and order revision. Hallam, Doyle, Selwyn, Gaskell, Pickering, Wilder, Law, Wentworth, are among them. We shall endeavour to secure all the fittest persons in the school. But the moral of this goodly narrative is, a request to you to assist and honour us with your contributions: the sooner the better, if you should accede at all to my request: and I trust, for the honour of Eton, which I have some fears for on this occasion, that you will do all which may be *conveniently* within your reach for us. Selwyn and I have been writing an introduction. Several contributions have been received, and many more are in their authors' hands. Two—one an original one, the other started in opposition, were to have gone on, but a junction has very happily though not very easily been effected. Hallam and Doyle were the chief promoters of one—Pickering and Gaskell of the other. I hope you will let me know what part of the world you are going into—and glad to hear you owe me a sovereign.

Eton College, Tuesday, July 3rd 1827 I have been allowing a considerable interval to elapse since I received your last letter without answering it on the score of your western tour. I should have supposed that you would not have been so curious about the supposed four heads of the men of Cornwall, as about their walking on all fours: according to your old idea. I hope you have satisfactorily elucidated this point, and returned to Iford still a biped. Keate has taken this opportunity of a regu-

[1] Paper torn.

lar week to send Hallam up for play; his exercise is on the force of nature; but he will have some thorns attending his roses; as, by way of preliminary to the process, which is a sufficiently troublesome one, the Doctor has marked about thirty places, which the author is to alter. Keate is somewhat fastidious; but Hallam does pick up odd expressions occasionally from Statius and his other more recondite friends. Selwyn has of course been sent up this time—he has had it four times in the sixth form: we are now full, and have got in Hanmer and Divett. A most pleasing effect has been produced on our worthy chief magistrate's temper lately, by some cause not well known, but supposed to be the birth of young Coleridge: or, as the Doctor himself expresses it, his 'having attained the honours of a grandfather.' He is becoming quite civilised: he patronises the *Miscellany* too, and says it is 'a good way for the boys to employ their time'. I do not know what the result of the Oxford and Cambridge match was: cricket has not been going on very well here—even though I am in the Upper Club. We have had two boat-matches, and there is to be one this week between the ten oar, and the ten best oars out of the other boats, in Roseaman's old ten-oar. I contemplate with anything but satisfaction the clearance which is about to take place at election. Doyle will be the only fellow here next term whom I know much of. Gaskell, I believe, goes to Oxford, and Hallam to Cambridge, next year: Selwyn to St. John's in October. Last week we had a dinner in celebration of a boat-match, at which Selwyn proposed 'Down with Canning'—which was opposed by some on account of the sentiment, by others on account of the unfitness of such an occasion for politics—and it failed. Wentworth goes up to Cambridge in October. My tutor, Berthomier, and other worthies in general, flourish. The Society is, I rejoice to say, in very good condition; we have seventeen members, with, I rejoice to say, a prospect of two or three more pretty soon. A few weeks ago we had Queen Elizabeth's penal laws against the Roman Catholics, and carried it against them, though with a majority of two. Gaskell was with us. We intend to . . . question of the rebellion against Charles the First[1]; and I hope that at any rate they will not muster more than three or four to vote for it. Puller was at the debate last Saturday; we had the character of Strafford, and carried it for him by a considerable majority—at least considerable in our pigmy numbers. I think the Whigs are getting in too much—thought

---

[1] Paper torn.

Todd would do well. Please to direct to Mrs. Ward's, and make use of my information as soon as you like.

The second number of our miscellany seems to have been liked better than the first, and the third as well as, or better than, the second. I think our fourth will be an improvement, and if each rises above the other in succession we must attain to something tolerable at last. The sale has been good—but our advertisements at first were rather unfortunate. Selwyn and I go through the bulk of the editing business— and the select committee have now quite enough power in their hands, if not too much. We shall have a list of names in the fifth, intended to be published on election Monday; and Doyle and I mean to carry it on till Christmas. I confess I should be sorry to outlive Bartholomew, such as he is—his health was drunk at the dinner, as was that of the Society. I breakfasted with Doyle's father on Sunday here, who is a very agreeable and gentlemanly man.

Seaforth, Wednesday, September 5th 1827 I ought to ask your pardon for having delayed so long to answer your last letter, which I received a few days before election. I got some numbers of the *Miscellany* to send you, but between the preparation with Keate etc for speeches, and seeing the last of so many friends, my time was so much taken up, that I did not hunt out your friend Tregonwell—I am sorry for this—but will you wait till your proposed visit to Eton (which I hope and trust nothing untoward will occur to prevent) or order them yourself? If you live in a civilized country, this will not be difficult. Kirby, Paternoster Row, is the London man.

So we northerners know nothing of scenery! Why, sir, we have scenery in the north the best of every kind: if you want such scenery as a rich and highly cultivated country affords, where will you find it more easily than in Yorkshire? and in the romantic—for in the other you may equal—perhaps excel us—go to the north of Lancashire, to Westmorland, to Cumberland, and then come back blushing partly from your own erroneous ideas, detected and exposed, and partly from the healthy breezes which will refresh you as you climb up our mountains. To compare a country made of tin to our's! Who ever goes to the south for scenery? How many thousands to the north? Who ever heard of a tour to the tin mines, any more than of a tour to the cotton mills?

With regard to 'Down with Canning'—that great statesman and magnificent orator is now laid low indeed by the hand of death. Notwithstanding your prejudices, for I can allow your feelings on the subject no better name, we have sustained in him a great, an almost irreparable loss. Best and greatest of the followers of 'his great master, Pitt,' his principles had not degenerated from the true, ancient, loyal stock of Toryism. He followed the real Pitt, the friend to liberal measures and the advocate of Catholic emancipation: not the imaginary one, whom bigotry has by some unaccountable process (I cannot say peculiar to itself, for the Whigs can do as much or more) converted into a deity for its temple, an image for its worship. He has died, in some respects, at an unhappy time: for the cloud which enveloped his administration had only been partially dissolved. If he sought place through Lady Conyngham, he did *very wrong*. If he intended to relax ought of his zeal for emancipation, he did *very wrong*. But these, I think, are hardly proved. His ridicule of Ogden was I fear unfeeling: his conduct to Lord Castlereagh in 1809 not justifiable. But, while *I* can look with pleasure on the whole of his career, *you*, one might hope, would favour with a smile of approbation the earlier part of it; the part when he . . . his voice against quailing before France; . . . when he exercised his pen in . . . opposition host.[1] Hallam has . . . because I do not wish to see more Whigs in power—you will probably do so because I look back with mingled reverence and sorrow on the life—and on the death, of Canning. Welcome both—if I feel that his politics were those of sound principles, and liberal measures—for why sound principle should bring with it exclusion, or liberality Whiggism, I do not know.

Our eighteen members are now reduced, I believe, to about ten, and we must look out for recruits. Chapman's pupils were, Taunton, Farquharson, Moss, Arabin, Kean, and Farquhar. Have you heard about the Harrow match? I have inquired in vain.

I go back to Eton I believe, and for the last time, on the twentieth or twenty-first of this month. I am not even yet tired of it, however unfashionable it may be to have been there six years, without being disgusted. The spelling of the name Ward is surely not very formidable. I fear the *Miscellany* men will run rather rusty before we get fairly through it. The circumstances which gave rise to it were very singular, and it came forth somewhat crude.

Liverpool, Friday, September 14th, 1827 Though I dare say you will be horrified at the very idea of receiving a letter from a country so near

---

[1] Paper torn.

to the land of cottontwist, and itself a country of tar, ships, rum, sugar, etc, I, remembering how ill I had behaved to you in delaying to write, and how well you have treated me in giving my epistle such a speedy answer, do sit down to indite a letter to you, though I fear that when I get back to Eton I shall not be able to keep up near so close a fire, as I expect to have plenty to do. Doyle, Law, and Rogers are my chief— almost my only, coadjutors: the first and last of the three are idle, particularly Doyle—and Law, though a steady going fellow, does not send in any great number of contributions or quantity of matter. I am *really obliged to you* for your critique, and should have been so still more if you had been a little less lenient. I like the Eton Dull Club, and always have liked it, very much: but it was not, surprising as it may be, *generally* admired. Most people thought it mere schoolboy wit. Selwyn's Art of Conversation, which though I thought it good, I never put on a par with the Dull Club, was, I think, more liked by our readers. He was indeed a most valuable working man: and as we were much together in our dame's of course we divided more equally the load which will now fall in greater proportion on my unfortunate and incompetent shoulders. I fear I must be content with a much lower rank than that which you have been pleased to assign to me: but Selwyn certainly had a claim to one of the first, if not the first, place. Hanmer's poetry was a good deal liked—though where there was a different opinion, it was usually in the extreme of condemnation. Skirrow was indeed bad: and his 'Lines to Contemplation' (he called them, and sent them in called '*Ode* to Contemplation') were, I assure you, much worse when they came in, than as they were published. But I do not call him 'indeed bad' on account of what *was* published of his, so much as on account of what *was not*. We were generally disappointed in Hallam. We have admitted things from old Etonians: and had accordingly about three pages and a half, or four pages, from them in our first five numbers. Their names need only be communicated (in case of acceptance—otherwise to no one) to me. With regard to the chorus from Euripides, it was a sugar plum for the higher powers: of course we would not go far in the same way. But, my good friend, it is not much more than nominally a translation, though so called: as you would perceive on referring to the original. We shall be very happy to have something from you.

The King has indeed made an excellent choice of a successor to Mr. Canning: and my Lord Goderich, by bringing Herries into the Cabinet in spite of the Whigs, has shown that he has not a tendency towards

Whiggism. Friend to emancipation, and reformed corn laws, and Free Trade (in general) as I am, though perhaps you may laugh at my saying it, I should be very sorry to see a preponderance, or even any considerable infusion, of Whig interest and influence in the British Cabinet ... not Whigs: we are Tories. I do not see ... involves any of the questions I have ... men ... [1] Toryism need not be ashamed of the maxim 'extend the blessings of the constitution to all who can enjoy them without endangering it'. It is a principle on which we cannot well disagree: it is in the application, in the particular case, that we are at defiance. Sorry I am that the particular case is of such awful importance, and the difference likely to produce such portentous consequences. I confess, and I ought to confess with regret that they exist at all—that my prejudices and predilections are all in favour of Toryism. While I have the period of the French Revolution stamped deeply on my memory, I cannot but feel distrust of the principles of Whiggism, and of its tendency. If Lyndhurst, Anglesea, and Herries are the sole means of keeping the Cabinet together, why is it that the Opposition and their papers have been doing every thing they can to dissolve it? As the natural inference would be that from respect to them their brother Tories refrained from attacking the Administration. I did not write the obnoxious phrase 'Fox chase': and beg pardon for not correcting it. I thought partridges had been considered pretty plentiful: they are so indeed, in the north, though hares have run short. I go to Oxford either one term before next long vacation, or in the term after it: I hope the former. I hope we shall then have opportunities of meeting. Thanks for your news about Eton and Harrow. I will inquire into the truth of the Wykhamite's allegation. Prithee what has the country suffered from the broad bottom? I am much obliged by the hatred you bear to my very name.

The members of the Society, after our election losses, which were very severe, were, Wright, Durnford, Law, Bacon, Sanders, Doyle, Canning, Telf, Handley, Gladstone. We lost Wilder, Hallam, Selwyn, Pickering, Gaskell, Wood, Wentworth, Cavendish. Last term the fun was *much better* than I ever remember it: and the debates generally from one to two hours. I fear I shall never see a renewal.

Eton College, Monday evening, November 26, 1827 I really should feel somewhat ashamed at seeing, on sitting down to write to you, two

---

[1] Paper torn.

unanswered letters of your's on my table, if I did not feel that I could in the present instance with some species of propriety assign my having been really much pressed and laden as the whole and sole reason for my not having written to you long ago. We had a press of matter, and consequently a proportionate increase of occupation, in getting up the tenth number; having then to clear off everything. We must put an additional sixpence on it, and it will be more than half as large again as they have usually been; if we could have avoided it without great loss we should not have altered the price.

I was heartily glad to receive your own favourable opinion, and your account of the general reception, of our ninth number. The eighth was liked well enough here—well, that is to say in proportion to the usual quantum of approbation which we enjoy.

With regard to the *Eton Miscellany*, my own I hope candid and un-prejudiced opinion—at any rate, it is one not formed without a good deal of practical experience, and reflection founded on it—is, that the design was rash and reprehensible, the execution extremely imperfect: that there are few things in it which rise above mediocrity, and many which sink below it; that Bartholomew Bouverie is not a worthy suc-cessor of Peregrine Courtenay, far less of the first and best of Etonian boy authors, Gregory Griffin. But I think we occupy a station somewhat higher than that of the Saltbearer—this idea however may arise from prej-udice in favour of myself and mine. I should have been glad to have had in the list [of] our contributors a very old companion and friend, in the person of yourself—but possibly you are better off unassociated with us.

My tutor asked me about you today. I told him I believed you spoke in the Union, and did not sap. With regard to Pickering's politics, I know nothing but from his letters. He tells me that we owe a debt of gratitude to Canning: and some one else, Handley I believe, that he should have been sorry to see the Eldonites come in again. I have not heard from him lately, but am expecting to do so almost daily.

Our tenth number will be out probably on Thursday: certainly, I believe, by Friday: on Saturday I shall take my leave of the Society; and on Monday I suppose I must bid farewell to poor old Eton. I shall depart with sincere regret: and I have long ago persuaded myself that I never can expect another period of my life to be so full of joys and so free from sorrows as that which I have passed here. Do you recollect, a day or two after our coming here, my meeting you in my tutor's dining room and our bowing to one another?

The Society flourishes: it has twenty-one members; and some promising young speakers; Chisholm minor, Bruce (Lord Elgin's son), Cowper, perhaps the most so. It is now in very good reputation.

My tutor still has few pupils. I dine with him on Friday. I have heard from Hallam and Gaskell, both in Italy, not very long ago. I am glad you like Bacon. What sort of figure does Chambers cut at Cambridge? With regard to the Colleger and Oppidan row, it stands, or rather stood, I believe, nearly as follow[s]. Crawshay, an Oppidan lower boy, quarrelled with a liberty Colleger, who is too a sixth form elect, i.e., within the number; there are disputes as to whether he had struck a blow; however, Sanders came up and gave Crawshay a tremendous knock down blow in the face. Keate said he would punish Sanders. The Oppidans went to him to make him beg C's pardon; he would not: a fight commenced: and Bethell, happening to come by, fortunately for the Collegers, stopped it. The Oppidans were severely punished—as was Sanders—but not the other Collegers, being considered as on the defensive.

I am told Todd has been writing on chronology. I dare say he will do well in the world.

I send this through Selwyn—as it is as quick.

Oxford, Wednesday, January 23, 1828 I am afraid that a considerable time has elapsed since I received your last letter; but in truth, now that I have left Eton, you cannot expect that I should have much intelligence of interest to communicate. I am indeed sitting down to write to you from the rival university, but what I can tell you, that you will care about, I really do not know—except, indeed, that I have seen your old friend Boughey here this morning; that however, as I believe you correspond with him, I fancy you have heard from himself. I matriculated today at Christ Church—by the same token I have got a great book of statutes to peruse. I am not to have rooms there till October, and, I am sorry to say, I am doomed to private tutorism for six months! I have however got a pretty good one, and, I believe, a pleasant man. You may remember Mr. Turner, such is his nomenclature, at Eton, as private tutor there to Lord Castlereagh, then Stewart. He is a very clever man: but had my opinion been the rule, I should not have wished any private tutoring to intervene between Eton and Oxford. But what must be must be, and what can't be cured must be endured. My direction, when you are disposed to favour me, will be to the care of the Rev. J. M.

Turner, Rectory, Wilmslow, near Manchester. Manchester is not the pleasantest place in the world to be stationed 'near', though Johnny Law might think so, but I believe the 'near' in this case means twelve or thirteen miles off. I heard from Pickering not long ago. I can feel for him in anticipation for myself.

I am not *altogether* displeased at the late change in the Ministry, though I wish much that a stronger body of those who advocate emancipation were retained. I think there are only five; Dudley, Melville, Huskisson, Grant, and Palmerston. Huskisson and Dudley are the two most considerable of these. I do not like to see the same man Commander-in-Chief and Prime Minister too, but I hope it will not be so. These Whigs never can keep in for any length of time; and indeed I am not sorry for it. They all swore that Mr. Huskisson would not remain with the Tories; but ecce signum! I suppose the general principles of Mr. Canning's Government, and those of Lord Liverpool's (for we have not any tangible difference *in acts* manifested, I think) will be continued in operation.

I sometimes see the *Standard,* which is very ably written: but extravagant in some of its articles(witness that about George Dawson the other day, whom they 'will not disgrace' by comparing, *in point of talent,* to Lord Lansdowne!), and very deficient in advertisements, without which or else a tremendous circulation, a London daily paper cannot I believe, answer well. Do you know anything of its circulation? I should suppose it very considerable.

I left the Eton Society in a very flourishing state. Both the Chisholms were among its members: they are remarkably fine fellows, I think. Chisholm major expected to be in the sixth form, but was not, on account of the rows, which was laid upon him: however, it was supposed settled that he was to leave, and he got leaving books to the extent of forty odd volumes—when, *on the Sunday night* (he was to leave on the Monday) down came his mother, and declared he should stay, to be put into the sixth form! He was placed in a very awkward situation, and much vexed about it: there, however, I believe, he still remains. Bruce, Lord Elgin's son, a new member, promised to be a good speaker. You have of course heard of Mrs. Canning's elevation to the peerage. I am very glad of it—here I can hardly hope you will at all participate in my feeling. I can hardly describe to you the feeling of joy with which I took no. 10 of *Miscellany* to send it to press. Now that it is finished, I must say, that I do not consider it on the whole a book creditable to

Eton; very inferior to the *Etonian*, and much more to the *Microcosm*. So abuse it to your heart's content. By your commendations of certain pieces I was much gratified.

Wilmslow, Tuesday, March 11, 1828 I fear that I have been for some time in your debt. The fact is, that it is more to fulfill the duty of a correspondent that I am now addressing you, than to give you any news. That is a commodity almost, if not altogether, unknown in this part of the world. Will you not be horrified when you call to mind, that I am writing to you from a place situated in the region of steam and smoke? within seven miles of Macclesfield, and twelve of Manchester? If not with that, you will at least, nec injuria, be horrified at my threatening to fill a sheet without promising to put into it a single syllable that shall conduce in the remotest degree either to instruct, interest, or amuse.

I cannot go any further without thanking you most sincerely for the very kind wishes expressed in your last letter. Whatever may be my lot for the future, I never can look back without pleasure and regret to the happy years which we have passed at Eton. For my own part, I found those pleasures progressively increase as I remained there longer and rose higher. Last term indeed, I had lost very nearly all my old friends: but the summer, and all preceding it, especially from the period of my entering the Society, was a time of very great and numerous delights. The change from the sixth form at Eton to a private tutor's is a very great one—certainly not on the whole a pleasant, though very frequently perhaps an useful one. My tutor is an Oxford first class man, and a very good mathematician. I do not however work hard at all here, and, except in mathematics, get through what is really a mere trifle: so that I am afraid when I leave this place I shall be rather worse in classics than better, than I was when I came to it. The country is a very pretty one, and though the *immediate* neighbourhood is not good, this being a manufacturing village, Cheshire is on the whole very well stocked with large landed proprietors and good society; much more so, I think, than the *generality* of counties in England. There is also a great deal of hunting and shooting, and some most thorough-going sportsmen are among its squires and clergymen. It is a remarkably fine county for farming, and the soil very rich. Some of the prettiest situations one could wish for are spoiled by the factories. Time rolls on here in the most monotonous manner imaginable, and one day is distinguished from another by little or nothing except the weather which is generally pretty variable at this season. I hope you enjoyed yourself in Hampshire in the vacation. Was not the season considered a very good one for hunting? My fellow pupils here are two: Wood, who was at Hawtrey's; and a brother of Powys at Okes's who was at St. John's about two years ago, has taken his degree, and is going to be ordained in the latter end of this year. I like them both very much. We have not much to do, and have resorted to gymnastics, as a time-killing and body-strengthening exercise.

There is nothing which enlivens a solitude like this more than receiving plenty of letters from Old Etonians and present Etonian correspondents; with them, I am happy to say, I am pretty well stocked. I heard a short time ago from Hallam and Gaskell. Both were at Rome. Hallam talks of coming home in June, Gaskell in September. Are you aware that Gaskell goes to Oxford? He is to be a fellow collegian of mine at Christ Church in October next, I believe. This I am very glad of. Hallam will, I suppose, join you at Cambridge. Have you read his father's book, or Southey's review of it in the *Quarterly*? I had a letter from Pickering some time ago. He is still at his private tutor's in Hertfordshire. From Doyle I hear pretty often. His mother Lady Doyle, died a short time ago, in a manner awfully sudden. She was taken ill one evening and died about ten o'clock at night! Selwyn writes to me that he is working very hard, and only means to allow himself by way of vacation, a week at Easter and the month of June. I wish you would write to me similar accounts, and hope most sincerely that you have not given up reading for, at any rate, classical honours. If you have, you are, in my humble opinion at least, doing yourself great injustice. How fares the Union? Do you speak much? I suppose Johnny Law has become conspicuous among the Radical luminaries of your assembly, who, by all accounts, are pretty numerous.

What is the adventure of Lord Aberdeen at Vienna to which you allude? I am very glad I have been able to keep off politics thus far; especially as in the first place I am very well pleased with the Government, in the second Huskisson does *not* support the repeal, and in the third you will not allow me to know my own sentiments with regard to Whig principles and a Whig Ministry. All I will say is, I hope it may be long before the country sees a specimen of the latter. I do not wish a repeal of all tests against the Dissenters, but shall be very glad if the use of the sacrament as one be removed, and some disclaimer of hostility to the Church substituted in its stead.

I may perhaps remain here till July—perhaps go next month as Mr. Turner has some thoughts of going up to London, in which case he cannot keep me. If he goes, I may perhaps go to Oxford before long vacation. A letter from you will at any time be acceptable.

25 Royal Circus, Edinburgh, Monday evening, May 5, 1828 My conscience tells me, as I sit down to write this letter, that I am sending you but a tardy reparation. I received your letter I fear as much as five perhaps six weeks ago, when at Wilmslow, which I have now left, for some time, if not for good. The examination of junior sophs was printed at full length in the London papers. I am indeed very sorry to see that you appear to have given up the intention at least of making considerable exertions at the university. It is, I think, if I may speak my mind, neither doing yourself nor Eton justice. However little inclined you may be to exert yourself for your own sake, however little disturbed by that jealousy which too often calls itself emulation, still you are surely bound to uphold her reputation to the utmost of your power. I rejoice to think she has lately sent such men to the universities as Durnford, Praed, Tennyson, Lofft, the Selwyns, etc. But, at least, if they had suffered 'the Ides of March' to pass as you have done, you must own she would have been no more indebted to or benefited by them than she usually is by the exertions or the honours of a Windsor bird. You will have Hallam upon your heels in October next. I am not without hope of seeing your name in the papers before that time though the Ides did pass. Of our contemporaries, each university will have, I think, about an equal share: for Doyle, Wood, Rogers, all do Eton great honour at Oxford. In addition to those, Hanmer may come in for a Newdigate or two: and Gaskell ought to be appointed *Public Orator* to the university, the present occupant of that station being pretty completely superannuated.

What do you think of the course which the Duke of Wellington, Peel, and, last not least, the bishops, have pursued with regard to the Corporation and Test Acts? I am in doubt as to what your decision will be: I am sure your judgement would lead you to hail the substitution of an unobjectionable (as at least it appears to them) for an highly objectionable test, yet I fear you will not much incline to desert my Lords Eldon and Redesdale, John Bull and his compatriots, etc. Lord Eldon's conduct has been bold, open, manly, candid: I wish I could add an humble testimony to its wisdom. I do really revere his sincere, though I think blind, attachment to the constitution: the principle we are bound to revere—the propriety of the method by which he reduces it to practice we may be allowed to doubt. It is a pity that Peel and Huskisson opposed the measure, and then had to give in: nor do I think the conduct of the former to Sir Thomas Acland was altogether fair: I mean in taking the matter out of his hands. But I do honour the bishops for their conduct exceedingly. I am sorry he of Winchester did not vote for the repeal, as it looks a little like his being afraid of the King. I hope you will soon let me have your opinion on these subjects. The Catholic question I fear we are not likely to approximate upon. But what say you to the Corn bill, and the modest request of *some*, that a remunerating price should be *secured* to them!!!!

Perhaps I ought now to tell you how I came into this land of Whigs and mountains. My tutor's wife was so unwell that he determined to take her up to London for the benefit of medical advice: and in consequence he was obliged to dissolve his engagement with us. He is a clever, agreeable, and good man: and I was sorry to leave him on sundry accounts, though I gained with him but little of what had been hoped for from the private tutoring ... My mother and sister have been here for the last ... months,[1] and I came to be with them during a journey of my father's to London. I may very probably, I think, go off to Paris pretty soon with one of my brothers who is in the Navy, and daily expected home from abroad. Should you write soon, please direct to Seaforth, as I expect to leave Edinburgh in about ten days. This is certainly a magnificent city; but Scotland is miserably poor; a great number of estates for sale, and about half its metropolis 'to sell or let'. It is a false and hollow grandeur, but grandeur there is, and in no ordinary degree. This is the letting season: but Edinburgh is always more abounding in sellers than buyers of houses.

Thus kindly have I been filling my sheet of paper with histories of Edinburgh and self, which you probably will not consider the most entertaining subjects in the world. I will tell you what I can of a more interesting kind. I heard a few days ago from Gaskell, who returns to England in September. He has been fortunate enough to see the eruption of Mount Vesuvius—which two of my brothers, who were residing at Naples at the time, also witnessed. Hallam has not written to me very lately, for in truth I could give him no direction: Pickering wrote some time ago, apparently in an uneasy state of mind, but working hard,

---

[1] Paper torn.

and determined to do his utmost at the university. Doyle is private tutoring near Stamford.

In the hurry of leaving Wilmslow I omitted bringing your letter with me, so I hope you will excuse my failing to reply to any particular part. Cheshire is really a nice country, the people kind and hospitable. What do you think of three Cheshire men being heard in a café near Paris, drinking 'The Cheshire fox hounds' with three times three? Is not that strange?

I hope your debating society flourishes. I should think you must find it much more agreeable than the Union.

Farr to Gladstone, Iford, 9 July 1828; ADD.MS 44352, ff. 60–61.
This is the earliest letter from Farr which is preserved in the Gladstone Papers.

Farr to Gladstone, Iford, 23 September 1828; ADD.MS 44352, ff. 77–78.

Cuddesdon, Thursday, September 25, 1828 If my leisure and ability kept pace with my inclinations, my letter by return of post would, I believe have communicated to you an entirely opposite answer[1]—however unimportant either way—to your kind and tantalising invitation, exactly the reverse of what this must convey. Perhaps when you recollect how much I should have been a gainer in all respects except one, which at present happens to be with me the main and almost sole one, by accepting, you will be induced to believe that it is with much regret that I decline. I know however you are fond of facts, and though I have not the power of manufacturing them ad libitum, the case as it stands with me happens to present some ready made ones which I trust you will consider sufficient. Christ Church meets on Friday fortnight: and between that meeting and the present time I have got, besides a good portion of Herodotus, which might easily have been managed, a great deal to get through in mathematics, in order to get myself even in any way prepared for that lecture into which Saunders means, I believe, to put me. Having Wood's (your head, I believe, is he not?) Mechanics to finish, and a whole book of questions on that treatise to work out, I have my hands quite full for every day: besides that, I have a good deal to do in the way of recapitulation. I have entered thus much

---

[1] The words 'entirely opposite answer' have been deleted in the MS.

into detail, not because I supposed such material would be very interesting as news to you, but simply to shew how different from an unfettered choice are the circumstances which compel me to come to the conclusion that I must remain where I am. I could have trusted the 'farmhouse' for at least endurable cheer, and with regard to gaiety, I feel that the talking over old times which you mention, and which I hope we may enjoy before any very long time passes, will when it comes be to me a source of much more delight. I have written by return of post in order that there may be no chance of you being put to inconvenience by expecting a guest who as 'he *can't* do as he *would, must* do as he *can*'. However, the account you have given, of the facility of intercourse between Oxford and Southampton, cuts both ways. I conjecture that it is as good from Southampton to Oxford, as from Oxford to Southampton. And I believe Oxford is not very much out of your way to Cambridge. My conscience twinges me however while I am writing this, and bids me fairly own, that I shall, unless rather in luck, have very little power of giving decent accommodation to a friend during my first term at Christ Church. The fashion at Oxford is *not* to build: the rush for rooms in consequence which has long been great and continually increasing, is now excessive. Consequently I am led to expect that I shall get none I can call my own till after Christmas, at any rate, but I *may* by chance get put into good ones for the term: in case I do, I shall venture humbly to submit the above named Oxford coach for your consideration, however little I may have to offer to make the place palatable. I think you do not go up to Cambridge till the end of October or November, so I shall be able to let you know how I am off. You will laugh at our affecting to talk of mathematics, I suppose: but in good truth I cannot there laugh with you. After disposing in this, to me at least, exceedingly unsatisfactory, way of your invitation, I proceed to other matters. First, Pickering has actually come *quite* round: whether permanently or not I dare not say. Perhaps vaga prorumpet froenis natura remotis. Your pun on Dawson I shall 'put about'. I think it is what a sable neighbour of our's at Eton would have called 'not so bad'. 'The character of Bellingham, Washington, and Grove' is to me indeed a sphinx (Buckinghamise sphinx)—though I have not had time to think much upon it. I never heard of any Bellingham but one, and he I do not think would be a favourite subject for the exercise of your descriptive powers. You will laugh at my blindness. I am sorry to see by your quotation from my letter that I omitted the word 'folly' in the list of 'testimonials' to the

Roman Catholic priests which I gave. For the present state of things those who advocate the R.C. cause are not, as I think, answerable. Had emancipation been granted when they first prayed it, they would have been so wholly. If it were conceded now, as they still continue to ask it, they would be at least partially responsible. But that they are to be judged for what is now done, I cannot allow. How did the notion of emancipation find its way into the British Parliament? It was not born in the head of a Fitzgerald, or even a Grattan: Irish clamour brought it there. Therefore, I should reverse your proposition and say the O' Connells, i.e. the Roman Catholics, created the Fitzgeralds, i.e. the Protestants who favour emancipation. I am sick of the question, and disgusted beyond measure with the priests and agitators. Still I think the primary cause lies at our door—I trust the Conyngham influence has not been the means of raising Dr. John B. Sumner to the bench, though it polluted the promotion of his brother. We see the *Sun* and *Standard* here: the latter is I think a very clever paper and good in point of news: more I cannot say. The present Bishop of Chester is if I mistake not in considerable reputation among the Oxford dons as a divine. Puller who is still here is a staunch Whig, and votes against Canning. He tells me the Whigs carry it in the Oxford Society which consists of about 120 members, being at present rather low. The country here is very pretty, and abounds very much in game, though that matters nought to us beyond the sight of them. How are you off this year for birds in Hampshire?

Farr to Gladstone, Iford, 29 September 1828; ADD.MS 44352, ff. 81–82.

Christ Church, Wednesday, October 29, 1828 I ought according to promise to have answered your kind letter some time back; and so I should have done, had it been in my power to offer you any allurements which might have succeeded in bringing you hither on your way to Cambridge. My habitation was in so unsettled and filthified a state, that I was far indeed from wishing to display its charms to a friend: so much so that I made myself scarce here as much as I could for some time. I have been obliged, as the lesser evil of two, to have operations performed on the walls whilst I have been inhabiting the rooms; which though not agreeable during their continuance, has left me with a sort of semblance of cleanliness about me. We are in such a state here, that I imagine myself in considerable luck, on account of having got rooms at all. You may guess at the number of freshmen when you learn that there are fifteen or sixteen from Eton alone. I think not above four or five have got rooms of their own, and several expect to be sent back almost immediately, and are in great doubt as to the possibility of keeping term. The Eton freshmen are Devereux, Farquharson, Hartopp, Riddell, Houston, Cholmondeley, Cockerell, Egerton, Barnard, Portman, Roberts, Tobin and sundry more. Rogers is come up to Oriel. I forgot however whether you knew him at Eton. I had seen almost nothing of him till the last term I was there: he appears to me a very likely subject for university honours. I admired much your considering yourself more a 'Xt Church' man than myself, when you did not even know how to write the word! not to mention that I dined in hall and slept in college before you had left Eton. I am a commoner: and a commoner's place is very much better suited for me, for many reasons, than the superior grade would be. I like Oxford very much, though not so well as Eton. We are not overworked by any means with lectures. Saunders, the mathematical lecturer, has a great deal of zeal in his department, and has put me into a differential calculus lecture: how fit I am for it let my companions and papers testify! Selkirk is in the same. He is considered likely, I believe, to make a very good mathematician. I am afraid that if I had accepted your repeated invitation the Herodotus you mention would still have enjoyed his otium cum dignitate; indeed though it was not agreeable, I am sure it would not have answered, after all my idleness, to come to you: nor will it now answer to solicit exeats for the same purpose. However if such things are known at Cambridge, since you seem to be thoroughly convinced of the ease with which they may be obtained, suppose you try the experiment, come over on some Thursday, and speak in the debating society in the evening? Hanmer (now Sir John) has promised to take me tomorrow, to hear him speak on the Corn Laws. I have offers to be *proposed*, but I do not yet know whether I shall try my chance. Gaskell and Doyle propose coming up next term. I have put about the former's fame, and I have no doubt he will be booked for the Society immediately. He is to come up for the purpose of being matriculated soon. Really it was most genteel in you to report me the heir of £13,000 a year; especially as I conceive regard for your own credit and veracity will seize you to make good the assertion. I met Todd the night I came up, and he gave me a long account of you all at Cambridge. I have heard about the Duke of Newcastle's scholarship with most unfeigned delight: I am in hopes it may do great good to Eton, as well as reflect great credit on his

Grace. With regard to his letter, I am in hopes that you Brunswickers may do good, though not quite in the way you intend, by enabling the Government to take higher ground in the settlement of the question, and making the agitators lower their tone: for settled it is to be, according to all the friends, I believe, and most of the opponents of emancipation. I shall rejoice in any settlement (consistent with justice) if such can be devised, by which the great body of Protestants may be reunited, instead of having a single question to separate men who so thoroughly agree as *some* of those on each side do in their general views. You have probably heard of Captain Canning's death. What a wreck that family has become! Believe me always (I believe it is an appellation which it is perfectly legitimate to use after a seven years intimacy) your friend most sincerely *etc.*

Farr to Gladstone, Cambridge, 10 November 1828; ADD.MS 44352, ff. 90–91.

Christ Church, Monday, January 26, 1829 Want of material and laziness, the usual obstacles to keeping up the character and performing the duties of a good correspondent, have prevented my answering your letter sooner. Did I read as I threatened and wished to do, my reading would excuse my delay; but the quantity and quality of my studies have hitherto not been such as to furnish me with any such justification. I wish you would even threaten reading, for I am sorry to see that you have given up even speaking about it. It appears even to me that the Cambridge system (if I have been rightly informed concerning it) of tying everything to mathematics, and making them a sine qua non to high classical honours must operate very prejudicially in many cases, as it has I believe done in your's, and in Selwyn's—to go no further. I presume you have not returned yet, as Christ Church, notorious for its short vacations, has only been up ten days, and the other colleges here three: and I believe Cambridge is later altogether than we are—indeed it may well be so, since staying up vacations is so much more encouraged and practised there. I have little to tell you concerning old friends, who have clustered more thickly in Cambridge than Oxford. Christ Church overflows with freshmen as usual, and many from Eton— Doyle, More, Thistlethwaite, Hope, Borough, etc. Poor Doyle expects to be sent down again almost immediately, as there will probably be no room for him when the possessor of the rooms he is in at present returns. He has been in six sets already, and has undergone much tribulation during the very cold weather we have had. Rogers is at Oriel, and they seem to have a very high opinion of him and disposed to make much of him there. Eton has got three or four heroes going in for the university scholarship here—none of whom are considered as having any chance —so much the more heroic in them. However she promises to do pretty well here on the whole, I think. The fame of last year's double and single classes must feed us for some time. I fear she will not be able to lay her finger on the scholarship. I hear the odds are three to two on Shrewsbury against the field.

I believe you are greatly pleased with the Newcastle scholarships—I am delighted too. At the bishop's the other day I heard the scholarship would be given not for divinity or classical proficiency alone, but to him who should be found to combine most of the latter with a stated quantity of the former—which stated quantity is to be made a sine qua non. The examination takes place I believe this term. Are you an admirer and supporter of King's College? What think you of the Marquis of Anglesea's return—or rather I should say dismissal? and what of that amazing production, the Duke's letter to Dr. Curtis? How goes High Toryism in the Union? It is in a very bad way here in the debating society, but at Commemoration in 1827, Peel was tremendously cheered and a partial shout for Canning met by an overwhelming proportion of hisses.

Gaskell came up here to be matriculated about ten days ago. He comes up as a gentleman commoner and will therefore have a smaller share of difficulty in getting rooms than poor Doyle. Gaskell expects to reside before the long vacation and talks of reading steadily here. The week before last I heard the new Bishop of Chester preach in Liverpool, and I was not then more inclined than I had previously been to acquiesce in your sentence against him of total unfitness for his office. If I might propose another reading it would be, to leave out the *un*. The anti-Catholics seem up in Devonshire—how do you like having the mob with you? Please remind Hallam if you see him soon that he is in my debt.

Farr to Gladstone, Cambridge, 14 February 1829; ADD.MS 44352, ff. 104–105.

Farr to Gladstone, Cambridge, 6 May 1829; ADD.MS 44352, ff. 118–119.

Farr to Gladstone, Iford, 15 October 1829; ADD.MS 44352, ff. 135–136.

Christ Church, Tuesday night, November 17, 1829 I allege to my conscience as an excuse for not having written to you sooner my knowledge that my place as a correspondent has been better supplied by Gaskell, who told me he had written to you, and I suppose by Doyle, who told me he meant to do so. We have not had much that could be interesting to you going on in the debating society. The week after you passed through Oxford we had a much better debate than that you heard, on the affairs of Portugal—it was carried against the Ministers by a very small majority—and I think had the question been put on the ground of our obligation to go to war, which Doyle and Gaskell maintained, on behalf of the young queen, they would certainly have lost it, the acts of interference, bearing at least the semblance of favour to the usurper, turning the scale. At least I think this was the state of feeling. However we have had some stir in our private business. The week before last a man named Maurice of Merton brought forward a motion that the *Sporting Magazine* be taken in, which excited an animated debate and a tremendous uproar. It was lost but only by a small majority, the numbers being 46 to 38. Since that time the opposite party have been canvassing actively, and notice has been given of a repetition of the same motion, the Society's laws admitting of a change of decision once within the term. The discussion was to have come on next Thursday night, but in consequence of a Woodstock ball at which some of our senators wish to kick their heels on that evening it has been postponed till Thursday the 26th. They are in great glee and expect to carry it, but it will not be without some struggle. The main objection raised against it has been, that our Society is purely literary and political, and has nothing to do with any publication further than as it conduces to the objects the attainment of which is proposed in these terms. Perhaps you may have heard that we are to discuss on that night the comparative merits of Lord Byron and Shelley. Doyle opens the question. It appears probable that Hallam, Milnes, and Sunderland, will come down to support the cause of the latter of the two. We do not hear of much speaking in favour of Lord Byron yet, but when we come to the 'dumb eloquence of votes' I suppose there is very little doubt that he will carry it by an immense majority. If I vote at all, I am inclined I think at present to Shelley. The interest excited about the *Sporting Magazine* is however so great that it will contribute I should think very greatly to shorten the debate. All the hunting men who will make their appearance in the room on that occasion, many probably for the first time, will listen I should think with little interest and less patience to a discussion so abstract as it is likely to be.

With reference to the matter of your last letter, I entirely agree with you as to the ultimate *identity*, or at least coincidence, of justice and expediency: but frequently they appear for a time disunited, and if present circumstances are unfavourable, and consequently inexpediency charged upon your measure, it is well to be able to allege that it was advocated not because it was expedient and therefore just, but because it was just and therefore expedient. I augur well, on the whole, from the resolutions of the Cork meeting, because if they have no other good effect I think they will at least supply an additional stimulus to activity on the part of the clergy. I am very sorry to hear of any clergyman who in the letter or spirit of his sermon commends 'Lord I thank thee etc' more than 'Lord be merciful to me a sinner'. I could not imagine any more unequivocal proof that a person was either an extremely foolish or a bad man. The very basis of all religion as it seems to me is this same 'Lord be merciful to me a sinner': an earnest and humble prayer for mercy, rested on no grounds whatever excepting our lamentable, God knows most lamentable, need, and the abundance of those means which his unbought favour towards us has provided. If as I am given to understand from the phraseology of your letter you so fully acquiesce in and applaud this as the foundation of all true religion by whatever name it may be called, I am happy to think that we are at least united and agreed in our theory of the fundamental condition of Christianity. I am astonished to hear that the Bishop of Winchester should have given money for the erection of an independent chapel; still more astonished that he should have refused it for a church. I hear, and that from persons not likely to be prejudiced in his favour, I think, that he gives away an immense proportion of his revenues—but to the manner of his promotion I must with you object. Ecclesiastical patronage has always appeared to me to be a very difficult subject. I think Huskisson will join the Administration before long. Your reading for [a] degree I hope has begun and prospers. Doyle and Gaskell—I cannot say do—but I have no doubt would if they knew I was writing, desire to be remembered.

Farr to Gladstone, Cambridge, 19 November 1829; ADD.MS 44352, ff. 139–140.

Farr to Gladstone, Cambridge, 1 January 1830; ADD.MS 44352, ff. 143–144.

Reading room, Oxford, Thursday, February 4, 1830 I had hoped to address you before this time, and I can assure you that my letter would have

followed the receipt of your paper more speedily, had I not been unwell
at the time it reached me. Doubtless it says much for you in one point
of view, that you should have taken so high a degree with what I presume I may fairly call a minimum of labour: but I must confess I think
it says much against you in another. The question naturally suggests
itself—if so little exertion, following such a college life, has done well,
how much more would a proportion of exertion better suited to the
prospects and opportunities of the party concerned have effected? In a
word my dear Farr I shall use the plainness of a friend in telling you that
while what you have now done bears testimony to those powers the
existence of which has never been for a moment doubted by any of your
friends; and while I would not remind your pride however that those
who do not know you will judge of you by your degree, and so judging
will assign you a much lower place than that which you ought to occupy:
yet I do desire to remind your sense of duty and of obligations as a
responsible being, that you have not done what God enabled you to do,
and you have not made a full use of those high and excellent abilities
for the employment of each and all of which you must answer before his
judgment seat. I do not know whether you will think a strain like this
inappropriate at the present moment, or absurd at any—unkind I
believe you will not suppose it: and the truth simply is that I could not
bring myself to utter the language of congratulation where, were these
the requisite view of matters on your part, I should think that of con-
dolence more applicable. I think you have more cause to regret that
having had such means and opportunities given you you have not done
more, than to rejoice that after so long continued a neglect of those
means and opportunities you have done so much. Perhaps however now
that you are freed from the shackles and trammels of college discipline
and college reading (for they have often power enough to annoy those
whom they cannot subjugate) that you will find some line of occupation
in which you will do yourself and your obligations more justice.

Last week Sir John Hanmer brought forward a motion which had for
its support to declare that the purity and independence of Parliament
was now better secured than it *would be under any* system of reform: this
seemed very strong as entirely denying the possibility of improvement:
Hanmer however withdrew it and a general anti-reform resolution was
carried by seventy-three to three! and this in a society where last year
the reformers had a decided majority. Tonight we are to have a motion
declaring the American government unstable and not suited to the

exigencies of a powerful nation—how it will be carried I do not know. Next Thursday we have a motion applauding the conduct of Mr. Fox and his friends on the treason and sedition bills—which I should think would be thrown out. After that comes a somewhat paradoxical dictum, 'that cheap justice is a national evil'. Gaskell wants to get elected President—he would fill the chair well and I dare say he will succeed. He does not however speak here so well as he did at Eton.

What do you think of the present condition of the Government and country? I do not like the Administration, which I think comprises no great share either of political or public principle: yet I think that they have some common sense and want in a straightforward way to keep the country afloat. I should like to see an Administration acting on higher principles. I wonder, who will be the new bishop. We have lost two of our eight canons within the last week—Dr. Hay (a great anti-Catholic) and Dr. Pitt, who was Mr. Canning's tutor and had a bishopric offered him on the occasion of his death. It is to be hoped their change has been a happy one and may we be ready when our appointed time shall come.

Farr to Gladstone, Iford, 12 February 1830; ADD.MS 44352, ff. 147–148.

Farr to Gladstone, 13 G.eat James Street, Bedford Row, London, 29 April 1830; ADD.MS 44352, ff. 151–152.

Oxford, Wednesday, June 2, 1830 On referring to your last letter I see that you charge me in it, and I fear but too truly, with being then in your debt. If however I were even then not free from blame I scarcely know how I dare write to you at all now. I have only to allege by way of excuse that occupations crowd thickly upon one, and although I am well aware that there is nothing in mine which would or ought to prevent any person blessed with regular habits of industry from doing his duty to his correspondents, yet I find they are sufficient not only to make *me* offend in that particular, but to come off but ill themselves—for they are but very inefficiently performed. You may perhaps laugh at my complaining of idleness—all Etonians will be lenient judges on such subjects—but the simple fact is that my industry was precisely of that mediocre character which rose somewhat above the standard of the general indolence there prevalent, but which unhappily falls far below that which is here considered requisite to reading for honours, at least to reading for them with any tolerable chance of success—especially as

I am anxious to go up at the very earliest time at which the statutes will permit me to do so—namely next Easter. However I must confess that giving you this long prose about myself is but a poor compensation, it may rather be called a considerable aggravation of my offence. I only left London a day or two before you got there as I was sorry to find by your letter. During the vacation I remained there but saw little of what was going on. I take it for granted that by this time you will have returned to Iford, to which place I shall therefore direct my letter. What do you think of the article in the *Edinburgh Review* on Eton? I confess with shame that there is too much truth in it—one part however I entirely dissent from—namely that about fagging which I consider to be one of the most salutary portions of the system—do not you agree with me? It is rather too much to conclude that the assistant masters have abundant leisure because Hawtrey who works nearly through the twenty-four hours found time to compile an atlas. On the whole however it seems to be the general opinion that the blow is not undeserved. But all alterations would be required to be introduced by a hand at once bold, delicate, and skilful, for if they went to work in the way these hard headed Scotchmen would have them I suspect they would speedily divest Eton of the main merit she has now—that of imbuing her children with a really classical taste and a perception of the spirit of ancient literature. I hope much may be done, especially as regards religious instruction—where something has been effected, thanks to the Duke of Newcastle. You will see that Lord Eldon has expended his testimonial money in founding a law scholarship here—very honourably to him I think. I should have liked much to go down to Eton as you proposed but time I fear would not allow. Gaskell is also very busy now, reading for his little go. Hallam has printed some poems (but not published them) which I think display uncommon talent though with one or two quite *minor* faults if I may be permitted to say so, of taste. Alfred Tennyson's are either out, or just about to make their appearance. We had the question of Jewish emancipation here a little while ago—and it was carried against them by 55 to 16. Gaskell spoke for them remarkably well. I do not know which way you are but should guess for them. We have questions put down against the Ministry, which is very unpopular here—they will probably come on in the beginning of next term—though it has been suggested that it is hard on the poor Duke to keep them suspended over his head through the whole vacation. I hope you liked the London Union, or Debating Society. As you ask me about

Manchester etc I reply albeit ill qualified and not even positive, contrary to my usual habits. I do not wish to see the numbers of the House increased for their sake. Again I ask pardon for my delinquencies and ever am most sincerely yours.

Farr to Gladstone, London, 22 June 1830; ADD.MS 44352, ff. 153–154.

Oxford, Monday, July 5, 1830 You will be surprised at my answering your last letter so soon, especially as I fear I have little to communicate: but the fact is that I wish to put myself into the good graces of all my correspondents as I am going to read at Cuddesdon, near Wheatley, about six miles from Oxford, all this long vacation so that I have little prospect, if at least my exertions in the reading line are at all what they ought to be, of keeping up correspondence with much diligence or regularity. I have been stealing (alack aday that one should be obliged to apply such a term to such an act) a matter of ten days vacation from my long vacation and have just returned from home to set to work. I suppose if I were in good 'condition' for my campaign I ought to have come up to the scratch with a large extra share of health and spirits, requiring a little Aristotle and mathematics to take me down. I lament however to say that the contrary of all this is the case—and I never did anything with a more wretchedly bad grace than bringing myself away from home. Opening my first book at Cuddesdon will however in all probability exceed this if anything can. My direction is Cuddesdon, near Wheatley, Oxfordshire. Gaskell is gone down into Yorkshire and threatens Thucydides mightily, but I do not think his exploits in that way will be great and if I were Thucydides I should not be much afraid of him. Doyle is coming up here to read till the middle of September— a very meritorious act for a person of his propensities. He is to have for a private tutor a very extraordinary man named Newman, who took about the most splendid double ever known here—his mathematics were so good that the examiners made him a present of books, though contrary to all rule (the Oxford constitutional principle being that all first classes are equal) and without precedent. He is going out as a missionary in October next, as he desires much to become a clergyman but has scruples about entering the Church in England on account I believe of his opinions about baptismal regenerations. I hear that when they are ordained as missionaries they are not required to declare their 'assent and consent'. This I think is very honourable to him. His case is almost an exact parallel to that of Henry Martyn. I trust his end may not be the same. Hallam's poems are not indeed in every place comprehensible, at least not to me, but I do not think it would be fair to call them obscure and I do think that they have uncommon merit. Tennyson's I am told are published. What do you think of the new King and the decrepid Ministry of the Duke? We are to have for our first question next term his foreign policy—and for our third the merits of his Administration in toto. Do you think you shall honour us with your presence at either of these debates? Both are expected to be carried by decided majorities against the Government. Their conduct on the measures which they have themselves introduced this session has been anything but dignified —neither law, spirits, nor sugar seem to be within their calibre. I am glad you have heard Chalmers. He must be magnificent indeed if he not only surpasses but eclipses Benson.

Farr to Gladstone, Iford, 10 August 1830; ADD.MS 44352, ff. 160–161

Oxford, Monday, September 13, 1830 I am afraid you have for some time been inclined to abuse me for negligence in performing the duties of a correspondent, and that you will now think instead of taking pity on a country gentleman in August I am rendering a tard[y] justice in September. But indeed I should not now have been sending you these hurried lines had I not been desirous of assuring you that it was not want of will that kept me from writing, but really the physical difficulties of keeping up that constant fire of letters to which I was in old times accustomed, together with the unintermitted succession of reading to which I have at last been compelled to resort. When ten or twelve hours a day have been spent in reading you will easily believe that sleep, meals, and exercise leave but a small fragment of the remainder of the twenty-four to be devoted to these duties. To this cause I hope you will attribute my past and I fear I must add my future intervals of silence. I never tried any really hard work before this long vacation, any thing I mean calculated to interfere materially with the pursuance of my own pleasure. I find it at times intolerably irksome but it gets lighter as I go on and perhaps my being so extremely indisposed to it only proves the necessity which existed of this or some similar discipline for my mind.

Gaskell has been accompanying Lord Morpeth on his canvass in the West Riding and proposed at Wakefield. We are to have some debates

about the Duke of Wellington at the beginning of next term. I have got
a motion against the Administration in general to bring forward. How
such a motion will be received I know not. I agree with you in looking
on the French Revolution with very mixed feelings—whether good or
evil may eventually come out of the present vast struggle on the Continent God only knows, but all see that it will be as Canning foretold, a
war of principles. I heard through the Bishop of Oxford of a letter from
Sir Arthur Paget who had been on board the ship where the ex-King was.
He told him that the ordinance had only accelerated the revolution by
a month for the plans of the liberals were all made—the Government
knew it—and thought the measures on which they ultimately ventured
were not indeed good or desirable but the last and only chance which
remained of checking the spirit which had gone abroad. I do think
however the French are entitled to the highest praises for their humanity
after the victory was gained. You will rejoice with me in the utter defeat
of the Government intrigues by the return of the two Grants for Inver-
nessshire and Norwich. Huskisson and the Duke are to meet at Liverpool
where they are to open the railway on Wednesday next.

One of my companions at Saunders's is Hamilton who was the elder
of the two at Holt's; he is a very clever man and goes up next time—expected to get his class—he was a pupil of Arnold's, now headmaster of
Rugby, who is a most superior man. Should you see his sermons look
at them and blame me if you do not find them worth the trouble.

I sincerely apologise for being obliged to write so hurriedly to you.

Farr to Gladstone, Iford, 17 October 1830; ADD.MS 44352, ff. 165–166.

Farr to Gladstone, Society Room, Eton College, 19 February 1831; ADD.MS
44352, ff. 181–182.

Farr to Gladstone, Regency Square, Brighton, 4 April 1831; ADD.MS 44352,
ff. 186–187.

Farr to Gladstone, Iford, 3 August 1832; ADD.MS 44352, ff. 233–234.

Leamington, Friday, December 21 [1832] I would have sent you an early
account of the result of our Newark election, had I been able to adorn
it with a frank, but as franks only began yesterday, I thought it might
as well be left to the newspaper announcements which are as speedy as
letters.

Our contest was most satisfactory throughout. In the first place, the return of a Member on the Duke's interest was the work of the people themselves exclusively: in the next, they have kept their hands clean as to means: and lastly, we took the lead during the first hour's polling, and kept it throughout. Our majority over Handley would have been considerably greater, had it been required—but our friends chose to bring him in, as preferring him to Wilde. My brother whom you may remember at Eton is also come in for Portarlington in Ireland.

But, agreeable as it is to enter Parliament in company with a large number of contemporaries and friends, it is very appalling to contemplate the results of the elections generally. I am sadly dismayed at those for Hampshire, where I thought you would at least have been strong enough to secure half the seats, inasmuch as the country is (is it not?) wholly agricultural. But we must leave the issue θεῶν ἐν γούνασι [1]—the human means prepared for the defence of our institutions are slender indeed.

I do not think the currency will become the engrossing question *yet* —because the Ministers, being themselves divided upon it, will not wish it to become so, and they will, I think, until the reform fever shall have been wholly dissipated, have power enough to determine *what* shall be the engrossing questions.

It were now perhaps folly to hope that, unless indeed some wholly unforeseen combination of circumstances should arise, the constitution can be preserved. The Dutch war might do it—the King might perhaps do it—one thing I believe would do it, and that is, the adoption of a broad national and Christian policy by the Conservative party—but how can this be expected, on a scale large enough to produce any powerful immediate results?

Lord Henley's conduct in retiring from Middlesex *seems* monstrous. We live in strange times, when *his* is called a mock reform.

Please write to me here when you can find time, and tell me more of what you are about.

Farr to Gladstone, Iford, 24 December 1832; ADD.MS 44353, ff 26–27.

No further correspondence has survived except one letter from Gladstone to Farr, Fasque, 30 October 1840 (ADD.MS 44357, f. 183), about Lord Lyttelton's candidature for High Steward of Cambridge University. It is docketed by Gladstone: 'Manqué and returned'.

---

[1] 'On the knees of the gods'.

APPENDIX 2

GLADSTONE'S CORRESPONDENCE WITH HIS FATHER ABOUT A CHOICE OF CAREER, 1830–1832

The following letters from Gladstone to his father deal with the choice of a career: 4 August 1830 (Morley, *Life of Gladstone*, i. 635-640); 29 August 1830 (D. C. Lathbury, *Correspondence on Church and Religion of William Ewart Gladstone*, ii. 223–226); 7 January 1832; 25 June 1832 (Lathbury, ii. 228). The original of the letter of 7 January 1832 has not been found, and the following is printed from Gladstone's draft in the Hawarden MSS.

Docketed: Very private and personal
          1830–5
          1832 January 7–16
          Draught of a letter to my father—private.

My beloved father,

Almost eighteen months have now elapsed since any communication has been made from me to you on the subject of my future destination: and it appears now to be high time that, if possible, it should be considered once for all.

Although under the same roof with you, I have preferred the form of a letter, to communication by word of mouth, because it seemed that my thoughts might thus be more fully and clearly expressed, while at the same time opportunity would remain for any additional explanation: and likewise because they might thus best be submitted not only to your own and my dear mother's consideration, but also to the remainder of those who feel so kind and affectionate an interest in this question—my dear brothers and sister. Nor do I hesitate to intrude upon your attention in the midst of your constant occupations, for I would fain hope that what I have to say will not afford you any new cause of anxiety, or of protracted thought.

It indeed sometimes appears to me that this course of proceeding may seem to give the subject an undue and ridiculous degree of importance, or rather of pretension to importance: yet as I trust such is not the motive which dictates it, it has on the whole seemed advisable to adhere to it for the reasons above mentioned. And perhaps the *nature* of what I have to communicate may afford an additional justification.

The letter which you received in the last summer but one is pretty fresh in my memory, though unfortunately I have not the draught of it with me for reference: and the subject to which it related has been to me, from that time to this, one of much anxiety and of almost incessant consideration, under many changes of circumstances and in various frames of mind.

Those variations of mental temperature and, particularly, those changes of external circumstances, have materially affected the conclusion to which I then (taking advantage of that more than parental kindness which had allowed me so full and so undeserved a liberty of choice) proposed to come: while they have never once suggested to my mind a doubt of the soundness of the principles on which I conceived it was founded. But to explain myself more specifically.

What was then written, I wrote under impressions of my judgment, associated perhaps with a larger share of emotion than is ordinarily incidental to my mind, regarding the condition of human nature at large, and the obligations of duty imposed upon individuals thereby. These impressions were summarily to the following effect.

That, looking abroad upon the world and taking its standard of principle and practice, and comparing it with that laid down by God in the revelation of his will, I could not shut my eyes to the existence of a portentous discrepancy: indicating nothing less than a fundamental perversion of the high capacities of man from those ennobling purposes to which they were destined by his Creator.

That in this perversion lay the parent evil of all that is sorrowful and all that is odious in the condition of mankind: and that he, who was most efficaciously occupied in resisting this evil, was filling the largest and the noblest sphere of duty, which God had assigned to man.

Thus far at least my mind remains precisely as it was.

But that letter went further, and stated, that it appeared to me, that the profession of a clergyman afforded by far the best opportunities of coming up to this high standard of duty. That God in his mercy and compassion for our lost estate had provided in his own Son an ample and free deliverance from our sin and therefore from our sorrows: and that, conceding to other occupations, without any disparagement, their proper dignity and honour, yet when a *comparison* came to be instituted that of a clergyman must transcend them all, inasmuch as it immediately involved, and involved too as its very sum and substance, the declaration of this message of love to perishing fellow creatures.

It is *here* that my mind has been shaken by the events with which the time has continually teemed since last July twelvemonth. And yet not with reference to any of the *general* sentiments which are even here expressed. It still remains intellectually at least as true relatively to my mind, as it is *essentially* in the everlasting counsels of Providence, that men have forgotten Him who never forgot them: and as often as my own inclinations suggest more modified notions, the words of Scripture seem to ring with fearful clearness in my ears—'Love not the world, neither the things that are in the world: for the friendship of the world is enmity with God'. Not indeed the persons but the *spirit* of the world: and not the spirit of that world alone which is designated the world in opposition to the religious world: too often it may be seen that this is still the world after that sense in which Scripture denounces it.[1] Simply, by the 'world' I understand those native tendencies of every human heart, which make us forget the true aim of our being—to do the will of God—and erect in its place another and an alien purpose—to do our own will.

Nor am I more able now than I was then to deny, or to evade, the declaration of our Saviour—'Wide is the gate and broad is the way, that leadeth to destruction, and many there be that go in thereat.' Nor would I willingly forget that the purpose of God in his dispensations of power and love is simply to *restore* the fallen race among which we are numbered to the glories of their forfeited inheritance: and that in that unseen world which is indeed our permanent sphere of action, highest in the scale of existence and most like to the Creator Himself will be those who have most effectually wrought the work of that Creator in this world, and under the habitual influence of that work have in themselves been assimilated to its character, and so to the character of its author. For 'they that turn many to righteousness shall shine as the stars for ever and ever'.

The question then to be answered in the choice of a profession, by the humblest man as well as the most highly gifted (and this is of course my justification for going thus much into detail) is, 'how shall I best be enabled to do in my sphere and calling the will of Him whose property

---

[1] This sentence is written above and replaces the following: 'And I trust it will not be thought I am so narrow-minded as to understand by the "world", properly and exclusively that body of persons who are so designated in opposition to the "religious" world. If I look to the ordinary world or to the political world or to the religious world, I cannot help apprehending that each of these is still *the world* in too many cases, after that sense in which Scripture denounces it.'

I absolutely am, that will being the extirpation of sin and misery from the world?'

Now it seems to me true beyond all question that in every calling, and in every station, this will, or in other words, our duty, may be performed, for even if I seem to use overstrained language, I would not have it thought that I wish to convey any other idea than this, and the character of a man under the habitual discipline of an obedience cheerfully performed, may grow up into that likeness to its original image, which may fit it to be transplanted from hence unto another and better vineyard.

It remains to state by what means my mind has been wholly unsettled as to the belief I formerly entertained, that duty might be most extensively and effectually performed in the clerical profession.

It is not from any mitigation in the idea which then possessed me as to the mass of sin and misery in the world: on the contrary, what has since that time passed has gone to convince me that there is cause for deeper and truer sympathy with the condition and prospects of mankind than ever; and that it ought to be the desire and prayer of every heart to feel with them and for them in sincerity and truth. For I cannot help believing, from circumstances around me, that the human race, or at least the civilised world, is rapidly approaching its crisis: that no very great number of years will in their revolutions bring the time when the whole fabric of human society shall be rocked to its very foundations, and when everywhere it shall be put to the test whether the house is built upon the rock or upon the sand, amidst the fury of the tempest and the flood.

The substance of these impressions was set down in some sheets which have already passed under your eye—and they remain to me vivid and convincing, though I have been long persuaded that it would have been most unbecoming in a person of my youth and inexperience to make them public, and therefore have to render you my best thanks for preventing the publication of the pamphlet which contained them.

In brief, they are founded on the following notions.

That intercourse *with subordination* forms the essence of what we understand by 'society' in its largest sense.

That society is essential to human happiness, and the performance of individual duty in the world.

That society has hitherto been *mainly* maintained and bound together not by the purely legitimate principle of action—duty to the

Almighty—but by a class of human and *secondary* principles: attachments founded on interest, affection, sympathy, and all other motives which influence man and man in their mutual intercourse. I would instance particularly those of parent and child: of landlord and tenant: of master and servant. These and a variety of other connections extending from the highest persons in states to the lowest, and involving an authority on the one side, and a subordination and obedience on the other, have by their intertwinings as it were connected every individual and every class with those above them and below them and thus has been formed a pervading bond of union, under whose constraint, sometimes more and sometimes less gentle, the lower classes of different communities have been retained for the most part content in their station, and have acquiesced in a life of labour from which others were, to their apprehensions at least, exempted.

But now a new philosophy is spreading, and a kind of calculation of interests, which is from its very nature necessarily short-sighted, is in every one of these connections, gradually and silently taking place of those feelings of obedience and attachment under whose influence men had hitherto been content to act. The extirpation of the ancient principles of political union is avowedly aimed at: not, as it seems to me, with the design and desire of substituting any thing better, but of leaving the human race in a greater degree than ever subject to what has been from the first its greatest scourge, namely the action of its own ungoverned and uninstructed self-will: seeking to put power into all men's hands, without teaching them how it is to be used (for is it not their boast that 'knowledge is power'?) and thereby furnishing abundant means for the work of destruction, to which only power is necessary, but none for the work of reconstruction, for which wisdom is likewise requisite.

But these are views of an abstract character perhaps, or at least relating to circumstances which must at all events be remote. However it seems to me that we may see the road to them somewhat as follows. Through measures now pending in Parliament and indeed elsewhere too, to the confiscation of the property of the Church: hence to its destruction as an establishment: through the destruction of the Church establishment to the overthrow of our own kingly government (at least as far as its *substance* is concerned): through the overthrow of kingly government in this country to the degradation of its national character: and through the degradation of the British nation to wide and irremediable ruin through the world.

Not indeed that I am convinced that all these miseries are certainly to come to pass: I hope in God none of them. But I do believe that it is about these that the battle must be fought: that men of this age who love their fellow men, and would have them happy, must consider themselves as fighting not so much against this or that particular act as against a deep laid game now in progress, and a spirit whose spread is awfully wide and whose influence as subtle as destructive. All the current and accepted notions of the present day seem to me tending, with terrible efficacy, to *systematise* and fulfill that selfishness which has ever been the curse of human nature: from the eruptions of which and their evil consequences, no age or time has been exempt: yet which has been on the whole materially checked by the influence of institutions and those secondary principles which were above adverted to—principles in their own nature most excellent, but by the perverseness of human nature exalted from their legitimate and appointed state and made to usurp the throne and province of God himself, by being rendered the ruling and *primary* motives of human action.

Now if the wayward will of human nature, acting as it has done by fits and starts, has been found by a melancholy experience powerful enough to introduce the hideous forms of evil into this beautiful creation, to dash every man's cup with sorrow, and communicate to some an almost unalloyed and unmingled bitterness, what I ask will be its results, and how tremendously multiplied its power when it has gained all that additional efficacy which is the result of design and combination? We see that things are tending unless the danger be boldly met and resisted to that state in which no bond of moral obligation will be acknowledged except what is founded on perceptions of individual expediency: old sympathies are daily falling into disrepute: in public matters, no man is to obey any laws but those which he himself has made: in private, who can say that even filial relations are looked upon now as importing the same degree of obligation to obedience or the same kind of obligation, that they once were, if at least we may credit men who have lived in other times, or that the same laws of discipline exist.

At least I do not doubt its being universally acknowledged that society may expect convulsions, even if the final issue be favourable to the happiness of the human race (which God grant) such as it has never seen before—for the simple reason that powers are now called into action such as it has never known before. When was there the same degree of knowledge without wisdom diffused? When was there the same facility of intercourse and combination among the people? Whole nations are like one mass: and in proportion as they become so will they be liable to those violent movements which result from the electric power of passion, from the force which opinion though uninvestigated gathers, by the mere result of progress, in the rapidity of its passage: from the destruction of the influence of shame, known to diminish continually as the numbers in whose hands the power of action is lodged increase. When were the abstract rights of man to political power, so fatal to organised communities, so unblushingly advanced and so universally and readily applied? When was there in a great crisis more disunion and hesitation among those at whose hands resistance to the work of ruin is to be looked for? When, above all, had the will and passion of multitudes afforded to them such a channel for the expression of their tendencies and for the concentration of their forces upon any given point, as now by the action of the public press?

Nor can I omit to name among the evil symptoms of the times the latitudinarian tone which all public and national expressions of religion have assumed. Is it a light matter, to quote *one case* out of many, and merely by way of example that the British Parliament should have been told that the cases of infidel blasphemies in this country were exactly on a par with those of Indian missionaries who attacked the established religion in that country, and that this prodigious statement should have passed unanswered?

Believing as I do that a great conflict for all that constitutes the happiness of man is rapidly approaching, a conflict not for details but principles and elements hitherto almost unassailed never openly or systematically—I am compelled to give up all peaceful anticipations of the comparative calm and ease of a professional life in any department whatever. Professions themselves were but a part of a system: and now perhaps the whole is to be contended for.

Yet I admit that now as heretofore no station is without its obligations, its honours, and its rewards. In public and in private alike, by the performance of all individual duties, both public and private, and by the unhesitating avowal and defence of sound though now comparatively despised principles in religion, in politics, in education—every man may perform his work under the Providence of God, and so pass away into rest. To such performance may we all without scruple and without ostentation be devoted.

But if it be true that designs of evil against mankind are now in progress on a more general and comprehensive scale than heretofore, it would seem to follow that while all stations are still to be filled and every kind of duty discharged, they perhaps may not be the worst of all qualified for performing their part who are not confined to a particular post and functions of a technical nature.

If then we suppose it granted that it is well on the whole that there should be some individuals, particularly in the present time, who should not be occupied in a manner strictly professional, then I am free and happy to own, that my own desires as to my future destination are exactly coincident with yours insofar as I am acquainted with them—believing them to be a profession of the law with a view substantially to studying the constitutional branch of it, and on experiment as time and circumstances might offer on what is called public life.

But to be a public man in any time and more especially in our own, requires (and I trust you will give me credit for sincerity in what I say) a zeal, a consistency, and a soleness of religious principle, of which I seem to recognise more and more the very reverses in my own character and conduct: together with intellectual powers and habits as to my attainment of which I have not as yet any confidence whatever, nor any ground of expectation from anything that has hitherto passed: for how many utter failures have there been under circumstances not only more promising, but more promising beyond all comparison? And therefore I trust that if any such plan, in conformity with your wishes, should now be put into execution—it might be with the understanding that in case it seemed impossible either to attain what is called success, or to uphold that tone of moral practice without which no success ought to be satisfactory, I might read the will of Providence in the lesson thus taught to a craving ambition, and seek a humbler and a safer walk of life.

So far as I individually am concerned, such an arrangement would meet all my wishes—and yet not so much because I flatter myself that I see my way through it, and feel treading on very sure ground, as because, the time being arrived when it is fit to do something, such a course seems on the whole most suitable and right: and because any steps taken in it seem easily revocable, should future circumstances seem to indicate an unfitness either in me for the condition, or in the condition for me: and I scarcely fear desiring a change on any other ground. And a strong general reason which influences me in relinquishing the desire of further delay is, that though I am by no means assured of the rectitude of my desires now, yet I do not see ground to expect that a further lapse of time would remove that degree of hesitation which I entertain.

If it be so, I trust that I have before me already ample material for study and work ready to my hands. Doubtless, such a disposition of time, without actual practice at the bar, would involve a sacrifice as to the prospects of emolument: but I trust that it would not bring with it any considerable occasions of expense: and that the scale of my individual wants, fostered though they may have been by liberality and indulgence, is not likely to be materially or rapidly enlarged.

And now may I [be] permitted to commend the consideration *and the decision* (for I dare not avail myself of so much liberty as you would give) of this matter to my parents? And in a matter of no small import, to me by necessity, to you by affection, may I not pray for the direction of God in devising and His blessing in executing, feeling as I am sure I ought to do from the evidence of facts, my own utter blindness and total incompetency either to discern or to pursue the line of duty in such a case—and being firmly persuaded, that under that supreme guidance, the question if lodged as above will be lodged in the best hands.

Nor am I apprehensive of *fundamental* error in the general principles which have been expressed in this letter—nor can I discern any absolute impropriety in the tone it adopts as to matters of religion, and the creed it professes—though I might indeed deeply blush, when called upon to show any traces of correspondence between so high a creed and so low a practice as mine. And yet I dare not on this account alter it, for the legitimate influence surely is, not to lower the creed, but to exalt the standard of daily conduct.

One word more and I have done. You may perhaps find much strangeness and perplexity in this letter, and much indistinctness of thought and reasoning: but of one thing I am sure, that it has not been owing to any desire on my part to hold back the most secret desire of my heart on this subject: such symptoms must be taken for a but too faithful transcript of difficulties existing within. Indeed it is my desire as I can say before God, to state all my thoughts, in such a place, and under such circumstances, just so that they may be made more clear and better known, if possible, to you than they are to me—and my [*word illegible*] object in going into this lengthened detail has been, not to influence immediately the minds of others, as though I were an advocate pleading a cause, but simply to give in as far as I was able a candid and a rational statement of those motives which have actuated my own.

APPENDIX 3

GLADSTONE'S ANTI-REFORM HANDBILLS OF 1831

People of England, REMEMBER!

The present Ministers are the men who voted *for* the address of 1830, stating that *slight and partial distress* existed in the country, *against* Sir Edward Knatchbull's amendment, stating that *severe and general distress* existed in the country.

People of England, remember!

The present Ministers are the men who voted *against* Mr. Davenport's motion last year for a committee to inquire into the causes of your distress.

Are they or their opponents most likely to administer practical relief? I say *practical* relief, for as to relief arising from TALK about liberty, the Ministers certainly beat them.

People of England, once more I say, REMEMBER!

These Ministers are the men who wished not to disfranchise *convicted Evesham*—but DARE NOT DIVIDE.
Who introduced the transfer stock duty, but DARE NOT DIVIDE.
Who introduced the timber duties and WERE BEATEN.
Who wished to give more Members to Ireland, and WERE BEATEN.

In a word: they have blundered at every step: they have failed in every measure they have brought forward: and they now seek to hide their incapacity, BY THROWING DUST IN YOUR EYES IN THE SHAPE OF PARLIAMENTARY REFORM.

GOD SAVE THE KING AND MEND THE MINISTERS!

People of England!

Your Parliament is dissolved, for having voted on Tuesday night that the Papists of Ireland should not be permitted to return a larger proportion of Members to Parliament, than that which was solemnly established at the Union between the two countries. We add no comment: nor is any needed. Do not for a moment believe it to be an act of your beloved King.

You are called on to exercise your suffrages in favour of men who wish to establish a NEW CONSTITUTION.

Before you vote, ask yourselves the following questions, and let no man

DIVERT YOUR ATTENTION FROM THEM.

1. What has *South America* gained by new constitutions? Confusion.
2. What has *France* gained by a new constitution? Disorganisation.
3. What has *Belgium* gained by a new constitution? Starvation.
4. What is 'Old England' to gain by a new constitution? and
5. What am *I* to gain by a new constitution?

Answer these for yourselves: vote for men who are solemnly pledged

1. To redress every grievance.
2. To remove every blemish.
3. TO RESIST REVOLUTION TO THE DEATH.

And may God send a happy issue!

Briton

Docketed by Gladstone: Strictly private. Draught of two handbills.

April 23, 1831.

ADD.MS 44721, ff. 20–21

APPENDIX 4

'TO VIOLETS
IN A VAUDOIS VALLEY'

MARCH 1832

Though couched beside the circling snow
I saw untroubled violets grow
Of odour soft and hue as deep
As where in balmy spring they sleep.
In the far Alpine vale imbreasted,
Through winter's dreariest months they rested,
Where some earthbank or shielding stone
Some unambitious nook and lone
Yea the stem pendent rocks did aid,
And the deep snow a shelter made,
To keep their shrinking fragile form
From the sharp wind and pelting storm.

O fragrant flowers of stainless hue,
Pleasant for perfume and for view,
Have ye no lesson for the heart,
Here dwelling, as ye dwell, apart
Where God had worship from his own
In temples unadorned and lone,
Pure worship of their prayers and tears,
Along a countless tale of years?

While yonder, on the sunny plain,
Stood many a huge and gorgeous fane,
Crowds on high marble altars gazed,
Tall solemn candles upward blazed,
And holy chant and incense rare,
Mingled and floated in the air,
Slow moving, that the people might
Taste all their sweetness and delight.

Here, by the *single* Word assured,
By bright temptation unallured,
A poorer simpler flock than they
Sought Heaven along a straighter way,
And offered at the Eternal Throne
A supplicating soul alone.

This people destitute and scorned,
These towers and temples unadorned,
Rested, as you ye violets, rest
In the far Alpine valley's breast,
And the deep snow and rugged rock,
That warns from you the tempest shock,
So guarded from the spoiler's rage
Their poor and peaceful heritage.

Nor such alone but deadlier foes
Were barred from their serene repose:
There was no native lust of pride
Upon the barren mountainside:
There was no wealth to tempt and win
The happy spirit into sin,
And virtue blossomed full and fair
In uncontaminated air.

16 September 1835
ADD.MS 44724, f. 51

APPENDIX 5

GLADSTONE'S CORRESPONDENCE WITH PEEL ABOUT HIS PROPOSED RESIGNATION IN 1842

Peel to Gladstone, Whitehall, 6 February 1842; ADD.MS 44275, f. 102
Will you be good enough to call here at half past eleven tomorrow on the subjects which we [have] been discussing yesterday, particularly that of flour, in relation to wheat, and the import of grain and flour from British colonies.
Docketed: Received 2½ p.m.

Gladstone to Peel, 13 Carlton House Terrace, 6 February 1842; ADD.MS 40469, ff. 156–157 (original), ADD.MS 44275, ff. 104–105 (draft)
With a view to diminishing as much as possible the annoyance which I most deeply regret to have caused you, I wish to lay summarily and clearly before you my view of the position in which I stand with respect to the corn scale.

Setting aside subsidiary causes, the root of the evil has been my misapprehension of the *capacity* in which I was called to attend your deliberations. I regarded myself as being there (and this I deemed a very high honour) to make myself useful, so far as I could, by giving information or suggestions to those who were to decide, and I never even remotely conceived that my assent or dissent would affect the proposition you were to make to the Cabinet, otherwise than as you might see force in the arguments which I presumed to urge. I do not discuss the justice of my impressions, but merely to state the fact.

My doubts upon the abstract question, how the scale will operate with respect to the relief of the *consumer* by the admission of foreign corn at lower prices than at present, will under the circumstances stated by you be kept so far as I am concerned profoundly secret. First, because of the extrinsic and some of them higher considerations which connect themselves with the immediate point of issue; secondly, because I see that the collateral regulations of your plan are in the nature of an actual good, that the diminution of duties is undeniably a diminution of certain of the evils at present felt, that it may also have the effect of introducing foreign corn at lower rates, that it is a step in the right direction, and one to be gained in concurrence with the feelings of the agricultural body, which I believe to be an essential element in the success of any such plan at the present time. If not therefore upon a deliberate approval of the scale in one aspect, yet upon a view of the whole case, I trust I may be enabled to give the measure an honourable and firm, or to use your own expression, a cordial support.

Peel to Gladstone, Whitehall, [6 February 1842]; ADD.MS 44275, f. 106

Since I wrote my first note I have been gratified by receiving your letter of today.

There are probably few persons who are not very much in the same position in which you are who would not (if their single voice could determine the question) modify the plan which I propose for the settlement of the corn question.

They consider, however, that alteration of the law is necessary, that the proposed alteration is an improvement, and they look to that point which must always be looked at by the members of a government, the prospect of carrying the measure they propose.

APPENDIX 6

'TWENTY-SEVEN PROPOSITIONS RELATING TO CURRENT QUESTIONS IN THEOLOGY'

Note The following fragment, which is bound with the autobiographica, appears to be from another statement of Gladstone's early religious beliefs, the remainder of which has been lost.

... here mention that, although I had known Dr. Pusey before my residence at Christ Church, in the days when it was the fashion to suspect him of rationalism, and although also, beginning with the Arians, I read several of Dr. Newman's works on their first appearance, I was not under any important theological influence at any time from the authors of the Tracts. The Prayer Book and then Palmer led me forward.

The course of the Oxford movement was prosperous on the whole, notwithstanding the storm justly raised by Froude's *Remains*, until the publication of Tract 90. It was then that the opposition began to be largely compact, broad, and solid. Reading the Tract at the time, I thought that at certain points (e.g., the argument on the fallibility of General Councils) it betrayed the existence of a sophistical element in the fine intellect of Newman. Apart from that, probably the opposition was grounded mainly not on deliberate or detailed objections to the interpretations but upon [a] general and rather blind aversion to the Roman Church. The principle of the Tract was sound: it was simply this, that in matters of religious controversy, among a variety of scales justly admirable, the one most favourable to concord ought to be adopted. But it was Newman's duty to have regard to the clouds on the horizon, already gathered in part by former imprudence, and to walk at every step with the utmost wariness.

I will now present in original the summary of religious beliefs and impressions which I drew up in 184[2] at a time when the controversy had anew been embittered by disputes concerning the doctrine of reserve, and by the excitement which from that source was imparted into the contest for the Poetry Professorship and the somewhat sectarian choice of Mr. Garbett.

Twenty-seven propositions relating to current questions in theology
W. E. G. 29 December 1842

ADD.MS 44731, ff. 44–56

I That Christ founded upon earth a perpetual visible Church: having a government and ordinances, which belong to a society as such: and having the essence of its unity, which is objective, in the identity of that government and those ordinances, and the proper subjective development of that unity in the universal and holy harmony of its parts.

II[1] Those ordinances were: (1) the preaching or declaration of the Word—by the Scriptures—by the Creeds—and by preaching properly so called and other authoritative teaching: and (2) the rites by which spiritual gifts are conveyed, particularly the two great and universal sacraments of union with Christ, Baptism and the Supper of the Lord.[2]

III To this society, acting according to its divine organisation, was attached the determinate dispensation of divine gifts upon earth in its ordinances; and also the general promise of the Spirit and of the indwelling presence of Christ belongs to its members.

IV Persons not in its communion are not to be covenant possessors of these blessings. But if the life of God be in them then they are actually possessors of them, although not through the known, appointed, and ordinary channels.

The gift of God to the Church does not tie His hands from giving in what way soever and to whom soever: but it deprives all, who are not partakers of that gift to the Church, of the title and pretension to impart that which they have not been authorised to impart, and seems to render their doing so to be in itself an act presumptuous and profane.

V In Baptism, duly ministered and not hindered from within, sin is pardoned and a new root of life implanted: not merely an impulse but continuous: not merely a change of state but of being.

---

[1] Article XIX [WEG].
[2] μαθητέμειν written opposite, i.e., 'to instruct' or 'to convert'.

VI Faith, or the belief of the truth, uniting the rational, percipient man as such to the truth, is the medium through which[1] he becomes a qualified subject of Baptism and all other spiritual blessings.

I can say conscientiously that we are justified by faith: but to say that faith justifies seems hazardous: it does not appear how faith is active in justification.

They that most insist upon the naked dogma of justification by faith, oftentimes most undermine it. For they are apt to give definitions of faith which make it in itself a moral quality and in itself a *work* as much as the outward acts that flow from such qualities.

VII In the Supper of the Lord are given, taken, and eaten, not carnally but sacramentally, in an heavenly and spiritual manner, the Body and Blood of Christ. Yet as Gelasius saith, the bread and the wine remain in their own nature: and on the other hand the Lord's Body and Blood are not figuratively but really present.

VIII The argument of Rome that under each species is contained the Body as well as the Blood: and the argument against Rome that the Lord's Body cannot be in two places at once seem to me incompetent arguments; rationalistic and irrational.

Transubstantiation, a definition in itself uncertain at the least: seemingly opposed to the truth of the nature of the elements: perhaps rationalistic, as limiting and tending to carnalise, our Lord's revelation: intolerable, when imposed as the normal and exclusive idea of the Lord's Supper: perilous in the way it is held by the Roman Church, as leading to idolatry.

A certain latitude seems to have prevailed in primitive belief as to the Eucharist. At the least a real and effective participation of the Lord's Body and Blood requires to be believed: but as to the mode of their presence in the elements, it can only be defined as supersensual.

IX I know not how the thank offering of the Eucharist hath any special gift of benefit except to those who take part in the offering: further than as the prayers of the faithful may be beneficial to others than those who put them up[2], which is not determinately nor sacramentally.

---

[1] δι'ῆς written opposite, i.e., 'through which'.

[2] only as the Eucharist may be considered as the very highest form of impe[ne]tration. W.E.G. December 29, 1844.

X   The rest and felicity of the dead in Christ may consist in some form or other with purgation in the intermediate state.

I do not know if it be absolutely against the doctrine of the Anglican Church, if a man should hold that such purgation might be not entirely without pain. There are pains in this life which are wholly subdued into, and which even form the ground of, an absorbing sense of joy: and these, I think, both of mind and body.

XI   This rest and felicity, if it admit purgation, seems to require progression.

The law of habit involves progression: and it is the law of our whole nature. The burden of proof is with those who would contend that it does not apply to the dead: and I know not how they are to bring such proof.

Again, the holy dead are part of the Church of Christ: yea, the greatest and most glorious part. It seems therefore that we must have sympathies with them: and it is presumable that we should pray for them. Again the burden of proof lies with the opponents of prayers for the dead: and I know not how it is to be found.

But again all this applies to the dead in Christ: and I know not what authority there is either to predicate *positively* of an individual soul that it is asleep in Christ: or yet further under the title of a saint to prefer it beyond the common lot of the holy departed.

If this be so then no prayer for individuals who have departed is warranted, unless conditioned by their having died in Christ, which we may not treat as certain.

XII   Those who say, we should not invocate saints or angels *because they cannot hear us*, seem to me to speak what is arbitrary and an assumption beyond our knowledge. The difficulty of hearing is a condition of space and matter, according to the laws of this present state: who knows that saints and angels are subject to any laws of space and matter, or if to any whether to the same as we are, or if not the same whether to laws which limit hearing and perception? The burden of proof lies with those, it seems, who say angels and saints generally cannot hear, *and* with those too who say the reverse: I know not how either can give proof: so that if the latter make any address whatever it must be *conditioned*, because the point seems to be indeterminate.

XIII Presuming it thus conditioned—what may without sin be asked of saints and angels? Surely not more than their prayers and aid in the same manner as from fellow creatures upon earth, with feelings the same in kind though with a proportionably and duly enhanced respect and veneration.

The Church of England has stopped her teaching which is public and authoritative at a point short of what is here indicated. (If these be the limits of what is allowable on prayers for the dead, and on invocation, yet it does not seem that the same things are necessary: and in recommending or using them, their past and present relation to neighbouring corruptions will behove to be remembered.

At the least, however, we may learn what we may not condemn.)

XIV So in the honouring of images. How is it possible to do otherwise than honour them? To use them as memorials is in idea a thing wholly and broadly distinct from that of worshipping the beings they represent, far more from that of worshipping themselves. It does not appear why an individual should not employ images as sacred tokens to awaken and assist him—provided

1. they be not images of Him Who may not be represented in an image;

2. the due relations be maintained between the several feelings suitable to those represented, that is to say to the Redeemer and to creatures;

3. the doctrine be repudiated that the same honour is to be to the image and to the person whose image it is;

4. no virtue of life be ascribed directly or indirectly to an image;

5. the brethren be not scandalised.

XV That it is exceedingly to be desired that the practice of open penance for open sin should be restored.

That we have great need of confession to one another for the relief of consciences and for spiritual help.

That especially, confession to priests, free communication with them on the direction of the conscience and life, the receiving of their advice and of absolution in cases such as the Church has indicated, might be used with benefit, provided this were always viewed as secondary and subsidiary to the primitive and public system of penance, it seeming to be more suited to subtler sins and to certain classes of minds: and provided the doctrine of compulsory auricular confession be avoided.

XVI   That in the Reformation of the Church of England and her subsequent history as connected therewith there are particulars to be regretted, as
    (a) the alterations of the communion in the second Prayer Book of Edward VI;
    (b) the occasional usurpations of the Sovereign—the indistinctness of some upon the limits of temporal and spiritual power—the severity of the penal laws which grew much out of the view of the ecclesiastical supremacy of the Crown:
    (c) the personal leanings of certain of the reformers, and the general heat against the Church of Rome, though scarcely less unavoidable than lamentable;
    (d) the loss of ascetic institutions;
    (e) the disparagement of the symbolical principle in worship;
    (f) above all, the disruption of communion and of hearts in Christendom: but this [is] a misfortune of which if there be blame, I dare not fix it.

XVII   That notwithstanding the Reformation was a signal blessing: and that it hath laid a ground for us, from which is cleared away whatever religious corruption had grown up—of which the lines and foundations are truly Catholic and primitive—upon which what lacketh may well be restored—and wherein the restorations needed are developments and not corrections of the spirit of the Church. The Church, however, seems to have left it free to her children to hold their own opinions this way or that upon the events of the Reformation.

XVIII   That cultivating thankfulness for our Reformation and a pious esteem of its instruments, we should imitate them least in that which was the result of circumstances and of human infirmities, and should cherish to the uttermost
a. our descent from and association with the ancient course of the Church from the beginning;
b. our brotherhood with all Churches of the world, though now unhappily we be separated.
Nor need we on this account undervalue community of faith or love,

or of particular doctrines, with those who have lost hold of the visible constitution of the Church.

But we have to guard against the insular feeling: and to draw our pedigree from beyond Henry VIII.

(I deplore the temper[1] towards the Reformers, towards the Reformation, and towards the name of Protestantism, of some whose *positive* teaching I admit to be eminently Christian and with whom I allow that Catholic is a far higher name, only I should say not incompatible.)

XIX   Idolatry seems to be tolerated in the present Church of Rome: but so is heresy, as in the denial of the visible Church and of the Sacraments, endured in the Church of England. (I mean of all life and power of the Sacraments, not of the outward part or visible sign.)

It may be said, however, that there is a more lively and continued protest in the Church of England against heresy than in the Church of Rome against idolatry. Likewise that her own witness is distinctly against it. As also that she is free from infinite abuses connected with purgatory, penances, and indulgences. And that she does not stint the word of God.

Upon the other hand the Church of Rome does more for the ascetic life, the doctrine of evangelical counsels, and the way of perfection.

I am not to compare them, but to be thankful beyond measure to be where I am.

XX   But the foregoing general view introduces a position which seems to me according to truth: viz. that great as are the evils in the Church of Rome, frightful and horrible as are the corruptions and idolatries which she endures, yet the abomination of desolation within the holy place doth not make the place unholy, the Spirit of God yet abides in her and I know nothing that ought to prevent our restoring communion with her on our side, provided she demanded of us no condition contrary to our conscience of the Truth.

XXI   More clearly then is it to be desired that our communion should be restored with the Greek Churches and others holding the Apostolic Faith. As well as that Protestant Societies generally should be reunited to us and to them, for the glory of the Redeemer and the conversion of the world.

---

1 See infra n. XXV [WEG].

XXII   That Holy Scripture is commonly clear for the purposes of practical religion to the single-minded and devout: and that where doubts have been raised as to its interpretation, those doubts so far as they concern matter of faith are sufficiently solved by the consent and witness of the Catholic Church: and that it is highly irrational and presumptuous in the individual to prefer his own construction to her's.

XXIII   That it is, however, of great importance that the line which the Church has drawn between matter of faith and matter of pious or probable opinion, and the limits thus defined for the liberty of the Christian be carefully guarded against encroachment on the part of those who moved by zeal or prejudice strive to enlarge continually the number of articles necessary to be believed by the intrusion of secondary or even of untrue notions.

XXIV   That we must be careful not to pride ourselves upon the simple fact of being in a theological mean between Romanism and latitudinarianism. That theological truth is often in a mean but not always or essentially: and that at all events the habit of contemplating it as a certain quantity, neither too much nor too little, is adverse to a true appreciation of its authority and its searching power neither of which are of a nature in any way restricted by measure: and is in fact a common and subtle form of accommodation to the spirit of the world and the flesh.

XXV   That while Protestantism in some mouths means the wantonness of private caprice, and never can compete, inasmuch as it is properly negative, with Catholicism, as a term designative of the true character of Christianity, yet
a. it has its own honour in that negative signification as a repudiation of what deserves to be repudiated, and
b. further it is in the minds of millions the traditional symbol of a positive, nay more of a Catholic, belief, so that to assail that which it indicates in them is to unsettle, by an incautious use of words, their Christianity itself.

XXVI   That we must hope to see a gradual progression in restoring the discipline, in adorning and so spiritualising the rites and worship, and in clearly and sharply defining the Catholic doctrines of the Church as well as in enlarging her borders: but that the elements within her which verge towards Protestantism more than towards Catholicism ought to be tenderly and gently dealt with, so that they may be repressed or modified or absorbed, not by substantive effort for the purpose, so much as by a genial development of the spirit and purposes of the Church herself; in order that they may stand or fall according to that test and not according to the humours of any particular class or time.

XXVII   That we have among us a school of divinity, represented mainly by the *British Critic,* which is become morbid in its views of the Roman Church and of the English Reformation; unable to see evil in the former or good in the latter. That the habit of discovering evil in the former or of fixing attention upon it is indeed for the individual a dangerous one but for teachers in a Church a sad necessity. If, however, it be excusable to overlook much in that kind, it is so much the more blameworthy to apply in a narrow, captious, or severe temper to the review of the deeds of our own immediate spiritual ancestry. This school is now so pronounced in its leanings towards Rome as such, that one would think it can hardly have a succession in the English Church: that it consists of individuals, and cannot be perpetuated in its present form: that it must come after a short time to be either less or more Roman than it is at this moment. That it is, however, as excellent in its faith, its devotion, its courage, its exhibition of the worship of God to the world in the beauty of holiness, its self-denial, its diligence and learning, its deep and tender tone of thought, that it were indeed most deeply to be lamented, if by a departure from the doctrine of the Church of England, or by the intolerance of any of their brethren, they should be driven out of its pale.

I have on this my birthday put down hastily the foregoing propositions, as a simple transfer to paper of the ordinary impressions upon my mind at the present time upon the great subjects now agitated among us. The spirits of most men seem to be more or less in motion with respect to them. I wish to have the means of measuring this motion in myself at a future time. For this reason I have arrested in this record the impressions of the time. I trust they may not be unstable. They have not been received by any violent or sudden process. Had I endeavoured to make them elaborate, they would hardly have secured their purpose as a simple representation.

They are stated categorically: but of course in so far as what they embrace is not matter of Christian faith,[1] they are held subject to correction by the judgment of the Church, as well as by any accession to my own mind of light or knowledge.

May God rule and overrule all to His glory.

W. E. G. December 29, 1842.
Perused in January 1844.
Re-perused on December 29, 1844.
And not again till August 13, 1888.

On re-perusing these memoranda after 44 years, I find nothing to demand change in what relates to positive belief.

In Proposition III the position of non-Anglican Protestants is crudely and hardily dealt with. The subject demands fuller, more circumspect, and more genial treatment.

In the autumn of 1845, visiting Munich for a domestic reason, I called on Dr. Döllinger whom I only knew of as the most distinguished Roman theologian of the country, or indeed of the generation (as I imagine his predecessor, Möhler, had been before him). He opened (I think) his own door in Von der Turn Strasse, and when I gave my name he said, to my surprise, 'Are you the distinguished statesman of that name?' I passed six days in Munich, much in his society: and I find recorded interviews of three and five hours, such was his bounty. It was a great stage in my religious education (posterior by nearly three years to the writing of these twenty-seven propositions). This I particularly desire to record.

Returning to them I think the most salient case of omission is that which relates to the Eucharistic sacrifice, rather feebly mentioned: to the doing by the priest on earth, and by the congregation through the priest, of what our Blessed Lord does in Heaven.

There are of course other *nuances* which I should vary.

Especially there is this. We have gained since that date in historical courage. I had not yet learned to recognise frankly that in the struggle of the Reformation, as in all great convulsive struggles, there were losses in regard to religious truth, as well as gains.

On the whole, perusing this paper, I think that when it was written, the education I had received was that of a man of thought, on the lines of theology, rather than that of a man of action. So I think Tholuck spoke of me: but no one knew how much I was *behind*.

W. E. G. August 13, 1888.

---

[1] i.e. and therefore not to be presumed open to doubt. W.E.G., August 1844.

APPENDIX 7

ALTERNATIVE VERSIONS OF 'RECORDED ERRORS'

ADD.MS 44790, ff. 131–141

July 14, 1894 Some of my errors

The errors that I here have in view are of course . . . separable content: . . . state of mind in which I entered public life.[1] Oxford had not taught me, nor had any other place or person, the value of liberty as an essential condition of excellence in human things. True, Oxford had supplied me with the means of applying a remedy to this mischief for she had undoubtedly infused into my mind the love of truth as a dominant and supreme motive of conduct. But this it took long to develop into its proper place and function.

It may perhaps be thought that among these errors I ought to record the publication in 1838 of my first work *The State in its relations with the Church*. Undoubtedly that work was written in total disregard or rather ignorance of the conditions under which alone political action was possible in matters of religion. It involved me personally in a good deal of embarrassment. It was deemed rather too moderate by my dear friend James Hope, then an ardent Churchman, afterwards Roman Catholic. In the sanguine fervour of youth, having now learned something about the nature of the Church and its office, and noting the many symptoms of revival and reform within her borders, I dreamed that she was capable of recovering lost ground and of bringing back the nation to unity in her communion. A notable projection from the declining state[2]

Sed falsa ad caelum mittunt insomnia Manes.

From these points of view the effort seems contemptible. But I think that there is more to be said. The land was overspread with a thick curtain of prejudice. The foundations of the historic Church of England except in the minds of a few divines were obscured. The Evangelical movement with all its virtues and merits had the vice of individualising religion in a degree perhaps unexampled and of rendering the language of Holy Scripture about Mount Zion and the Kingdom of Heaven little better than a jargon. The antagonism of Protestantism to Popery

---

[1] This sentence has been overwritten and is largely illegible.

[2] The last word appears to be 'gate'.

246

which had [been] taken by Dr. Chalmers in his recent lectures on Church establishments, the wretched error of which confounds Church and world and introverts their positions, was not indeed the creed—for the idea of a creed implies something like systematic thought—and seems to deny the habitual view of our public men with few exceptions (such as Mr. Burke) from the Revolution downwards. To meet the demands of the coming time it was a matter of vital necessity to cut a way through all this darkness to a clearer and more solid position. Immense progress has been made in that direction during my lifetime and I am inclined to hope that my book imparted a certain amount of stimulus to the public mind, and made some small contribution to the needful process in its earliest stage. The total change in thought within the last sixty years has been immense and highly beneficial. With these remarks I pass on.

I have had occasion to mention elsewhere that before the session of 1842 began I had been dissatisfied with the provisions of Sir R. Peel's bill for the mitigation of the Corn Laws, and had begged him in consequence to accept my resignation. In my non-approval I was probably right but certainly wrong in my request. I had not yet acquired experience, and I knew not how the provisions of measures were inseparably associated with the characters, position, and authority of those who were to carry them. I really put myself down in making this proposal as equal to zero. But although in myself a very insignificant personage I was the organ and representative of the Government as to its commercial department and its commercial department was about to be the most important of all public departments for the time. My failure to perceive the true bearings of the case was one among many proofs of the tardy growth of my mind.

About the time of my resignation (January 1845) on account of the contemplated increase of the grant to the college of Maynooth, or at some period not remote from it, I became possessed with the idea that there was about to be a renewal in some shape of our diplomatic [relations] with the see of Rome, and I believe that I committed the gross error of tendering myself to Sir Robert Peel to fill the post of Envoy. I have difficulty at this date (1894) in conceiving by what obliquity of view I could have come to imagine that this was a rational or any way excusable proposal; and this although I vaguely think that my friend James Hope had some hand in it serves to show me that there existed in my mind a strong element of fanaticism. I was an ideologist:

but my ideology was feeble and inconsequent. I believe that I left it to Sir R. Peel to make me any answer or none as he might think fit: and he with great propriety chose the latter alternative.

In December 1845 I became Secretary of State for the Colonies: a resumption of office which led to my temporary absence from Parliament as I could not honourably seek re-election at Newark when my conduct could have been nothing but gall and wormwood to the Duke of Newcastle. While I held this office, it was represented to me that the conduct of the gentleman who was then Governor (of Van Diemen's Land?) in regard to women constituted a notorious scandal in the colony. I remember that the bishop of the diocese (Dr. Nixon) was very prominen[t] in urging upon me the necessity of taking some step to abate this scandal. I inquired what was the evidence upon which I was to proceed; and I received the answer that there was no need more of evidence in such a case than for establishing the existence of the sun on a bright noonday. So positive were these assurances that I addressed a letter to the Governor on the subject of them. He replied by challenging me to the proof. I fell back on those who had urged me on. They and the Bishop in particular entirely disclaimed any concern in the matter, and left me in a hopeless position which they had almost compelled me to assume in the interest of public order and morality. There was on my part in this matter a singular absence of worldly wisdom. My mind contemplated all things in the abstract (but I was now thirty-five years of age) and could not grasp or estimate the element of flesh and blood which counts for so much in them.

I pass on, however, to an error which was more inexcusable and which had a bearing by no means unimport[ant] upon the course of public affairs.

Early in 1855 the sufferings of the British army before Sebastopol led to the proposal of a hostile motion in the House of Commons which destroyed the Government of Lord Aberdeen, the immediate resignations, however, being only those of Lord Aberdeen, Lord John Russell, and the Duke of Newcastle. On one of the turns of the political wheel which followed, the Queen sent for Lord Lansdowne. I received a summons one morning to Lansdowne House where Lord Lansdowne made known to me this intelligence. He put to me the question whether I was willing to continue under him in the office of Chancellor of the Exchequer. He said, 'If you consent I think I shall persevere with the commission: but if not I shall probably abandon it'. From motives which it is not now easy to analyse I declined. I stated that I had been perfectly satisfied with the Coalition which had subsisted up to that time, but that I was not disposed to a Coalition in any other form. I was extremely sore at the treatment which my friend Lord Aberdeen had received. And I think that though perfectly satisfied to be in a Peelite government which had Whigs or Radicals in it, I was not ready to be in a Whig government which had Peelites in it. It took a long time with my slow-moving and tenacious character for the Ethiopian to change his skin.

I can hardly suppose that the eventual failure of the Queen's overture to Lord Lansdowne was due to my refusal. But that refusal undoubtedly constituted one of his difficulties and helped to bring about the result. I have always looked back upon it with pain as a serious and even gross error of judgment. It was I think injurious to the public if it contributed to the substitution as Prime Minister of Lord Palmerston for Lord Lansdowne: a personage of greater dignity and I think a higher level of political principle.

There followed almost immediately a step which drew down upon me and upon the other parties to it, who were (in the Cabinet) Sir James Graham and Mr. Sidney Herbert. We had in the Aberdeen Government resisted the reference of the question concerning the army before Sebastopol to a committee of the House of Commons. It was an instrument grossly inadequate; and to acquiesce in its appointment appeared to be, and I think eventually proved, a gross fraud upon the country. Lord Palmerston gave in to the proposal without having the authority of the Cabinet for the act. We resigned: and for resigning were universally condemned as deserters of the public cause at a moment of difficulty. The error, if error it were, was a joint one. And there may be two sides to the question. But I think our course was one which has much to commend it to high minded men. The course actually taken resulted in the appointment of three separate tribunals of inquiry: the committee to satisfy public opinion, a commission sent to the Crimea to establish the facts, and a military board which sat at Chelsea to whitewash the officers of the army. The public were put off with shams, and the result obtained was nil, I fear, from the subject leaving open the question whether the retiring Ministers were or were not in error.

I have yet, however, to record an undoubted error, the most singular and palpable, I may add the least excusable of them all, especially because it was committed so late as in the year 1862 when I had over lived half a century. In the autumn of that year, and in a speech delivered after a public dinner at Newcastle-upon-Tyne, I declared in the heat of the American struggle that Jefferson Davis had made a nation, that is to say that the division of the American Republic by the establishment of a Southern or Secessionsist state was an accomplished fact.

Strange to say this declaration, most unwarrantable to be made by a Minister of the Crown with no authority other than his own was not due to any feeling of partisanship for the South, or hostility to the North. The fortunes of the South were at their zenith. Many who wished well to the Northern cause despaired of its success. Not only was this a misjudgment of the case but even if it had been otherwise, I was not the person to make the declaration. I really, though most strangely, believed that it was an act of friendliness to all America to recognise that the struggle was virtually at an end and I was so fortunate as at a subsequent date to obtain from the American government a most handsome acquittal so far as the motive of my imprudent and reprehensible act was concerned.

In looking back upon such an act as this, the reasons which condemn it appear to be so glaring, and the absence of any countervailing reasons so palpable, that it seems absolutely incomprehensible how they could have been overlooked. And I am the more pained and grieved at my offence because I have for the last five and twenty years received from the government and people of America tokens of goodwill which could not fail to win my undying gratitude.

July 14, 1894

ADD.MS 44791, ff. 45–48
1896 Mistakes—certain, doubtful, or suppositious.[1]

Let me now place clearly on record the list, or lists, of my political mistakes: and let me take first those of which I am vividly conscious. In some cases they were common to me with my colleagues: in most they were wholly my own.

I divide them into (1) the certain, (2) the doubtful, (3) the suppositious. But before touching on particulars, I must refer to causes with which I connect these errors. These are two in particular—one, a singular slowness in the development of my mind, so far as regarded its opening out into the ordinary aptitudes of the man of the world. For

---

[1] 'Real, reputed, or arguable' was crossed out and the above substituted.

years and years, even into advanced middle life, I seem to have considered actions simply as they were in themselves and did not take into account the way in which they would be taken and understood by others. I did not perceive that their natural or probable effect upon and in minds other than my own formed part of the considerations determining the propriety of each act in itself, and not unfrequently, at any rate in public life, supplied the decisive criterion to determine what ought and what ought not to be done. In truth the dominant tendencies of my mind were those of a recluse; and I might, in most respects with ease, have accommodated myself to the education of the cloister. All the mental apparatus requisite to constitute what we call the 'public man' had to be purchased by a slow experience, and inserted piecemeal into the composition of my character. I remember for example that when (in 1848 or 1849) the repeal of the Navigation Laws was before Parliament, I, although strongly favourable in principle to the measure, yet was so struck with the enormous waste which would be caused by the want of reciprocity in this particular class of cases, that I gave notice of a motion in favour of making the grant of full equality for ships conditional upon like conduct on the other side. But when I learned from the Government that they (very properly) would on no terms accept the motion, which was not unlikely to be carried, rather than run any risk of wrecking the entire measure, I withdrew my notice. At this the Tories, with whom I was not in consultation, were much put about: and I, who had thought of things only and not taken persons into view, was surprised at their surprise, and failed to perceive that, as my personal position at the time was one which would greatly have helped the chances in their favour, I had in effect given them a kind of vested interest in my conduct. This was a clear error; but, as it had no public consequences, it was a minor one, and I do not admit it into my list.

The other cause was my very marked temperament with regard to religion. I had in me more fanaticism than piety: the fanaticism in me was not held in check by such piety as there was to hand. My opinions, though they had been to some extent qualified, and rather seriously shaken, by the study of Butler at Oxford, were still when I entered Parliament the rigidly narrow opinions of the Evangelical school in which I had been bred. I had not (thanks probably to Mr. Canning, whom I idolised) ever applied them in hostility to what was called Roman Catholic emancipation, but in the religious arena they were as against Popery very thoroughgoing—and the support of Protestantism in Ireland seemed to me the most sacred perhaps of all public duties. My mind was a dark place, and the light for a long time only came in through crevices. Hence a transition period during which I dealt in artificialities, and allowed myself mistakes which now appear to me gross. What this support of Protestantism really meant and was, I perhaps could not, certainly did not, ascertain.

I will take care broadly to distinguish from the rest such of my errors as now stand forth both in my memory and in my understanding as gross and palpable.

Most probably, who know the history of my life, may expect me to begin with the publication in 1838 of my first book on the relations of the Church to the State. Certainly that publication was undertaken without any consideration of what I may call the case all round. I did not weigh, it never crossed my mind to weigh, the effect which the book might have on my personal advancement. It was an attempt to set forth in good faith what seemed to me the truth: and as I had not yet intelligently attained to the principles of self-government for a nation (here I think Mr. Burke and the French Revolution were partly responsible) I did not question the title of the State to uphold it, whatever might be the state of opinion outside.

The proposal of what was termed the appropriation clause forced the question into prominence: and it began to be considered beyond the walls of studies what was the proper basis of the system briefly represented by the *dictum* of 'Church and State'.

About the year 1835 that noble-hearted man Dr. Chalmers, in my view the flower and cream of Presbyterianism, came up to London, and in his broad and most unmusical Scotch, set forth, through a series of lectures at the Hanover Square Rooms, his doctrine of Church and State. In my view the sum and substance of them (they were shortly afterwards published) was this. The State has a limited competency in the matter of religion. It is not competent to draw the minuter distinctions, such as those between the English and the Scotch Establishment Acts, between one form of Protestantism and another, for either of these it is entitled to regard as the word of God. But there are also broad distinctions which it is competent to draw. Such is the distinction between Protestantism, which is the word of God, and Popery, which is the word of man. The State ought therefore to refuse its support to Popery but it should establish some form of Protestantism.

I was already educated into ideas which made this theory insufferable to me and was gradually embracing the historical idea of the Church, so that this theory was in my eyes insufferable, and the desire to offer a better one was I think the *raison d'être* of my book.

I probably did not understand that governing opinion had already drifted long past any philosophical or historical theory of the relations between the Church and State: for the doctrine so eloquently set out by Macaulay, in his article on my volume, can hardly be called a philosophical theory. Accordingly, I did not know what a gap I was placing between myself and my political friends and leaders; although, when I did come to perceive it, I was perfectly ready to accept the consequences. Peel never said or wrote to me one word upon the subject. But I remember that peculiar embarrassed shyness of his on the first occasion when I met him after the publication, and I do not doubt that he regarded it with horror on its own merits, and on my account with dismay. When the 'Bedchamber' affair happened, or on some occasion about that period, Lord Russell had referred to strange opinions lately promulgated, he took the opportunity of saying that he and those with whom he had been in consultation had no concern with such opinions.

Why is it that I do not set down the book among my gross and palpable errors? Now for my answer. Down to the time of my entrance into public life the prevailing creed of public men as to the Church was the Erastian system. I think that Lord Aberdeen, and in a degree Mr. Stanley (Lord Derby) were on better lines, but generally the assertion holds. To get rid of this debasing system I even then felt an unconquerable desire, and one of the chief satisfactions of my political life has been to witness its progressive decay, which has now I trust nearly reached the stage of the last gasp. Now I make bold to say that my book on Church and State was the first manifestation from a political quarter of what was eventually to be a revolution in opinion. It was anti-Erastian from beginning to the end. The work was one most necessary to be done, and though my effort may in itself have been insignificant it helped to set thought in motion and was the small starting point of a process really great. Viewed from without it was a mistake: but I think it subserved high and necessary purposes, so that I have never been disposed to give it any utter condemnation.

APPENDIX 8

GLADSTONE'S LISTS OF HIS CRITICS

Gladstone's autobiographical writings include two lists of his critics.

ADD.MS 44790, f. 169   *September 1894*

I do not know if it has happened to any other man to be so contemptuously or severely censured as myself by such a number of persons undoubtedly able, conspicuous, and distinguished: above all so remarkably diversified. I will name such of them as occur to me.

> Mr. Carlyle (Froude's Life)
> Mr. Froude
> Mr. Clark Maxwell
> Lord Shaftesbury (Hodder's biography)
> Mr. Lecky
> Mr. Goldwin Smith
> Sir Francis Doyle (Reminiscences)
>
> Mr. Swinburne
> Lord Grey
> Mr. Swinburne[1]

Nothing one would incline to say, could have united such a body of independent witnesses as this, except that what they said was the truth.

ADD.MS 44791, f.21   *1895*

It has certainly been my fate, in a peculiar degree, to be the recipient of praise I did not deserve. On the other hand I have been visited with censures, I do not say undeserved, but remarkable for their severity, for the variety of quarters from whence they come, and for the eminence of those who have delivered them. Even at the moment I remember them.

> Lord Shaftesbury
> Mr. Froude

---

[1] The last three names are added in a later hand.

Mr. Carlyle
Sir Francis Doyle
Mr. Swinburne
Pope Pius IX (officially, 1874)
Mr. Lecky
Mr. Ruskin (who altered)
Dr. Hook
Mr. Goldwin Smith
Archbishop Magee

It is curious that this list should not contain the name of any one of my political opponents.

INDEX